PATRICK
MOWER

PATRICK MOWER

MY STORY

BY PATRICK MOWER

JB

JOHN BLAKE

Published by John Blake Publishing Ltd,
3 Bramber Court, 2 Bramber Road,
London W14 9PB, England

www.blake.co.uk

First published in hardback in 2007

ISBN: 978-1-84454-447-9

British Library Cataloguing-in-Publication Data:

A catalogue record for this book is available from the British Library.

Design by www.envydesign.co.uk

Printed in Great Britain by William Clowes Ltd, Beccles, Suffolk

1 3 5 7 9 10 8 6 4 2

Papers used by John Blake Publishing are natural, recyclable products
made from wood grown in sustainable forests. The manufacturing processes
conform to the environmental regulations of the country of origin.

Every attempt has been made to contact the relevant copyright-holders,
but some were unobtainable. We would be grateful if the appropriate
people could contact us.

To FWD (Frank Dibb), theatre critic of the *Oxford Times* who sowed the first seed.

Acknowledgements

My eternal thanks to my dear friend, Patrick 'The Major'
Codd, who has pushed and prodded, poked and praised.
His exhortations and promptings have helped me over
many a brick wall. I thank him for his faith and patience
when I was losing mine. Also thanks to my editor Mark
Hanks for his direction and advice. I would like to thank
Anya and Maxim for locking me in a darkened room in
order that I finish this autobiography – 'so we can get on
with *The Most Glub Snaggling Bling In The Uniblub*'
(the children's book we are writing together). My thanks
to Sandra Kocinski, whose red eyes bear witness to the
hours spent deciphering my longhand and typing my
words into legibility. Also, thanks to John Blake for letting
me write the book I wanted to!

Contents

Prologue

THE KNIFE SLICED through my hand.

It cut deeply into my palm and nicked the index finger. The second and third fingers of my left hand were almost severed.

I felt no pain. I remember thinking how fragile the bones looked in the gaping wounds.

And then the blood came. And with it the pain.

My brother Don screamed, 'Don't be stupid, you little idiot!' as he forced my right hand off the shaft of the bread knife. In the struggle we knocked over the table and with it the tea things. I was still trying to plunge the knife into my chest. He ripped it from my grasp, pulling the razor-sharp blade through my clenched left hand.

The pain in my hand still couldn't stop the torment in my mind. The smash of a broken plate came from the scullery, followed by another sickening thud.

Above my mother's sobbing, the familiar slurred, pitiful Welsh voice of my father pleaded, 'I didn't mean it, Peg.'

These nightmare sounds that stopped my sleep were now invading my daytime. My little nine-year-old mind could take no more.

I had tried to kill myself

The scream of agony about to burst from my throat was stopped by the thick voice of my father in the hallway. 'Now look what you've done.' I could see the anger in his eyes as he bent down to pick up the broken jam jar. The tea that the jar had contained now mingled with my blood on the dirty linoleum-covered floor.

My head started spinning and I fell back against the chimney breast. Blood spurted from my hand, splashing crimson on the wall. Two belts hung there on separate nails. One for the dog – and one for the boys. For certain one of them would be used tonight.

1

Sins of The Father

LOOKING BACK, I still find it hard to believe just how far I've travelled since my childhood in the hard, mean crucible of impoverished streets tucked away just a couple of miles from the Dreaming Spires of Oxford.

But my story begins in the depressed valleys of South Wales, with my father Archie, a superb athlete, risking his reputation to fleece the bookies out of a bob or two of their ill-earned bounty.

Archie Mower was the fastest collier afoot in the Rhondda, a valley of despair since the closure of the Pontypridd pit, and the soul-destroying hardship that accompanied it, six weeks earlier. But Archie had already seen a way out – if he could swing the gamble that would, years later, shape my early life.

In 1928 there was precious little Roaring Twenties glamour to spare as Archie, carefully glancing to left and right, slipped the improvised lead weights from the soles of his battered running 'daps' – the weights that had sufficiently slowed him in the preliminary heats to trick the bookies into lengthening the odds on him winning.

'What price am I?' breathed Archie, bending down to retie his laces.

'I can still get 5–1 with Bythan the Book,' replied his brother, Walt, palming the lead weights into his pocket.

'Put it all on then,' said Archie.

Glancing at the coins shining brightly against the black lines of life and heart etched deep in his palm by years at the coalface, Walt hesitated.

'You sure you can beat Iean in the final? You came a bad second in the heats...' A cough rattled through his chest, stopping his words.

Archie's face broke into the smile that had itself broken so many hearts. He knew it would be at least two minutes before Walt's wheezing would allow him to continue speaking. Silicosis was remorseless.

'Put it on, Walt – I'm as fit as a butcher's dog,' he said, his eyes focused on the running track laid out on the valley floor as the first of the competitors began making their way to the start through the throng of expectant miners all dressed up in their stiff white collars and Sunday suits.

Because of the lack of horses and dogs to gamble on, it was common practice for valley communities to bet on local athletes.

'Better make yourself scarce, Walt.'

As he watched his brother leave, still spluttering, Archie knew that if he stayed in this God-forsaken place it would not be long before he too would become as bent and racked.

A flag snapping in the wind brought him out of his reverie. Looking up, he saw the banner proclaiming 'The Cambrian Dash'. This would be the last time the 75-year-old race was run, but Archie knew none of this as he adjusted his laces yet again. He just knew he had to win – and pull off their betting coup.

With the pit closing, he had joined the hundreds of other miners who now, instead of the daily 6am ritual of staring into a cat-black coalface, were looking into an equally unforgiving future. His weekly wage of £2.50 had stopped but the tallyman still called; the rent man still knocked; his three daughters still needed feeding. They still couldn't understand why Pa didn't come home with a black face any more and scrub himself white in the bath in front of the fire. But, more important than all that, the birth of his son was imminent.

'Runners for the Cambrian Dash.'

The megaphone startled Walt. He stepped back into the gathering crowd as two officials pulled the finishing tape across the track in the middle of the valley nestling between the Twyn-y-Fan Henlog and the YDavallt hills. Tugging his cap well down over his eyes and with his hands thrust deep into his pockets, he could feel the lead weights in one and the betting slip in the other. So far so good.

He glanced across to where Archie stood shaking his legs to relax the muscles. No wonder he was so successful with the girls, thought Walt. Archie was five feet nine inches tall, with broad, powerful shoulders, slim hips and strong muscular legs, and now as he jogged to the starting line, keeping his head well down, he shook it so that the black slicked hair fell over his face. It was a fiercely proud Celtic face. Black brows protected black laughing eyes. His nostrils flared above the smile that was always lurking, ready to get him into – and out – of trouble, a smile that might well be needed today.

Archie knew he was the fastest runner, and in order to reach this stage without becoming favourite, thereby shortening his odds, he had persuaded Walt to run in the heats and quarter-final as A. Mower.

The heats for the Cambrian Dash were held in all the valleys around the Rhondda and the victors in the semi-finals were now, like Archie, making their way to the starting line. As there was little communication between the valleys the chances of anyone knowing the brothers was very remote. But now, with all the officials and competitors gathering for the big day, they had to be careful. Even though the brothers were similar in look and stature, they were by no means identical.

The lead soles had enabled Archie to run flat out in his semi-final and come a poor second. He knew he would win today and the only people to suffer would be the bookmakers – and they'd certainly made him suffer in the past.

At the crack of the starting pistol, Archie felt he was not so much running towards the tape as running away from something. He could feel Dai Llewellyn at his elbow as he powered even harder.

Each step seemed to push his life further behind him. It was as if he was climbing out of the present into his future. His left foot pushed away the mines... Then, with his right, he kicked away his debts... His miserable house... The mouths to feed... Smug mine managers... Abandoned miners...

His wife Jean was about to give birth. His son!

He became aware of Jonas Pugh drawing alongside. It was the smell.

The thought flashed through Archie's brain, Pugh's the right name for you – you stinking bugger. Just because we no longer have to wash the coal dust off us every day doesn't mean you never have to use your tin bath.

He drove his arms to punch the air even harder. His legs responded. Now he was running towards something. His son!

His feet barely touched the newly mown grass. 'This is for you, *bach*!' The words forced their way through Archie's bared teeth as he breasted the tape.

Of course he had won. He knew he would. His momentum carried him though the cheering, back-slapping miners. Still keeping his head down, Archie jogged through the throng until he got to the old pit shaft.

'Good lad, Arch,' wheezed Walt, handing him his clothes. 'I think we got away with it.'

'I'm sure we did.' Archie smiled up at his brother as he squatted on his haunches to catch his breath. 'But I'm not taking any chances. I'm not going back for the trophy, much as I'd like my picture in the *Porth Post*. Somebody's bound to remember your ugly mug.'

'I can't have the brains and beauty,' laughed Walt. 'I'll go and see Bythan and pick up our winnings. Meet you in the Colliers?'

'Sure,' beamed Archie. 'We've got a lot to celebrate. A lot to celebrate.'

Later, as he stood swaying on the doorstep of his two-up, two-down cottage, Archie heard the baby cry. He placed the remains of his £14 winnings on the kitchen table and made his way unsteadily to the foot of the stairs.

'Is it a boy or a girl?' he called.

'A girl,' replied the midwife.

'Fuck it, I'm off,' slurred Archie.

And he was.

2

The Other Oxford

TEN YEARS AFTER he quietly closed the front door in the Rhondda Valley, we rejoin Archie equally carefully easing open a kitchen door in Cowley, Oxford.

But, if I may, I will leave until later the explanation as to how and why Archie Mower has now metamorphosed into Pat Mower. Because, as the inebriated Wilfred Lawson said to the man sitting next to him in the audience at the Old Vic Theatre, 'You'll like this bit. This is where I come in.'

To be precise, this is where I came out – straight on to an old brown sofa, fortunately missing the spring that had burst through a seat that had seen better days.

Archie – sorry, Pat – sat nervously smoking one of his Capstan Full Strength cigarettes in the kitchen of the three-bedroom semi while his wife, Peggy, gave birth in the front room. Hearing the baby's cries, Pat called out, 'Is she all right?'

'No, *she* is not,' replied Peggy. 'But *he* is. It's not a Patricia after all. It'll have to be a Patrick.'

Perversely, already having two sons – trust me – if my father had had a pair of scissors handy at that moment I think I may have spent my life as a Patricia!

But, spared the snip, I made my first appearance on 12 September 1938, or somewhere around that date. There is no record of my birth, As my delightful mother told me some 20 years later when I called her in a sweat from Somerset House. 'Mother, I've just been told I don't exist.'

'Don't be silly, Patrick,' she laughed. 'Of course you do.'

I was to learn throughout my life that such trivialities as birth certificates, and whether fathers were fathers or brothers brothers and sisters sisters, were a minor consideration.

Sisters! I haven't got any sisters. At least I didn't have for 30 years – until five of them turned up at the stage door of the New Theatre one stormy night in Cardiff.

And, strangely, it was rather reassuring to discover that the accusation, made by more than one fair maiden, that I was a bastard was, in fact, correct.

Such irrelevancies as these have helped to make me now, at the ripe young age of 60-odd, still completely prepared for the unpredictable.

But let us return to that leather sofa in Oxford in the year 1938 – or was it '39?

And to my father Pat, who was really Archie. And my mother Peggy, who was really Harriet. And, of course, a certain Mr Hitler.

Although, naturally, I was completely unimpressed by Neville Chamberlain waving his piece of paper, I could sense that all was not well. My earliest recollections were of lots of banging and shouting, and indeed peace didn't really break out in our house until my father went off to war in 1941.

I soon caught on that those two other boys in my life were my big brother Donald, who was two years older than me, and the very big Derek, who was eight years older. We were three happy, blond-haired children. My eyes were brown like my father's and theirs blue, like Peggy's.

I appreciate now that life for my mother, having no money, three young children and a husband away at war, could not have been easy. In those days the memories of the First World War were still etched deep into the psyche of the working class. Between 1914 and 1918 young men went off to war to die, with only the lucky few coming back. So it was understandable that if your man, be it husband, son, lover or brother, was going off to combat the German painter with the Charlie Chaplin moustache, the odds on him returning in a box were very high.

Life expectancy was low so that life had to be lived to the full. And my mother certainly appeared to be determined to make the most of hers. As I heard one American airman say on kissing her goodnight on the doorstep, 'Peggy, you sure are a looker.'

And so she was, with her cornflower-blue eyes and naturally blonde hair, kept in its 1940s wave by the 'Tony perm' that Iris Murphy from across the street administered every Friday afternoon. She was terribly proud of her fine figure and her much-admired legs.

'Are my seams straight, Patrick?' That was the last thing she always said when she was ready to go out. She would light up another Craven 'A' cigarette, examine herself once more in the bevelled mirror and, with a sweet 'Be good' thrown over her shoulder, the door would close.

I can still hear her high heels as she clip-clopped down the path and crossed the road to Mrs Murphy's. As my mother approached, without fail the front door would open and out would pop Mrs Murphy, like the wet-weather lady on a weather house. My mother would then about-turn, give Don and me a little wave, have another puff on her fag and then the two of them would totter to the main road to catch the bus 'up town'. Marlene Dietrich and Hilda Baker.

Behind the net curtains in a road like ours, eyes constantly peeped. As there was no television, their soap stars were the people who made up the day-to-day traffic along the road. And I'm sure these two painted ladies played leading roles in many of their stories.

To most people, I'm sure, Oxford would seem to be the ideal birthplace, with its beautiful colleges, the sound of willow striking leather in the Parks, earnest undergrads, gowns billowing from their shoulders, striding purposefully down the 'High', that celebrated High Street bordered to the west by the Gothic splendour of the University Church of St Mary the Virgin and to the east by the Baroque grandeur of Queen's College.

Queen's was founded in 1341 and if, 600 years later, you were to take the number 73 bus out past All Souls over Magdalen Bridge you would notice that the High Street became the Cowley Road. The elegant limestone of the colleges is replaced by the grim concrete of the Cowley 'works'. Like a scene from Ridley Scott's *Blade Runner*, they straddled the road. On one side was the monstrosity that was Morris Motors and on the other the Pressed Steel Company, an equally hideous eyesore with its chimneys incessantly belching sulphurous smoke.

It was here, at this end of the town, that I made my first entrance. At 86 Ridgefield Road, Cowley, to be precise.

In the 1940s Oxford was far more 'Town and Gown' than it is today. The university and its inhabitants were as alien to us 'down the Cowley Road' as were the American officers with their chewing gum, Camel cigarettes and seemingly bottomless pockets full of money. There was never any aspiration on our part to go to 'University' because there was never the remotest possibility that we could ever go there. They were 'them' and we were 'us'. It was the natural order of things. We never questioned it. Especially if you were the offspring of a Welsh coal miner and a mill girl from Oldham.

So my young life seemed perfectly normal. It wasn't until I was 15 and had to talk about the 'Dreaming Spires' when playing Morgan Evans in *The Corn Is Green* that I even realised there were any.

In fact, Don and I had a rather good time running wild in the streets, digging trenches, fighting the 'Jerries' – as our German foe were universally known – in the back garden or playing in our local 'rec'. I couldn't count the number of times we were left on our own, but it seemed it was always Derek who came to find us to put us to bed.

Even when the ambulance came to take Don and I to an isolation hospital, we thought it was an adventure. We didn't know that, because of our lack of general cleanliness and decent food, we had contracted scabies. We really were dirty and smelly and, by today's standards, our diet – which seemed to consist largely of bread and jam – would have sent Jamie Oliver and the food police into a state of permanent shock. But we didn't know any better.

What we did know was that we had horrible itches that, quite naturally, we scratched until they wept. They then formed mighty scabs, which we picked off with even greater relish.

We were in hospital for several weeks and, after the initial pain and discomfort of being soaked in disgusting, smelly baths for several days, we adapted quite quickly. Being well looked after and having regular baths was a new experience for both of us and we readily became accustomed to this new life.

There were some important-looking people in suits waiting for us when the ambulance took us home. I suppose they were from the Council – social workers, perhaps. Where Derek was during this period is all blurred, but it became clearer in light of what I was to learn much later.

I was now five and Don, being two years older, had the responsibility of taking me to school with him. He was always complaining about having to look after me and he had some very original methods of teaching me to stand on my own two feet. One thing about my first day at St Mary and St John's Infants School I recall very clearly. As we arrived at the school gates, Don, having made me walk ten paces behind him all the way as he chattered to his older friends, turned to me and said, 'Right, Moany, you're on your own. You're in Reception, I'm in Class Two. Don't talk to me. Meet me back here at the end of school.'

I can't recall much else about the first day at school, but I do remember waiting, a skinny little waif, for two hours at the gate afterwards. Whether Don forgot, or, more likely, thought it would do me good to find my own way home, I never knew.

Feeling very cold in my little shorts and short-sleeved shirt, I started to cry. I didn't even know the name of our road, so I couldn't ask. I hadn't been looking around me on my way there, just following my hero as I had been ordered. One of Don's favourite games was to take me up to the woods at the nearby golf course to play hide and seek. I would hide and he, with brotherly malice, would go home.

I wasn't scared. It was just that it was the second time I felt I had been let down that day. The first time was in the Head-mistress's office. After Don had left me I'd wandered in there by accident.

'What do you want? Are you a new boy?' a voice barked down at me.

I was very small for my age and the Headmistress was extremely tall. In her long black dress she seemed to go on and on. In the middle of a thin pink face was a quite scarily hooked nose upon which were perched a pair of glasses with bright-red frames.

She peered down at me. 'Well... Are you new?'

'Yes, I think so.' I felt a butterfly stir in my stomach.

'What interesting shoes,' she said.

I looked down at my feet. 'They're clogs,' I announced.

'So I see. How sweet,' she chuckled. 'What class are you in?'

'I don't know,' I said, trembling now. The other butterflies had awoken. I didn't like this lady. She was very posh.

'Oh dear, what's your name?' she asked.

'Patrick.'

'Patrick what, dear?'

'Patrick Mower.'

What she said next allayed all my fears. 'Well, Patrick Mower, wait here for the present.'

Oh, it's not going to be so bad after all, I thought. Even so, I did what I still do to this day. In times of boredom or if I find myself in a situation I'm not comfortable with, I fantasise. I take myself off to a more green and pleasant land.

The butterflies settled down, and I sat down. The clogs had made the sides of my ankles really sore, so I took them off. The right one now became a destroyer, sailing off to rescue my uncle Stanley from those 'slant-eyed Nips'. He had been a prisoner of war for three years, working on the notorious Burma Railway, and would later tell us of the horror and butchery he experienced there, burying comrades where they collapsed.

Of course, at five years of age, I didn't realise that my description of his captors was pejorative. Everyone called the Japanese 'Japs' or 'Nips'.

My left clog was now a giant sea serpent about to devour

my right clog, when a new voice brought me back. It was a different lady.

'Would you like to come with me, Patrick?'

I stood up. 'I can't,' I said.

'Why not?'

'I'm waiting for my present.'

'Your what?' she exclaimed.

'The tall lady told me to wait here for the present.'

Mrs Livingstone, my form teacher, burst out laughing and took my hand. 'Come on, Patrick,' she smiled. 'Let's see if we can find you one.'

In fact, despite the traumas of Day One, I soon thought school was a wonderful place. I enjoyed learning – I still do – and made the most of it.

But Don was always up to his old tricks of 'mitching' at every opportunity. He would go to any lengths to avoid school, even down to pouring an inch of salt into a cup of water, stirring it vigorously and then making me swallow it down without pausing once for breath. As a result, before we had walked halfway to school, I would have turned green and been violently sick.

My crafty brother was not satisfied with me just being ill. He would hold me so that I retched all over my shirt – as proof of how 'poorly' I was. He would then march me home and, naturally, stay to look after me. He was full of tricks like that and it's a small miracle that I did as well at school as I did, as Don had only one ambition as far as school was concerned – never to go near the place, and that inevitably involved me missing lessons too.

At the time I didn't realise – we were kids and didn't even think about it – but we must have looked a pretty bad sight. As well as being dirty and smelly, we always wore the most awful tatty clothes. To save money, as there never seemed to be a penny in the house, our mother knitted trousers for Don and I to wear to school.

That's how she came up with the cash-saving brain wave – clogs.

Before moving down south to Oxford, my mother had been a 'clog girl' herself, working in the Lancashire cotton mills. So when she saw an advertisement in the *Daily Mirror* for 'Genuine Wooden Clogs – They Never Wear Out!' she thought it a brilliant idea. In her childhood it had been quite normal to wear clogs. But in Oxford they were a source of amusement and even ridicule.

When the clogs arrived they were four of the same size and shape. No left or right foot. Don's seemed to fit him, but the toes of mine had to be stuffed with newspaper as they were far too big for my little feet. Even when they were packed with paper it was still quite an art to keep my feet in them as I walked.

Fortunately this experiment didn't last long.

Don, who was always one step ahead of me, often literally, took to stuffing our sandals in his shirt and as soon as we turned the corner into Howard Street he would pull me into the allotments. We would then swap the clogs for our sandals. We would leave the clogs in an old shed, go to school and then retrieve them on the way home. This worked well for quite a few weeks until one day after school I arrived at the shed to find Don still there.

'We're in trouble, Bruv,' he said, concern for once furrowing his brow. 'The clogs have gone.'

I can imagine to this day some old gardener still telling his grandchildren all about those strange garden gnomes who left their magic clogs behind. And I hope he had some enjoyment out of them because, apart from the pain they caused to our feet, we both got a good whacking from our mother. For some reason she didn't believe us when we arrived home, crocodile tears streaming down our faces, saying we had been set upon by a gang of bigger boys who had stolen our 'precious' clogs. We had forgotten we were wearing our sandals. Maybe that had something to do with it.

There really was no money. Mother didn't work and our father was away in the Army. In fact, I don't know how we survived. I didn't think we were poor and never really noticed other children's clothes, but they noticed the smelly Mowers.

We had an outside toilet and I remember my surprise at school at the sight of toilet paper. We always wiped our bottoms on newspaper, torn up and left on the floor. That was what the *Daily Mirror* was for, I thought.

Don and I were far more interested in racing out into the street at every opportunity to join the gang of boys we always played with. We were all about the same age and, in those pre-television days and long before kids became brainwashed with video games and the internet, our main recreation was playing football.

There must have been 20 of us and, like all boys, we could be pretty cruel. One lad, called Ashley Alexander, lived next door to us and everyone in our gang treated him really badly, calling him 'Jewbag' and tormenting him at every chance that came our way.

On one occasion we pushed him into a concrete coal bunker, slammed the door shut on him and then barricaded it with a sack of earth so that he couldn't open it. I remember his mother calling him, 'Ashley… Ashley…' and then asking us whether we had seen him. 'No,' we all replied, looking, we hoped, the picture of innocence. We left him in there for five hours, and I haven't a clue why we did it. We didn't know what a Jew was, even though some of the gang must have been told by their parents, but he was different, and to us he was always 'Jewbag'.

Another day, in one of those bitter wartime winters, we nearly froze Ashley to death. There had been a very heavy snowfall and we made an igloo in the street out of big chunks of ice and snow. It was a magnificent igloo, round and with a proper entrance, and because so few cars ever came down our street it was perfectly safe to leave it gleaming white as a star attraction. Naturally it was poor old Ashley who was made to go inside – and then we blocked up the entrance behind him and left him there. He was frozen with the cold, but he didn't dare cry out for fear of what we might do. Again we smirked as his mother, becoming increasingly frantic, called for him in vain. And again we denied all knowledge of her son's whereabouts.

Just before dark my conscience started to prick and I sneaked out of our house in my bare feet because I didn't dare let Don know what I was up to. I could hear Ashley's mother calling up and down the street as I dug a hole in the side of the igloo with a sharp stick and pulled Ashley's hand through. It was blue with the cold, but, by pulling as hard as I could with one hand and digging at the frozen igloo with the stick gripped in the other, I managed to pull him through. When he finally came crashing out in a spray of snow and ice, his teeth were chattering and his body was shaking uncontrollably. He was unable to speak, but I said, 'Your mum wants you,' and ran into my home.

We persecuted Ashley because he was different, and if those tiny bigoted incidents are magnified many, many times, it is no wonder the Jewish race feels persecuted. I am happy to say that Ashley is now a firm friend and I have apologised many times for our 'innocent' childish behaviour.

When we weren't playing football, our gang would go up the street to the golf course, where our favourite occupations were jumping the brook with its eight-foot-high banks, climbing up trees ten times as tall as that and stealing golf balls. We delighted in watching the proud golfer looking for the evidence of his perfect drive, mystified as to where his ball had gone. It was not the fairies who had made his ball vanish but the scruffy little boys hanging from the branches of the trees and hiding in the bunkers.

The golf course was to be the scene of my first sexual encounter, with a girl who lived opposite us. Two fumbling innocents on the magical mystery tour of sex.

In all the childish scrapes and shenanigans Don and I got up to, we were watched over with a kindly eye but a firm hand by our big brother Derek, who, at 13, was already a strapping six-footer.

As Hitler's Germany crumbled towards defeat, we three boys were looking forward to the end of the war and our father's return. Our mother less so, I fear, because, in his absence and to her children's detriment, she was having such a good time with her heady flings with high-flying Flying Officers.

I said earlier that peace only broke out in our house when my father went to war. Now the opposite was to be true.

3

A Light in My Head

I VIVIDLY REMEMBER MY father's return. It was VE Day, 8 May 1945. A street party the like of which I had never seen before, nor witnessed since, was in full swing. Acrimonious neighbours sat grinning side by side. Old enmities were literally brushed under the table which spread 200 yards down the middle of Ridgefield Road. Home-made cakes and jellies, paper hats, balloons, incessant cheering, laughter, and the whole street singing Vera Lynn's wartime hit: 'There'll be bluebirds over the white cliffs of Dover.'

I was sharing a kitchen chair with Ashley Alexander when the cheering started at the far end of the table.

A soldier was walking down the middle of the road with a kitbag slung over his shoulder. The women, as one, leaped up to kiss this returning hero. It was as if this lone uniformed figure had won the war single-handed.

As the figure strode towards our end of the street,

acknowledging the cheers and kisses bestowed upon him, I heard my mother gasp, 'Oh my God, I don't believe it, Pat... It's your father.'

She went to him and, pushing away the other women trying to congratulate him, threw her arms around his neck.

We three boys remained at the table. To me this was a stranger. He had left when I was three years old. I was now nearly seven.

The street resumed cheering and singing as my mother and father walked into number 86. Derek said, 'Pat, Don, come on...' and we followed them down the path.

With this stranger in the house the next few days were confusing, particularly as it was difficult to understand what he was saying, his Welsh accent was so pronounced. In fairness to my father, he hadn't spoken English until he was 12.

But at last I had a father. It was every lonely boy's little dream: someone to really look up to.

For the first few weeks after his demob from the Army, my father seemed a pleasant man. Relieved to be back home, and, with the odd pint of beer to help him, he appeared to enjoy civilian life.

I don't know whether it was his discovery of my mother's infidelities or the responsibility of suddenly having four mouths to feed, but the atmosphere suddenly changed dramatically. He made it very clear that he was the master and we boys learned fear.

One day he brought home a white bull terrier from the pub. The dog's name was Silver and it was extremely dangerous. It would obey no one but my father – obedience having been beaten into him by the belt that my father hung over the fireplace.

A few months later a second nail was banged into the wall alongside Silver's. On this was hung another belt – for his sons.

My father's lessons in life had been in the hot, claustrophobic, dangerous and male-dominated world of the coal face so deep underground – a hard, unrelenting school. And then he had been thrown into the equally savage world of war. He knew no better. That's my excuse for him.

He started to look in on himself, and the more he did so the more resentful, bitter and introverted he became. Since the first Gulf War we have heard a lot about Post Traumatic Stress Syndrome. I think my father discovered it in 1945. I am sure he was blaming the world for his present situation. Unfortunately I was part of that world.

There was no money coming into the house. My father would stand at the gate of our three-bedroom semi staring into the road, the bull terrier at his feet growling and snarling at passers-by. My father was equally bellicose.

On two occasions the gate was 'accidentally' left open. The first time Silver returned covered in blood. The second time he killed Mrs Goodwin's white poodle.

When Mr Goodwin knocked at our front door to remonstrate, my father, as usual wearing just a scruffy pair of trousers and his old Army vest, called Silver to heel and, fixing Mr Goodwin with a look to kill, told our irate neighbour, 'Sod off or the dog will do the same to you.'

After Silver killed another dog the local policeman came round on his bicycle one morning to tell my father that a van would be coming that afternoon to take Silver away. When the van arrived Silver had mysteriously disappeared, I know not where, but, knowing my father, it was probably in a hole at the bottom of the garden.

Our poverty eventually forced him, with great reluctance, to look for work. Another cause for resentment.

One morning as Don and I were walking to school we saw a

dustbin lorry on the other side of the road and with youthful exuberance Don yelled, 'Look, it's Dad!' And there he was with a heavy dustbin on his shoulder. As we crossed the road to greet him, he saw us, turned his back on us and, as he dumped the garbage into the back of the truck, snarled, 'Fuck off.'

Was he ashamed? Did he hate us? He probably hated himself for being in that position, that's all I can think.

Looking back, the conditions we lived in were appalling. The house was constantly filled with cigarette smoke, the thick fug blackening the ceilings, because both my parents smoked incessantly, my father the acrid Capstan Full Strength and my mother her beloved Craven 'A'. Don and I shared a bed, top to tail, Don with his head at the top, of course, and our smelly feet poked under each other's nose.

The slightest disobedience from either of us would result in the belt that hung alongside Silver's being lashed across our bare buttocks or the backs of our legs, after which we would be ordered to bed.

But the strongest words and lashes were left for Derek, who had a little bedroom to himself. As I was to learn, there was something more in my father's animosity towards our big brother. Don and I had 'Archibald' as our middle name but we discovered that Derek's was 'Stanton'. When I innocently asked why, my father's response was a tremendous whack across the ear that sent me flying across the room. Enraged, he stood over me growling, 'Don't ask stupid questions.'

Needless to say, the question never came up again and I would not discover the truth for another 15 years.

We did not have cups and saucers. To save money, we drank our tea out of jam jars, usually without any milk – and certainly without sugar.

The few plates we possessed were always in peril in the constant rows that were fermenting between my parents. For both of them had affairs, and we boys were caught in the cross-fire.

One afternoon my mother dragged Don and I to the stop to wait for the number 9 bus to the centre of Oxford, which my father, having left 'the bins', was now driving.

When the bus arrived, my mother pushed in front of the rest of the queue and pulled the blonde conductress off the platform, whacking her round the head with the handbag without which she never left home.

'These are his children, you dirty whore,' she screamed, pointing at Don and I.

I stood mesmerised as the conductress yelled back, 'Whose children?'

'Don't give me that, you tart!' my mother yelled, pushing a letter into her face.

'Look, "ALL my love, Beryl"!' she screeched, giving the poor woman another clout around the ear.

'But my name's Margaret – and I only started on the buses this morning!' protested the woman, frightened now.

I'll never forget my father's face when he came round to the back of the bus to see what was causing the hold-up. He took less than two seconds to sum up the situation before wordlessly scurrying back to his cab.

The engine burst into life and I swear the double-decker almost did a 'wheelie' as it roared off, leaving the conductress sobbing on her knees, my mother, now gobsmacked, still brandishing the letter, Don and I crying our eyes out and everyone else wondering where their bus had gone.

Despite the tension that so often hung in the air, far thicker than the fug from my parents' cigarettes, there were moments of happiness. I can still recall the words of the Doris Day songs I sang with my mother as she bumped me on her knee while gazing wistfully out of the window. But those moments were fleeting. Too soon I would be brutally brought back to earth by the regular funerals in our garden as we buried litter after litter of kittens, each one individually drowned in the rain barrel by my father, who treated our cats with the same studied callousness as he did his dogs.

Yet he did have a genuine fondness for canaries and always kept one, a constant reminder of the perils he had faced down in the pits. He seldom mentioned those far-off days, but, looking back later on the things he did say then, I realised how they had moulded him into the man he had become. I remember him telling us of how, when he was lying on his side hacking at the rich anthracite seams in the baking and claustrophobic heat, he would keep an ear out for the canaries whistling. If they stopped it meant they were suffocating from noxious gases.

It was dirty, hazardous work with the constant risk of cave-ins and gas explosions. Crippling injuries were commonplace and if you escaped those there was always 'the dust', the deadly side effect of mining the hard but top-quality anthracite. The clinging black dust that so often brought the killer disease silicosis was everywhere, not just underground, entering the lungs of the miners, but also permeating the very pores of your skin and caking the villages with its toxic grime.

And for relief there was only rugby, the chapel, with its firebrand hell and brimstone preachers, or the trades and Labour clubs for recreation. You made your choice. My father soon made his. The Labour club had been his second home and it was there that he became a committed Socialist with a hatred of the 'top-hatted' mine owners and their 'lackeys' – a hatred he was later to visit upon we boys.

The full horror was brought home to me when we went by coach down to South Wales to see my uncle, Bythan Price, who was in hospital dying from silicosis. In my innocence I asked what the polished brass pot on the floor was for, putting my hand inside to feel its contents. It was my first – and last – encounter with a spittoon. My hand was covered in the disgusting green and yellow phlegm that my uncle would hack up constantly from his lungs and spit, with unerring accuracy, five feet into its heart.

As we got off the coach back in Oxford, my mother pulled me out of my father's hearing and, pushing the front-door key into my hand, said quietly, 'Run home and see if there are any letters to Harriet Mower. If there are, put them under the mat.'

I ran ahead to find there were indeed three letters to Harriet, which I dutifully hid.

My father took to staying in the pub after work, finally rolling home full of drink and ill humour at closing time. By now the atmosphere had become so poisonous that Derek, observing more and understanding more than we younger boys did, couldn't stand any more of it. He signed up to the Royal Navy under the Boy Entrants scheme. Derek was only 14, but it was his way out.

Every night I would cry myself to sleep, Don's smelly feet constantly kicking me as he told me, 'Shut up and don't be a baby!'

The incessant rowing, the accusations, the swearing, the beatings, the sight of my father regularly hitting my mother. I was a sensitive little boy and these humiliating and bewildering scenes, which had become commonplace, were taking their toll. My head seemed to be full, of what I didn't know, and would accept no more. I could hear noises – screaming, shouting – but they seemed to bounce off my head instead of sinking into my mind.

I don't know where the thought of what I was about to do came from, but I knew I could take no more. I'd been told many times by my brothers not to play with the bread knife, which my mother sharpened on the back-door step, because it was so dangerous.

It seemed so simple. It wasn't pre-planned and I hadn't got the idea from seeing something on TV as we didn't have a television. As Tom Jones sings in Delilah, 'I felt the knife in my hand…'

I know now, of course, that people who commit suicide invariably make sure that someone knows and I remember saying to Don, 'I can't take any more. I'm going to kill myself…'

I put the knife to my chest. I was going to do it.

'Don't be so stupid, you little idiot. Give that to me,' Don screamed, lunging at me.

Forcing my fingers off the handle of the knife, he seized it and, as he pulled it from my clenched grip, it sliced through my left hand.

In the struggle one of the jam jars full of tea went flying off the table.

Don, believing he had caused the horrific cut, ran to the scullery, shouting at my parents, 'Pat's cut himself…'

Seeing the scene in the front room, my father had no concern for the blood streaming from his young son's hand. It was the broken jam jar and spilled tea on the floor that put him into a fury.

My mother, seeing the blood pumping out from the cut, pulled off her cardigan and pressed it into my hand, staunching the flow.

She rushed me next door, to the home of the local midwife. With great care, but causing me tremendous pain, the midwife cleaned the wound and put on a bandage, telling my mother, 'Patrick should go to hospital.'

But, as my parents didn't have a car, I didn't go.

Instead, the bandage stayed on unchanged, getting filthier every day, until it fell to bits.

The horror of that day has never left me. Yet, amazingly, my school work didn't suffer because of everything that was going on at home and to this day I still have a glowing report from St Mary and St John's Infants School. It lists the eight subjects we were taught and for seven of them the assessment was 'Excellent'. The only one that let me down was Religious Instruction, against which the teacher's terse comment was 'Must pay more attention.'

So, apart from letting my mind wander to less godly but far more interesting subjects as I gazed out of the window in RI classes, I was the perfect pupil.

And, although by any standards life in our home was appalling, being a mere nine years old I thought it was normal. I hated it and was intimidated by the rows and beatings that continued unabated, but I didn't feel hard done by. I thought all parents drank heavily and were brutally strict. I thought everyone was unhappy.

But, as the days passed, I became more self-sufficient. To escape the atmosphere at home, I spent more and more time in the street with the rest of our gang. One of our favourite pastimes was trawling through the gutters looking for 'dog ends' – usually half-smoked American cigarettes that the troops had given to local girls in return for feminine favours.

Smoking was so commonplace that I don't remember a single boy of our age in the neighbourhood who didn't puff on a cigarette. It was what you did. Mind you, I don't think I ever smoked a full cigarette – just those dog ends, which we would light up and drag on with a manly swagger as we hung around the street corners. It made us feel grown up and tough – a complete contrast to my life at home.

Around that time I discovered St Mary and St John's Boys' Club. I'd had enough of just hanging around street corners smoking and when I heard about the club, which was only half a mile away, I persuaded four of the other boys to join me in checking it out.

It was well worth the visit. We found they had table tennis, and upstairs, above the main hall, they even had indoor football. This was exciting stuff to boys bored rigid and longing for something different. It was run by the austere Cowley Fathers, a very strict High Church of England sect who dressed in long black robes and had shaven heads. The look might have street cred nowadays but back then it seemed very unusual.

One of the club rules was that you had to attend the church on Sunday morning. This was a completely new world to us, but the following Sunday we duly turned up at the church. The other four boys lasted half a service before running out giggling. I stuck it out and began attending both the club and the church every week.

Then, when I was 11, two things happened that were to change my life. The first came as a bolt from the blue. I returned from school one day to be greeted by my mother, looking downcast and holding a letter from the Education Authority.

'I don't think your father is going to be too pleased,' she said anxiously. She was right.

My father, who was now working at the Morris Motors factory in Cowley as a storeman, was furious when he read the letter, which informed him that I had passed the Eleven-Plus examination and therefore could go to the local grammar school. Scrunching the letter up and throwing it into the grate, he shouted, 'I knew you were a bloody snob. You'll go to the same school as your brothers.'

Other boys who had passed this magical examination, with

the opportunities it offered, were rewarded with a bicycle or new football boots, and one was even taken on holiday to Brighton. They were made to feel special about their achievement. But in our house I was made to feel that I had done something wrong. They were greeted with enthusiasm; I was treated with disdain. Instead of a cause for celebration it was a cause for more misery.

I hadn't even realised that I had sat the exam, let alone knew what type of school was now open to me. But I soon learned the reason for my father's displeasure: it would entail buying me a school uniform. Despite the opposition of my father and brother Don, who was attending the local secondary modern school, when I understood the opportunity I was being offered I was determined to seize it.

Fortunately, my mother felt the same. She acquired second-hand a Southfield Grammar School blazer – several sizes too big – and a tie from a family who lived down the road, and somehow scraped together the money to buy me a cap. Luckily I had a pair of short grey trousers, although they were going to prove not so lucky.

For my first day at Southfield Grammar I had nervously arranged to meet up with another new boy, Colin Gammon. As we walked up the hill towards the school, which loomed intimidatingly before us, my observant little brain noticed that mine were the only thin white legs on view. Long trousers, I was to learn, were worn for the winter term.

We were placed in Mr Cross's form, 1C, and were seated alphabetically. Each boy had to stand up in turn for the register and give his Christian and middle names.

'Mower!' our form teacher's voice rasped.

With trepidation I slowly rose.

'Christian name?'

'Patrick.'

'Any other names?'

'Archie,' I whispered.

'Speak up, Mower. What did you say?'

'Archie,' I repeated.

A few titters ran around the classroom.

Mr Cross sat up. 'Archie or Archibald?'

'Archibald,' I heard my voice say.

More laughter.

'Archibold or Archibald?'

I took a deep breath. '*Archibald*,' I courageously informed him.

He allowed the class a full minute's laughter before slapping a ruler down on his desk for silence.

For the rest of my days at Southfield Grammar School, and even to this day in Oxford, I am still fondly called Archie or Arch Mower. And in the photographs of me in school teams I am described as 'A. Mower'.

The second event of huge significance started with my discovery that the youth club was entering a play in a local drama festival.

Roy Copeman, who was to become a very good friend, was to direct this play and he asked me if I could do an American accent. Whether it is because I have a very good ear for accents or I had picked it up from hearing my mother's many GI admirers, we discovered that I could, and Roy cast me.

'Silas B Fortescue of the Baltimore Small Arms Company,' were the first words I ever spoke on stage, and I was hooked immediately. I found being someone else seemed to be the answer.

For two never-to-be-forgotten weeks, I was Silas B. Fortescue and the unhappiness that had constantly pervaded my soul disappeared. It was as though someone had switched on a light in my head.

'Acting,' it has famously been said, 'is the art of putting ourselves in a parallel universe.' At the tender age of 11, I discovered that I could do precisely that. I had found my escape.

The youth club performed three one-act plays a year and I was in all of them. It was my own special heaven.

By the time I was 15 I was in four different drama groups in Oxford, riding between performances and rehearsals at breakneck speed on the bicycle I had finally acquired.

But that was still in the future.

4

Love-struck

O N ONLY MY second day at Southfield Grammar School,
I discovered another humiliating fact of life. The third
lesson of the day was gym and, being athletic, I was fairly
confident as I walked along to the changing room with my
white shorts and plimsolls. I had taken off my trousers and was
stepping into my shorts when one of the other boys called out,
'Mower – you forgot to put your pants on.'

'What do you mean?'

'Your underpants.'

'What are they?' I was genuinely bemused.

Again laughter at me filled the room.

I didn't know that men and boys wore pants under their
trousers, but I had enough sense not to let the others know. And
happily they thought my innocence was feigned and I was
simply being humorous. But I swore to myself that it would
never happen again. Before the next gym class, I used the money
I earned from the paper round I did before school each day to

buy a pair of pants. But even that severely stretched my resources as the few shillings I got from the local newsagent each week had to be shared with my father.

My skinny legs, sadly, had to withstand the icy blasts of November and December before they were finally cosseted by a pair of long trousers. Fortunately, by the time they covered my legs I had grown enough to fit the blazer.

At the same time my school days and early acting adventures were all happiness. I enjoyed school. I devoured Latin and French – maybe I was once again escaping into foreign worlds.

I discovered the wonder of William Shakespeare's words and, while my classmates hated English literature, I couldn't wait to engage with Shakespeare and Wordsworth and Keats and Tennyson – each one transporting me with his own individual magic.

Even Don caught the reading bug when our mother put her treasured copy of *Forever Amber* up in the top cupboard, warning us, 'You boys must *not* read this.' That was just too tempting, and whenever she went out we found the book and eventually read all 600 pages twice, but, disappointingly, we never found anything in it we thought the least bit naughty.

Like my brother Derek, I discovered that the safest route to take – although not as drastic as his escape to sea – was to spend as little time as possible at home and became involved with every activity on offer at school. I was a very keen sportsman and eventually played basketball, cricket and rugby for Southfield. I was also in a bicycle speedway team called the Bats and can still recall painting bright-yellow bats on our speedway coveralls.

And with the youth club I really did escape. On one occasion we camped at St Ives on the north Cornish coast, high on a hill overlooking the most spectacular bay I had ever seen. Not that we saw anything of it when we first arrived. We spent the first couple of days peering into a thick mist that blotted out everything beyond a few yards, lost in a grey world in which Ken, the youth-club leader, and the Cowley Fathers desperately tried to keep us amused singing roundelays around a roaring camp fire.

Relief came on the third morning when Gordon Russell and a boy named Tim were sent down to the nearby farm to fetch a bucket of milk. As they disappeared into the fog we could hear the clunk, clunk, clunk of the bucket swaying between them. No sooner was the noise out of earshot than a jubilant voice could be heard. The two boys were racing back up the hill, shouting excitedly, 'Hey, it's sunny down here.' And it was.

We had pitched our tents on the top of a hill which, the locals later assured us, was more or less permanently covered in sea mist. If the boys hadn't gone for the milk we could have spent the week getting ever more miserable in our cocoon of fog. As it was, we spent the rest of the week in glorious sunshine on Porthminster Beach, a memory I still treasure.

It was while camping in Jersey the following year that I discovered a quality I had that, I am happy to say, is still with me. Girls found me rather attractive. Whether it is pheromones, long legs or long hair, I have something they like, and so, at the ripe old age of 13, my interest in Latin ladies was first kindled. And I had a very interesting French lesson.

We were playing football on the beach when a tall, golden-tanned girl with dark, curly hair strolled towards us. She was wearing a bright-red swimming costume and, even at the tender age of 13, she filled it remarkably well. At the end of the game some of the older boys were soon chatting to the dark-haired beauty and her friends while I held back, waiting with the football.

Eventually, the girl in the red costume left the crowd and slowly walked towards me. 'Are you on holiday?' she asked.

'Yes,' I replied.

'So am I,' she said. 'I am from France, and my name is Yvette, but I go home tomorrow,' she continued without a trace of an accent. We chatted for hardly a minute, then she told me that she had to go back for her tea, but asked, as it was her last night, if I would like to meet her later.

'Yes,' I gulped. 'Where?'

'There.' She smiled and pointed at a German anti-aircraft bunker overlooking the bay.

In the tent later I splashed Old Spice on my face.

'You'd better take my johnny,' laughed Gordon Russell as I combed my hair in the mirror hanging from the tent pole.

'Have you got one?' I said nervously.

'Yes. Look, it's unused,' he proudly proclaimed, producing a tatty square envelope with the word 'Durex' printed prominently above the words, 'Warning. Do not perforate.'

The evening was a great success for me, although I fear not for Yvette.

After daring to hold hands in the fading sunlight as we looked at the twinkling sea, I became aware that Yvette was determined to make the last night of her stay memorable. She told me that she was a virgin but, pressing her thigh against me, added that she didn't want to remain one any longer.

As I led her into the bunker my knees were knocking. It was not the sweetest-smelling place to take the first steps of a misspent youth, but it was dark enough to conceal my inexperienced fumblings.

That evening I encountered my first brassiere. After much kissing and hugging I dared to move my hand from her back towards her front. This obviously triggered something in

A rare picture of the Mower men. My Dad, me, Don and Derek. With my beloved mother in the back garden at Ridgefield Road. Mum and Dad enjoying a joke together, with dad smoking one of his ever-present Capstan Full-Strength cigarettes. Me with my first car, aged 17. Me as Elvis singing 'Blue Suede Shoes' with my band, The OXO's, and an early photo of my mother, a real beauty.

Above: On stage in my pink tights, aged fourteen. It was when playing Claudius in *Much Ado About Nothing* at All Souls College, Oxford, that I realised acting was my destiny.

Below: The baby-faced youth who plucked up the courage to ask Audrey to dance. Here I am in another early amateur production.

Early days. Audrey and I starred in *The Corn is Green* in Oxford at the tender age of fifteen (*top left*), but before long I'd left the dreaming spires for the rooftops of London – here I am at twenty atop RADA (*top right*). Straight out of RADA I landed a part in the ill-fated musical *House of Cards* (*bottom left*). I'm pictured here with Stella Moray. Dedicated to the stage, I turned down many TV offers for the privilege of playing Mortimer the Younger in *Edward II* at the Birmingham Rep, the place to be in those days (*bottom right*).

Young love.
Audrey, the beauty I doffed my cap at every day until she spoke to me! We were happily married, and soon with two beautiful children, Simon and Claudia.

This Sporting life. Sport had always been a grand passion, and fame has given me the opportunity to meet some of the greats. I'm pictured here with Geoffrey Boycott (*top right*) and (*below, from left to right in the foreground*) Brian Rix, Don Wilson, Colin Milburn and Bill Edrich.

Above: Creating drama on the cricket pitch with the *Emmerdale* team.

Below: Partnering up to play tennis with Trevor MacDonald in La Manga, Spain.

Golf is one of my true loves. I've worked for years on my swing and even when the weather's grim on the green you'll find me singing in the rain! In 2000 I took part in the Sir John Mills Celebrity Golf Classic, and am pictured here (*bottom left*) with Sir John and Dennis Waterman. My son Maxim helped me stay on par too (*bottom right*)!

Above: : In 1966, I played at White City in front of 10,000 against Jack Charlton, Bobby Moore and George Cohen (*all pictured*) and the rest of World Cup-winners' team. The TV showbiz team included the likes of Dennis Waterman, Robert Lindsay and Richard O'Sullivan.

Below: Winners! After nutmegging Bobby Charlton, I lift Britt Eckland and the cup at the Empire Pool, Wembley, with Brendan Price and pop star Eddie Grant.

Yvette's plan. She promptly grabbed my hand, lifted her jumper and replaced my hand on her left breast, which was protected by a strong pre-war bra. As I attempted to put my hand inside the cup, she murmured, 'Un moment' and reached behind her back to unhook it.

My hand slid up under the now loosened bra, desperate to caress my first breast. But, instead of the firm rise of a silky mound I had so often encountered in my dreams, I felt a handful of cotton wool. Yvette was not such a big girl as she appeared to be.

By this time I was very excited – and so was a particular part of my body.

With even more daring and a lot of kissing, I undid the zip on the side of Yvette's skirt and, with her guiding my hand, slid it down the front of her knickers.

She was moaning and writhing, her tongue in my ear, hoping she would achieve her desire and go home a sophisticated woman.

It was at this point that, just as Dr Kinsey had helpfully told the world, I discovered the G spot. I touched something with my finger that caused an explosion in Yvette and an eruption from Patrick.

We were both shocked. We gazed into each other's eyes amazed. Little did we know that we had achieved something many married couples go through their whole lives never attaining – simultaneous orgasm.

As I walked back to the camp, with a broad grin on my face, I was tempted to throw Gordon's present into the sea and pretend to him that I had done the dirty deed. But I suppose it was a sign of my growing up that I owned up that I hadn't used it. I handed it back to Gordon, who carefully inspected it to make sure I was telling the truth.

At the youth club, my skill as an actor improved with every new play we performed and I was soon winning Best Actor awards at amateur drama festivals. I even went on a drama course with Gordon Russell at Chepstow, in Monmouthshire. Gordon was also a good actor and we had done, to critical acclaim, a two-hander of *Death on the Line*, an adaptation by Eric Jones-Evans of Dickens's short story *The Signalman*. I still have a cutting of the review in the *Oxford Times*, which appeared under the headline 'Fine acting by Patrick Mower'.

But my success cut no ice with my father. He never once came to see me on stage and showed not the slightest interest in my work. My mother, God bless her, saw every performance.

In fact, my father loathed everything to do with the theatre and my school. One day when I was tidying my hair in the mirror he came up behind me and growled to my mother, 'Look at him, the bloody ponce. No arse on him.'

Every day was like that and the bullying was constant. The physical beatings had mercifully stopped. Judy, a bulldog, the latest in a long line of dogs that my father brought home, now bore the brunt of his boot and belt.

Yet there was always the threat of the belt and on another occasion when I was setting off for the drama club he exploded, 'That's where you belong – with all those bloody queens.'

He made it clear that he was desperately disappointed in the way I was turning out. I didn't smoke any more, I didn't swear. I played rugby union and, although that had been the great sporting god of his youth in the Valleys, perversely he wanted me to play football like all the boys at the secondary modern schools. He also felt that I should still want to hang around the street corners looking for mischief – and drink, despite the fact that I was far too young to go to a pub legally. In his eyes, real men boozed. Only sissies and poofs didn't.

I'll never forget the disgust in his eyes as he peered at me: a look cuts deeper than a welt.

I was doing well at school and, to my surprise, found that I was popular. In my second year I was elected Form Captain, a position I was to continue to hold for the rest of my years at Southfield. As a very fast sprinter, I was made captain of my house's athletics team, and I was also in the house cross-country team after making the mistake of turning in too good a performance on one crucial occasion. The cross-country runs were obligatory for everyone, and I was usually to be found dawdling with the ne'er-do-wells, having a puff on a cigarette. But one day in my third year I was jogging along on my own when I came to the entrance to the rugby pitch.

'Come on, Mower, you can do it,' shouted the geography master, who was checking the boys through the gate.

'Do what, sir?' I called back.

'You're third,' he shouted encouragingly.

Looking up, I saw a boy toiling across the pitch 200 yards away, heading towards the running track and the finishing line. I accelerated and easily overtook him, leaving only the sports master's son ahead of me. I tried to catch him and, if I had realised earlier how close I was to the leaders, I could have won easily, but I had left my effort too late.

My reward was to spend many an afternoon in purgatory representing Southfield Grammar against distant teams like Burford High School. That's when I learned all about the loneliness of the long-distance runner plodding round the rain-splattered streets of Burford or dragging my weary limbs round Magdalen College playing fields with not a soul to cheer me on. How I often wished I had stayed behind smoking those fags.

I also made my mark at cricket, which continues to be one of my great passions. It was while I was a member of the school's

First XI that Danny Plymm, the sports master, took me on one side to tell me, 'I want you to do me a favour and step down from the First XI to captain the Second XI.'

Obviously it wasn't as prestigious, but I agreed and we had a fantastic season, winning all our matches. Sadly, however, just like the cross-country races, no one bothered to watch us.

My brief encounter in the bunker on the beach had awoken all the correct desires and longings, which were bursting forth not only in my loins but also over my 14-year-old face. Thank God for Clearasil.

To reach my school I had to cross over the Cowley Road. Each morning, at exactly four minutes to nine, I had noticed a very beautiful, black-haired girl, pedalling her bicycle furiously as she swept past me on her way to Milham Ford School, the local girls' grammar. With her long dark hair flowing from beneath her boater, she took my breath away.

I was so enchanted that I took to hiding behind a fence until this apparition rode towards me. I would then step to the kerb and just happen to be waiting to cross the road as she passed. I would doff my cap to her, which made her laugh. I became besotted with this girl.

I discovered that she was called Audrey Giles, was in the fifth form at Milham Ford and lived over her father's shop, the Corner Stores, two miles away. She was more than a year older than me, but my obsession was so great that I was prepared to be late for my own classes in order to catch that fleeting smile.

As any 14-year-old boy will remember, a girl of 15 or 16 is way out of reach. But Eros had lodged an arrow deep in my heart. Now I had to find a way into hers.

Audrey, I discovered, was taking ballroom-dancing lessons in the centre of Oxford. This was my chance. Freshly scrubbed and shaved – although the fluff on my chin could have been blown off – and wearing a thin tie of the kind worn by the American singer Guy Mitchell, a heartthrob of the day, I enrolled at the dancing school.

Although my musical taste at the time was more for Johnny Ray and Frankie Laine, I soon found myself treading on the toes of many very unfortunate maidens as we attempted to quickstep to Glen Miller and Ted Heath.

It took me four weeks to pluck up the courage to ask Audrey to dance. Over those previous weeks I had become painfully aware that she didn't recognise this schoolboy without his cap.

She was always surrounded by older, bigger, taller, better-dressed and even more handsome boys than me. So, not surprisingly, the answer to my request was, 'Sorry, no.'

Another four weeks went by before I asked again. But by now I was at least on nodding acquaintance with her, no doubt helped each morning by raising my cap as she rode by and calling out, 'May I have this dance, please?' She just laughed, but at least she recognised me.

My spots were also better and so, thankfully, was my quickstep.

Finally, I decided to seize the moment one more.

The dance ended and the couples left the floor. Audrey, looking radiant in an emerald-green dress and white high heels, sat back among her friends.

Two very deep breaths and I strode purposefully across the floor to her.

'May I have this dance?' I asked politely.

She smiled. 'Yes, of course,' came the reply.

As we stood there, Glen Miller's 'In The Mood' broke out from the loudspeakers and Audrey asked, 'Do you jive?'

I looked blank.

Jive! I thought. I've only just learned to quickstep.

She took my hand and spun on to the floor, her skirt floating out around her.

I had dreamed of this moment. I had rehearsed it in my mind. I wanted to hold her, embrace her... I wanted her close... I wanted to talk to her... Instead, she was looping my arm over her head and spinning away from me. I pretended I knew what I was doing, but I felt clumsy and could find no rhythm. I attempted to make conversation, but the music was so loud she couldn't hear me.

All too soon the number ended. She thanked me and returned to her seat. I sleepwalked to my side of the room. What a disaster.

But they say forbidden fruit tastes sweeter.

To get to Brett's Dance Academy I always took the number 9 bus. I knew Audrey would have to catch the same bus around the same time as me. Brett's opened at 8pm on a Tuesday, so for weeks on every Tuesday I waited for each number 9 between 5.30 and 8.30pm.

But no Audrey!

The mystery was solved one evening as I entered Brett's and a tantalisingly familiar voice said, 'Hello.'

I looked around and Audrey was leaning her bike outside the side wall of the academy. She used to cycle there.

It wasn't just my emotions that were dancing romantically; my feelings were doing the quickstep too.

My life was changing.

Going to church ceased to be a penance I had to endure in order to remain a member of the youth club. One man in particular had a major influence in the way my life was taking shape: Father Joe Hemming. He was an impressive sight. Very tall, with grey hair sprouting an inch and a half out of his ears, he had a handsome, rugged face beneath his shaven skull. I never saw him dressed in anything except the black cassock he wore to take the services. He was a very good man who taught me the difference between right and wrong, and not only did I look up to him then, but, in retrospect, I realise he was the father figure I had yearned for.

St John's was very high Anglican, almost Catholic, and the air was thick with incense. Sitting at the back of that beautiful church half listening to the chorales and descants, I learned the power of contemplation as I started to get my life in order, asking God to make my father, whom I really disliked, better towards us, especially my mother. I used God as a personal psychiatrist and I suppose in a way it helped.

I used to say my prayers regularly and still do. I think we all do in times of crisis. I'm sure God listened to me years later, when I was living in London, when the wife of my best friend, Michael Latimer, had a brain haemorrhage and, as I slipped into the local church to pray for her, I ran into Roger Bannister, who was a regular worshipper there. I again sought divine help when the photographer John Paul's girlfriend, Angie, developed breast cancer.

With Audrey, however, I realised I was going to need more than prayers if I was going to make my dream real. I forced the fickle finger of fate to point at the two of us.

Two weeks later as Audrey was leaving she found that her front tyre was flat – and her pump had been stolen.

It was five miles to her home, but, luckily for Audrey, a knight in shining armour appeared and I heard myself offering to walk her home. As I pushed her bike down Longwall, past All Souls College into the High and over Magdalen Bridge, I swear the nightingales had left Berkeley Square that night.

We just chatted but my dream had come true.

As I wheeled her bike along on that fateful night, we talked about many things, but I was soon to learn that looking younger than your age – and I always have – is not a great help when you are a teenager. Even though I had shot up to five feet ten, that night I looked about 12. Not a great help in the romance stakes, although to this day I don't know my real age. My mother just plucked a number from the air. Many years later, while trying to get a passport, I found that my birth had not been registered, so I rang her from Somerset House panicking that I didn't officially exist, and asked her which year I was born.

'Oh, I don't know, Patrick,' she said testily. 'Let me speak to the man.'

I watched the Registrar's eyebrows rise higher and higher as he listened to my mother. I never discovered what she told him but whatever it was it worked.

The year 1938 was chosen.

When I told Audrey my age she didn't say very much except, 'That young?' I didn't realise the significance of that phrase initially. I soon did.

I had already discovered that my baby-faced looks were quite appealing and at the dancing school I was no wallflower. When I politely asked young ladies for a dance, I was never refused, and you soon realise when someone likes you. So, although Audrey had seemed unattainable, I had remained quietly confident of winning her over.

Having reached her home, I politely wished her goodnight. As a gentleman – and, I trust, I still am – I made no attempt to kiss her – it was more serious than that. I didn't even ask her for a date. I was on my very best behaviour, acting as though it really was an 'accident' that I had been on hand to walk her home. I simply said I would see her at Brett's the following week.

I then walked home with a spring in my step and love in my heart and knew that this was the girl I was going to marry.

By the way, I still have that bicycle pump.

The next day at school I confided in my lantern-jawed best friend Dickie Dunford that I had 'broken the ice' with the boated bicycling beauty. I told him I had walked her the whole five miles home and had told her my age.

His response was far from reassuring. 'You've no chance there, Arch. She's too old for you.'

That was what he thought. And so it turned out did Audrey.

At Brett's the following Tuesday, having liberally doused my newly shaved baby fluff in the latest aftershave, Aqua da Silva, I stood reeking in the doorway, waiting for Audrey to park her bike.

As she arrived, I nipped back inside and then 'by chance' came to the door as she walked up the steps.

'Oh, hello, Audrey,' I said, using my well-honed acting skills to feign surprise.

She said, 'Hello ... uhhh.'

To save her embarrassment I quickly added, 'Patrick.'

'I'm sorry. I was out of breath. I'm a bit late.'

My ego had a slight puncture.

It was soon to became a full blow-out when I made my first request, 'May I have the pleasure of this dance?'

'Sorry, no...' she replied.

She refused me twice more that night.

It took my pathetic love-struck brain three weeks of refusals to get the message that Audrey simply didn't want to know.

It must have been obvious to her, from the baleful look on my face as I sat across the ballroom floor looking at her like an untrained puppy waiting for a titbit, that I was smitten.

I persuaded Dickie to ask one of Audrey's friends, Jean, if I stood a chance with her. He came back and said, 'I told you so, Arch, she thinks you are far too young.'

At 14 this was indeed a major blow, but I was in love and I persevered.

The following week I boldly crossed the ballroom floor and said, 'I may be too young to go out with you, but does that mean I can't ask you to dance?'

'No, of course not,' she said.

'Well, may I have the pleasure?'

And to my joy she said, 'Yes.'

Luckily this time it was a waltz, 'I'm In The Mood For Love', and, although I was tongue-tied with my partner, I found myself singing along with Ella Fitzgerald.

'How do you know the words?' asked Audrey.

'My mother taught them to me,' I replied with an inner smile, sensing that perhaps Audrey might warm to me after all.

Being a very beautiful girl, Audrey was not lacking in dance partners or admirers and one tall 17-year-old lad seemed to be constantly around. The swine was also a brilliant dancer. Taking an instant dislike to this handsome rival, I resolved that he wouldn't thwart my scheme to woo Audrey.

I knew I had to be very cunning if my plans as regards Audrey were to work. I limited myself to two dances a session at Brett's. I no longer watched her with baleful eyes. Instead, I laughed and flirted and danced with many a lovely girl.

On my occasional dances with Audrey – when I always made sure that the position of my hand on her waist was never anything less than strictly ballroom – I revealed my keen interest in amateur dramatics, from which I was getting nearly as much excitement and pleasure as I got every morning from doffing my cap to her, except by now it was, 'Good morning, Audrey,' and, to her peels of laughter, 'Morning, Patrick.'

She had also realised that my crossing the road in front of her at exactly the right moment every day was stretching coincidence to breaking point. Challenged, I boldly owned up, 'I hide behind the fence waiting for you.' That tickled her fancy and I felt there still was a glimmer of hope. So, having confessed my ruse, I continued with it, but we now shared the joke every morning.

The next major step in my campaign began when, with my newspaper-round earnings, I finally bought a second-hand bike. My intention, of course, was to be able to 'accidentally' accompany Audrey as she rode along to my beloved Brett's.

But James, my dashing dancing rival quickstepped in front of me. I saw this beautiful, brand-new, multi-speed, red Raleigh racing cycle leaned, entwined with Audrey's, against the passage wall outside Brett's. It had drop handlebars. The bastard!

I parked my rusting sit-up-and-beg bike deep in the shadows and left early. I was so fed up that, to Dickie's annoyance, I insisted on cycling the long way home down Longwall to avoid seeing Audrey and my rival. A few months later, I must admit, I had almost given up hope. I'd even stopped bothering to ask Audrey to dance. My courage had deserted me. I could act nonchalantly no more. My heart was raw on my sleeve.

But a tin-tack was to come to my rescue.

Dickie deserted me on Magdalen Bridge saying, as he rode off, 'Hard luck, Arch. See you in school tomorrow.'

I looked down at my flat tyre and, bending over, pulled out the offending sliver of metal. I wheeled the bike on to the pavement and looked down into the Isis flowing gently beneath me. This is the famous bridge from which, on May Day morning, undergraduates leap, champagne bottles clutched in their fists, hopefully missing their college chums cheering in their punts below.

I threw the tin-tack as far out into the river as I could. I saw a tiny splash and started singing, in my best Johnnie Ray falsetto, 'If your sweetheart sends a letter of goodbye it's no secret if you sit right down and cry...'

Just then a voice called out, 'Don't do it!'

I turned round to see Audrey.

'It's all right, I'm not going to jump,' I said.

'No, don't sing – it's awful!'

We both laughed.

'You don't normally go this way,' I said.

'No, I'm trying to hide from James.'

My heart skipped a beat.

I couldn't believe my luck. In one fell swoop the subject of my envy was dismissed and the object of my desire before me.

I felt like diving in after that tin-tack.

Audrey walked home with me. She could have ridden off but she didn't. She walked with me. That gesture told me more than any words.

After that I started waiting with my bike at the end of the road where my school was, so that I could cycle with Audrey on her way home from school to her father's shop. We would then stand with our bikes and talk about anything and everything.

5

The Fuse is Lit

IT WAS MY success in one of the amateur theatrical
productions that was to eventually lead me into a life in the
theatre. FW Dibb, in the *Oxford Times*, said of my performance in
a Chekhov play, 'Patrick Mower plays Flauvert with the delicacy of
a pastry cook...' Today the review would probably say, 'Patrick
Mower was very camp,' but by good fortune one of the judges at
the drama festival was the highly influential Daphne Levens, one
of the main directors of the Oxford University Dramatic Society.
She liked my style and wrote a very complimentary letter to Roy
Copeman, my director at the youth theatre.

She asked Roy if I would audition for Claudio in an open-air
production of Shakespeare's *Much Ado About Nothing* that she
was directing. Shakespeare! Roy gave me the play to read and
to my unsophisticated brain it might as well have been in
Chinese. I was completely unprepared for this plunge into
literary genius. But there was something about it that made me
tremble. Shakespeare still does.

Luckily, Audrey, being a year ahead of me at school, was already doing Shakespeare for her English literature O-level, and she readily came to my assistance. With her help I began to understand the beauty of the writing.

The auditions were held in the most beautiful house I had ever been in. Large Georgian windows overlooked magnificent manicured lawns. Cream carpets complemented deep white sofas and the rich bold colours of huge oil paintings warmed the rooms – all a million miles from my own semi in Ridgefield Road – and I got the part as Daphne wanted her Claudio to be 14, the same age as Shakespeare's character. But the rest of the cast were undergraduates, graduates and professors from various colleges in the university, highly articulate and intelligent. It was a huge leap for me to act at this level.

At the first rehearsal Daphne introduced me to the rest of the cast with the bold announcement that I was one of the finest young actors she had seen. This gave me supreme confidence and I was accepted as an equal. Once again I found myself transported to an imaginary place where I really felt at home – only this time Audrey was starting to share the journey with me.

She helped me to read my lines and we both discovered the iambic pentameter (what joy!) with its five pairs of syllables, one short, or unstressed, followed by one long, or stressed – the bedrock of so much wonderful verse and dramatic writing. There are a few actors at the RSC who are yet to discover this pleasure! Audrey was the first human to see my long, athletic legs in tights, and pale-pink ones at that. Luckily, as a rugby player, I already had a jockstrap. No padding required!

Much Ado was performed in the open air at All Souls College, fortunately then unpolluted by aircraft noise.

By this time I had been introduced to Audrey's parents and we were starting to be a serious couple, seeing each other almost every night. Audrey had gone against the advice of many of her friends but, as we discovered, the age difference was irrelevant and soon forgotten – except when I had to lower my voice as she sneaked me into an X-rated movie.

Audrey shared my excitement and the success of the show, but she didn't enjoy my first stage kiss as much as I did: the 18-year-old girl playing Hero insisted on sticking her tongue down my throat.

My awareness that I was not unattractive to the opposite sex sometimes had embarrassing consequences as when the family got together at Christmas 1954.

Big Derek, who was home on leave, had a voluptuous girlfriend called Greeta, whose claim to fame was that she walked the greyhounds around the dog track in Oxford, beaming happily to the punters. Brother Don also had an attractive girlfriend, called Sue. The girls, along with Audrey, all came round for tea, but, when Audrey left to go home to her parents, Greeta and Sue turned their attentions on me. As they had both been imbibing Derek's navy-issue rum a little too enthusiastically they followed Hero's lead as they searched for my tonsils while proffering mistletoe drunkenly above my head.

I can still hear my father dismissively snort, 'Look at that tart,' as Greeta wrapped me tightly in her arms. Both girls were older and far more worldly-wise than me, so I found it totally overwhelming and, wanting only my Audrey, struggled to break free. I'm sure my reluctance served only to prove to my father that his suspicions were correct, because he growled to my mother, 'You see, I told you he was a queer.'

On one occasion at Brett's, Audrey's friend Jean came up to me and asked if I would walk her home because the battery on one of her bike lights had failed. But, instead of going straight down the High, she guided us down an alley where you had to squeeze together rather tight. As we walked through the passage chatting away she pressed herself against me and put her arm round my waist. There's a green light going on here, I thought. I was in love with Audrey, but I have often wondered whether Jean was trying to pull me, or whether she had been sent by Audrey to test if I was being the faithful boy I said I was.

I was still enjoying school, especially English literature, in which I studied *Romeo and Juliet* for my O-levels. History was not my strong subject but by good fortune I'd studied five topics well enough and questions on all of them came up. My other passes included French and maths and I was keen to stay on to do A-levels and eventually go to university. My father had other ideas.

Apart from sleeping there, I was spending very little time at home. I was either at the youth club doing drama productions, playing basketball or with Audrey. We used to sit holding hands and talking about our future together. And then there was my other ambition: to become an actor, which was strengthened after the graduate who played Benedict in *Much Ado* told me he thought I had a real future in the theatre. I discovered there was a place called the Royal Academy of Dramatic Art, and urged on by Audrey – who was the only other person who knew my plan – I applied for an audition. Unfortunately at 15, I was too young, but the fuse had been lit.

I think it was because of the unhappy childhood from which I was trying to escape that I was always seeking to better myself – and I feel I still do. By now, my mother seemed to have become a nicer person, possibly because I no longer associated her with my father and their betrayal and indifference. I forgive them now because I realise that they didn't know any better, although that is not really any excuse.

But my father was still very much a figure of authority in the house and, after many arguments, a lot of shouting and recrimination, he told me I could forget any fancy ideas of staying at school, let alone going on to university. He said he had kept me for long enough and it was high time I went out to work and brought some money into the home.

In those days there was no argument – and that was what I did.

With my qualifications and, I suppose, my artistic bent, I was given an apprenticeship as a mechanical engineering draughtsman at the dreaded and monolithic Pressed Steel Company in Cowley. A lot of people would say I was very lucky, but I didn't feel it. Abandon hope all ye who enter here.

And so began the daily bike ride past Audrey's parents' corner stores and up the hill to the huge factory, where the hooter beckoned you in and the hooter turned you out. In between, the ants made cars.

The apprenticeship was scheduled to last five years, with six months spent in each of the various departments of car construction. There was the pattern shop, where wooden shapes were created to form car panels. The paint shop. The machine shop. The jig and die shop, where you lay on your back grinding away surplus metal under a massive 50-ton cast-iron press with only a two-foot-high cylindrical jack stopping it from crushing you. It was very dangerous work – two men lost arms in the six months I was in that department. And, of course, the drawing office, where we were allocated our drawing boards. The cartridge paper that lay on mine was covered in two words: 'AUDREY MOWER'.

I had been at Pressed Steel a year when, one night after basketball practice with my old boys' team, the New John's, I was almost at my front door when I was startled by a huge commotion on the other side of our street. Seven or eight neighbours, each clutching some sort of makeshift weapon – planks of wood, brooms, even a golf club – were shouting as they prodded a large bush in the garden of a pretty woman called Molly.

For weeks, the street had been alive with rumours that a peeping Tom was lurking in the neighbourhood and that night they had set a trap. Molly had pretended to take a bath with the curtains open and, as the peeping Tom had sidled up for a look, the trap had been sprung and he was caught in the bush.

Suddenly, with a mighty roar, the man leaped out and, taking advantage of the vigilantes' surprise, slipped past them and raced off down the street. Their shouts of surprise turning to anger, they tore after him, waving their weapons in the air. I joined in. The peeping Tom kept up a furious pace and one by one his pursuers dropped out of the chase. As we sped along, winding through street after street, I suddenly realised that I, as a fit young man, was the only one still in pursuit. What was worse, I was gaining on him.

When I was about ten yards from him, he looked back over his shoulder and I saw his face clearly. I knew him. He was a tough nut, who worked on one of the milling machines at Pressed Steel and had a brother.

The thought flashed through my brain, What on earth am I doing? I can catch him but what then? Cowardice or common sense slowed my pace and I allowed the distance between us to lengthen. I watched him disappear into the darkness.

Six months of my apprenticeship had to be spent in the very machine shop where he and his brother worked. They were identical twins but the threatening eyes that followed me every day in the first two weeks betrayed their owner.

And then, one day, just after the hooter had blown for lunch, he came over to me. Grabbing the lapels of my overalls, he pushed me back, forcing my head dangerously close to the still spinning blades of a milling machine.

'One word and you're a dead man,' he spat. 'You saw nothing.'

It was like being in an old black-and-white movie. Threats like that worked for Edward G Robinson – and they certainly worked for him.

I had now grown up so fast that I was prepared to take on a major responsibility at the youth club in a bid to save it from folding. A bad bunch had invaded the place. Led by a boy I'll simply call Ricky Edwards, a hulking brute with tight, curly black hair, who, like me, had a Welsh father, the five-strong gang were deliberately obstructive, negative and sometimes destructive, breaking chairs and windows. This proved too much for Ken, the club leader. He decided he could take no more and the club closed.

Father Hemming was determined to keep the club going and appealed to me to reopen it, convincing me that I commanded enough respect from the majority of members to become leader. I have found throughout my life that I am pretty good in an emergency. I was the chap who leaped forward at a Paddington Station coffee bar to extract a poor woman's tongue from the back of her throat while she lay, her arms and legs twitching, heaving in an epileptic fit, as 50 or so travellers backed away, still sipping their beverages. Their reluctance to get involved was justified. For the following eight days as I went to catch my train, the woman had a fit at exactly the same time each day and, if left to her own devices for a minute, miraculously got up and carried on eating her sandwich. So, after consulting Audrey about Father Hemming's request, fearless Patrick said, 'Yes.'

Every Tuesday, Wednesday and Friday, I would ride home from Pressed Steel, meet Audrey on the corner of her street for half an hour, cycle home for my tea and then set off to open St John's Boys' Club.

All went well for the first two nights. On the Friday, after I had welcomed a few of the young early arrivals, the double doors burst back open and Ricky Edwards stood looking down at me like Jack Palance in *Shane*. Behind him stood his four henchmen.

'I've been told you're barred, Ricky,' I heard myself saying rather bravely. 'So you can't come any more.'

He grabbed the front of my shirt with both hands and pulled me to him. We're now in a scene from *Little Caesar* in which he is Edward G Robinson and I'm the punk.

'Who's going to stop me?' he hissed.

I stared into his eyes. Was he really angry or was he acting? I plumped for the latter. 'I am,' I said. *Wrong!*

He pushed me back across the room and all five of them stepped inside.

'I'm going to stop you.'

They spun round to see Father Hemming, stern of face, bald of head.

'Do you want him to go, Patrick?' he asked me.

'You can stay if you behave,' I told Edwards and his gang. 'You're ruining the enjoyment for the other children. They're terrified of you, Ricky. It's not fair. Just because you don't want to join in and have fun like the younger ones. You're ruining it for everyone.'

In the silence that followed, I expected to hear the 'ping' of the enemy submarine being spotted by Jack Hawkins in *The Cruel Sea*. Instead, Ricky just said, 'I'll get you, Mower.'

He turned and left with his sidekicks.

Father Hemming put his hand on my shoulder and said, 'Thank you, Patrick. I don't think he will be back.' And he wasn't.

I ran the club for two years, although Ricky Edwards did 'get

56

me' – at the St Giles Fair nine months later, when I was only saved, I'm sure, by another movie.

I had developed an irritation of the skin from the chemicals we were using in the paint shop to test the paint's quality and viscosity. The back of my left hand had turned into an even more scabrous mess than I remember from the pustular eruptions that covered my skin in my revolting scabies days. Although I was not really suffering from any pain, my hand had to be covered up to the wrist in a thick cold-tar bandage 24 hours a day, giving me a faint resemblance to some Frankenstein figure.

So, when, at the fair, Ricky Edwards spun me round to meet his face, hissing, 'Where's your priest now, Mower?', I slowly raised my left hand, like Boris Karloff in *The Mummy*, and held it between us as though this bandaged hand was a badge of courage. It wasn't a threatening gesture, and I wasn't asking for pity. It was more a warning: 'You touch this and you catch whatever I've got!'

Edwards's eyes left mine and looked at the black tar which was seeping out between my fingers. No words were exchanged. I could almost hear his brain asking, 'Is it leprosy, or what?' Whatever he decided the threat was, it was enough for him to back away and quickly disappear into the throng of merrymakers.

Years later I had Graham Crowden in fits of laughter as I regaled him with that story while we were filming *The Curse of the Mummy's Tomb* with the delicious Isabelle Black.

The evenings I spent running the youth club were among the happiest of my early life. I found that I really enjoyed being a father figure to the young boys and girls. I discovered the truth of the name Patrick, which derives from 'Patrician', meaning 'a born leader'. I liked the responsibility and found dealing with the myriad problems of teenagers exhilarating. I also directed them in plays and would find time at work to track down pieces that I felt would be suitable.

One afternoon, while pretending to be engrossed in some drawings of Alec Issigonis's Morris Mini, I wrote a half-hour play specifically for the youngsters and I'm happy to say that it won an award at a drama festival.

The first night was not without its own special drama. My leading man, or rather boy, a little ginger-haired ragamuffin named Eddie Nevitt, hadn't appeared at 7pm, with the curtain due to go up in half an hour. We had sold a hundred tickets and parents and friends were already pouring into the hall.

With disaster looming, I pedalled furiously round to Eddie's home – to be greeted on the doorstep by Eddie in 40 years' time – dirty vest and a shock of bright-red hair above a freckled face.

'He's not coming. I've sent him to bed for being cheeky,' I was informed by his father.

I pleaded. I cajoled. I offered free tickets. I asked to see Eddie's mother and explained that we had a theatre full of people and he was the star.

'He's a terrific actor,' I told his parents.

'I know he is. He runs bloody rings round me,' said his father.

'Please, Mam. Please, Dad…' said a plaintive little voice from the top of the stairs.

Fortunately, the pyjama-clad Eddie's appeal worked and, with him on my crossbar, I tore back to the club in time to stick on his bright-red moustache and push him on to the stage. Another success.

I was also having much more success with my love life. I was in love. And so, gradually, was Audrey.

My own theatrical career was also moving forward. Another Oxford amateur dramatic group, the Haddow Players, having seen me on the stage, asked me to be in one of their productions.

I agreed, on condition that Audrey could also be in the play. She was, and this led to our doing more productions together at the Gladiators, a company that was the natural progression from the youth club but also affiliated to St Mary and St John's Church.

I saw Audrey every day. She too had now left school, and was working for an insurance company. We would meet on our bikes at 5.15pm, gaze into each other's eyes and talk sweet nothings, oblivious to the busy Cowley Road traffic. Later that evening, unless I was at the youth club or in a rehearsal, we would meet again at her home and sit holding hands on her sofa, making small talk with her parents. We were becoming very serious. So much so that I, theatrical to the last, asked her father if I could have his daughter's hand. I remember the lovely, gentle Bill Giles being lost for words. 'Ah... I'll... I'll have to ask her mother...'

Luckily, Audrey's mother, although expressing concern at our tender years, said she was pleased that my intentions were honourable.

My mother was delighted. My father, stuck deeply in his usual leather armchair, Capstan Full Strength clutched in his fist, merely turned the radio up a bit louder and went back to his *Daily Mirror*.

So, at 17, I found myself engaged to be married.

Strangely enough, in the next six months, two of my friends, Dickie Dunford and Fuzz Youngman, also became engaged. It was obviously catching.

It's worth recalling that in the 1950s sex before marriage was very much frowned upon, although Audrey and I, both passionate and hot-blooded individuals, took great delight in discovering the wonderful secrets of each other's body.

Fortunately, I was now able to take Audrey out in style, having passed my driving test and bought a Morris 8 from my brother Don for £25. This was freedom, although I still used my bike for speeding around Oxford.

I was now in five different drama groups, which entailed a lot of bicycling to play some very serious roles. In Henry Miller's *The Crucible* I played John Proctor with stick-on beard – my bum fluff still not having grown into stubble – and Audrey was the leading lady. Then, in Emlyn Williams's *The Corn Is Green*, I played Morgan Evans, the part Richard Burton made his own, with Audrey as my schoolteacher.

I was so obsessed with acting that once again I secretly auditioned for RADA. This time I was accepted.

Now friends, Romans and countrymen rallied around to tell me what a fool I would be if I packed in my apprenticeship halfway through. I only had two-and-a-half years to run and then I would be a fully qualified mechanical engineering draughtsman. 'Something to fall back on,' everyone cried. I was still putting part of my salary into the family pot in Ridgefield Road, so my father's only concern was that I would stop earning.

Audrey wanted me to go for it.

I had reached the first key crossroads in my life, and I took the wrong turning. I accepted other people's well-meaning advice and stayed at Pressed Steel.

But, faced with my father's cutting indifference – he still refused to see me 'poncing around in make-up with all those other queers' – I was determined to make at least one major break. I couldn't wait to leave home.

Audrey and I set a wedding date – American Independence Day, 4 July 1957.

It was a white wedding, of course, with Audrey looking absolutely stunning, while I wore a dark-lovat suit. The service at St Mary and St John's Church was conducted, at his own request, by Father Joe Hemming. I had never been happier.

After spending our wedding night in the Strand Palace Hotel in London, we caught the ferry to Jersey for our honeymoon. Bliss!

Our first home was a rented one-bedroom flat on the ground floor of a lovely old house in north Oxford. It was a time of tremendous joie de vivre. Life through rose-tinted spectacles. For us it was idyllic. We were both still involved with the church and the Gladiators and counted the priests – Brothers and the Fathers in the Mission House of St John's – as our friends. We had become so much a part of their family that they offered, and we gratefully accepted, a low-rent top-floor flat next to the church that overlooked the Iffley Road running track. It was on this track that Roger Bannister, in one of athletics' great milestones, had become the first man to break the four-minute mile, on 6 May 1954.

Enter stage left: the union militants whose wrecking tactics brought companies to their knees. The late 1950s was a time of massive industrial unrest, with wildcat strikes over petty grievances constantly disrupting production, as militant communists and socialists strove to set the agenda for Britain's workers. In those days of the 'closed shop', everyone had to be a member of a union and as draughtsmen I and my immediate colleagues were members of the Amalgamated Shipbuilding and Engineering Union. All the workers dutifully attended union meetings – in company time – which became more and more frequent. But one such meeting held in secrecy behind closed doors guarded by hatchet-faced stewards was very different.

When the special speaker, a notorious firebrand, stepped on to the podium we all had to raise our hands in a vow of secrecy and agree the meeting had never taken place. Then came the punch line. Our branch had been chosen to spearhead a union drive to break the management. We were to demand a massive pay rise and shorter working hours as well as better conditions.

The reason for the absolute secrecy was that from the very first day of the strike the union would pay our salaries in full so that no worker would suffer. That way we could stay on strike indefinitely – until the 'fat cat' bosses caved in.

At that time I was on a day-release course at Oxford Polytechnic, which is now called Oxford Brookes University, so maybe my dream of attending Oxford University had technically been fulfilled. I was studying Applied Maths and Applied Heat and Thermodynamics, not a scintilla of which is now left in my brain.

So, for eight weeks in that glorious English summer we lounged around wearing our best 'hard done by' expressions. It certainly beat work – and, more importantly, it enabled me to pass my Higher Certificate of Education, the equivalent of a Bachelor of Science.

The workers also won. Whether democracy did is another story.

Now a highly educated and very good draughtsman, I worked on massive drawings, some of them 60 feet long, from which cars, including the Austin Princess and the Morris Mini, were eventually made. I was earning a very good salary. I had a job for life. I was the envy of my friends.

I had a blissfully happy marriage and a lovely home. What more could a man ask?

The answer had never been in doubt. I wanted to be an actor.

In 1957, a year before my apprenticeship ended, I auditioned once more for RADA – and was offered a scholarship to start on 1 October, a week after I became fully qualified.

Mr Charles White, the head draughtsman, gave me my indentures. I gave him my notice.

Another crossroads. This time I took the right turn.

6

Adoration

IN OXFORD I was a confident young man, but as I boarded the 7.15 steam train to Paddington Station on my first day at the Royal Academy of Dramatic Art the wicked city of London seemed a daunting proposition.

From Paddington I caught the Tube to Euston – my first ride on the Underground – my confidence draining with every hiss of the closing doors.

I walked through a slight drizzle down Gower Street to the disappointing entrance to the Academy. Surely, I thought, it should be pillared and porticoed. Instead, there were just two strangely carved figures above the double doors. Having only entered through the back door for my auditions, I hesitated.

A brash American voice shattered my reverie. 'Hi, are you new? C'mon, I'm as nervous as hell. What's your name?' The voice belonged to a tall, large-breasted, pneumatic beauty with long red hair, who I soon discovered was Carol Cleveland, later to achieve fame as the butt of many a jest in the brilliant *Monty Python* television series.

Not wishing to be away from Audrey, who meanwhile carried on working for the Alliance Assurance Company, I was to make this journey back and forth for the next year. It made for very long days as I left home at 6.45 each morning and often didn't return until 10pm. Yet it seemed a small price to pay, and I put the many hours I was spending on the train to good use.

I was either reading plays or writing my second play, this time in longhand on an A4 pad. It was quite a therapeutic exercise, strangely containing a scene where a boy teaches a robin to eat bread from the palm of his hand – and then one day crushes the bird. To my amazement, years later I was to read a very similar scene in a Chekhov play, but there was no way I would have had any knowledge of it when I wrote mine. To my chagrin I left the play – a year's work – on the train, never to be seen again. Now in my attempts at writing, I make sure I have a copy of every sweated word.

I also moved up in the motoring world to become the proud owner of an MG sports car. With Audrey working at the Alliance and with my grant and the money I had saved while working, we weren't short of cash. So I traded in my Morris to buy the classic PA model in British Racing Green with the splendid registration number MG 35. Today, it would be worth a small fortune, but some years later I was forced to get rid of it when they brought in the MOT. The ratchet handbrake, which worked on wires, became too worn to use. Sadly the cost of repairing it, because it was so specialised, was prohibitive and I gave the car away.

During the holidays, I was also earning money myself. Terry Taplin, a fellow student at RADA, used to stay with us in Oxford and he and I got a variety of jobs, from selling vacuum cleaners to hoeing between the plants at a rose farm wearing only our underpants. We weren't very successful at any of them but we literally drove into trouble when we joined the construction crew building the M40. With my motoring skills I was promoted to driving a dumper truck and after two days I fancied I was rather good at it. So much so that on the third day I gave Terry a driving lesson in the truck. Disaster swiftly followed. Terry lost control and in agonisingly slow motion demolished all the kerb stones it had taken the crew two days to lay. We were both sacked.

Before the Christmas break, RADA mounted a production of George Bernard Shaw's *Caesar and Cleopatra* which was to tour Cambridge and Oxford during the holiday. The director, Waris Hussein, offered me the part of Achilles, the leader of the Roman legions, but I, big-headedly, declined it, telling him I wanted to play the handsome hero Apollodorus. He turned me down flat, saying he was giving it to Curt Dawson, a very good-looking American.

However, I was to get my big break when the production came to Oxford. After watching the performance at the New Theatre with Ian McKellen playing Achilles, Audrey and I invited the cast back to our flat for a party. With the party in full swing, Waris told me he had been asked to take the production to the Duchess Theatre in London's West End for six weeks. But he had a problem. Ian, who was also playing the Major-Domo, had to go back to Cambridge University, so, please, would I take over in London? I didn't need asking twice. 'I would be delighted,' I told him. It was a wonderful opportunity Ian had afforded me and we have been firm friends ever since.

So, at 22, I made my first West End appearance at the Duchess. Little did I know that I would be starring in the same theatre twice more in the next three years – in the riotous *Alfie* and in Ibsen's *John Gabriel Borkman* alongside Sir Donald Wolfit and Dame Flora Robson.

In the New Year of 1961, Audrey managed to get a transfer to the Alliance office in London and we rented a two-bedroom, second-floor flat above a postman in Finchley. This vastly improved my travel arrangements and Audrey easily fitted in with my born-again-student lifestyle. She happily provided an open house for impecunious students running low on cash towards the end of each term. 'There's always a spare room back at Pat and Auders" became a well-honed phase at the Academy.

Many a midnight thumping was heard on the floor as the postman banged his ceiling with a broom in a bid to quell the noise, as starving students, heavily fuelled on halves of bitter, raided our fridge for the remains of Audrey's succulent cooking.

And then there were the parties, happy, full-of-fun events with raucous sing-songs which inevitably ended in students not only 'crashing' in the spare room but wherever they happened to fall.

At the parties were the usual suspects – John Hurt, very shy and introspective until a few glasses of beer had been consumed and then, look out, world! Ian McShane, flashingly handsome and knowing it. David Warner, lanky, moody and spotty. Tony Hopkins with no Welsh accent. Mike Leigh, a little gnome even then, like a naughty schoolboy, fiercely intelligent, always pricking pomposity. Gemma Jones, serene, composed, gentle and talented. Lynda Titchmarsh, affectionately known as 'Tits', who became the actress Lynda Marchal, who in turn became the famous writer and TV dramatist Lynda La Plante. Hywel Bennett, who was thought destined to be the next Richard Burton. Roger Hammond, round and benign even then. Simon Ward, blond and doe-eyed. And our closest friends and fellow students Michael Latimer and, 'from Leeds and proud of it!', Terry Taplin, the best actor at RADA.

In October 1961, I was in my last term and, like all final-year students, I had written to every theatrical agent in London. The agents were invited to attend the nightly performances at the Vanbrugh Theatre in Gower Street and I was disappointed in my casting. I had wanted Thersites so I could be covered in syphilitic scabs and crawl moaning around the stage – something to get my teeth into. Instead, I was given the Inspector in Agatha Christie's *The Hollow*. Oh no! I also had an angry young man in a new play set in South Africa called *The Day of the Lion*, directed by a very young, very good Moira Armstrong. But, to top my displeasure, the Academy had, for the first time, decided to do a pantomime, *Cinderella*, and I was to be the wicked Baron Bruticus. And I had to sing. But I was tone deaf – RADA had told me I was.

At the beginning of the second year, all students had the chance to audition for a musical scholarship, which turned out to be free singing lessons. The notice on the board announcing this had in heavy type and underlined: 'Auditionees must wear jackets and ties. No jeans.'

My audition time was 3.30pm and I raced down from a rehearsal of *Troilus and Cressida* – in which, being rather precocious and always after a bit of pizzazz on the lines of 'inspiration whirls me around' – I had done a few spins, ending up on the floor, from where I finished my speech. Pretty advanced stuff for those days, I can tell you. So I arrived at the audition rather grubby and sweaty, and knocked on the door.

A somewhat high-pitched voice called, 'Come in.'

I entered to see a small, effete-looking man dressed – I could hardly believe my eyes – in white tie and tails, sitting at a grand piano.

'Patrick Mower?' he asked without looking at me. 'You're late...' He turned slowly. His eyes started at my trainers and continued upwards until they reached my sweating brow. With a lip curl and nostril flare that I'm sure Kenneth Williams stole to make a fortune, he continued without waiting for breath '...and improperly dressed. Sing this!' His finger disdainfully prodded a note I would later learn to identify as middle C.

'Aaah!' I sang.

'You're tone deaf. Tell the next student to come in.'

And that was that.

I had always loved singing. I used to know all the words of the Doris Day and Guy Mitchell songs, while, as a draughtsman, I sang in a group impersonating the Kingston Trio. I had even sung a few Elvis numbers. So to be told I was tone deaf and in so cursory a manner was rather painful.

But being 'tone deaf' didn't stop me joining in the singing at our parties and it was then that I began harmonising with Michael Latimer, or rather I would sing the melody and he would harmonise. Mike was a tall, very handsome 'debs' delight' whom nobody took terribly serious as an actor. To this day, our mutual friend Terry Taplin calls him a 'Hooray Henry' and a 'toff'. And a toff he was. Charterhouse and Cambridge, with very rich parents – his father did 'something' in the City – he had a cut-glass public-school accent and lived in Kensington. He was extremely confident, very popular with the ladies and had friends with names like Bacchus, Santa Cruz and Squidgy. He even went out with a famous fashion model but, more importantly, in the evenings he was half of a cabaret act. To Patrick from Cowley, this was extremely glamorous.

Over a period of weeks in the early, half-stoned hours of the morning, Mike had taught me a few of his cabaret songs from the act and I had picked up some of the patter. The double act was Mike and a rather portly chap called Ian Hamilton who, as the Debs' Delights, sang witty songs, strummed guitars and told some rather dubious jokes which went down extremely well.

I was sitting outside the rehearsal room talking to a very beautiful black-eyed student called Alexandra Malcolm, who went on to marry Simon Ward – lucky man – when a breathless Mike Latimer burst out on to the stairs.

'Ah, Patrick, there you are. Do you want to earn £100 tomorrow night?'

Now in those days £100 was a lot of money, especially to a student, so I swiftly said, 'Yes please.'

'Right, we'll need to rehearse then,' said Mike.

'Rehearse what?'

'My cabaret act. We've got a booking for Quaglino's and Ian is ill.'

Luckily, I'd never heard of Quaglino's and didn't know that it was one of the top clubs in Mayfair. The obliging Dr Jekyll in me stood up. 'OK. Then I'd better learn it,' I said.

That evening and all the next day, in our flat in Finchley, with Audrey making endless cups of tea, my personality veered recklessly between the cool, charming Dr Jekyll and the angry, frustrated Mr Hyde, an appalling combination for others to cope with as I learned to strum the simple chords on the guitar and sing the words of eight songs.

At 6pm on the fateful day, Mike said, 'We've got to be there at nine o'clock. If in doubt, make it up. In cabaret you cannot stop. And don't worry. Remember, they don't know the act either. I know you can pull it off, Patrick, or I wouldn't have asked you. I'll pick you up at 7.45. Don't forget your DJ.'

'My what?'

'Your dress suit.'

'He's only got his wedding suit,' said Auders. 'It's a really lovely lovat colour.'

'Bloody hell,' said Mike. 'I never thought. We'll have to borrow Ian's. Can you meet me at the Hamilton pad at 7.45?'

He gave me the address off Sloane Square. It was a joyful June evening as we tootled in our MG PA down Park Lane. I looked across at the beautiful Auders, her lovely black hair blowing in the wind. I was wearing a pale-blue suit and a red-and-white polka-dot bandanna round my neck. I put my arm around her shoulder. 'My first professional job,' I beamed. 'Aren't you glad we left Oxford?'

In the tiny pause that followed I looked at her. Love poured from her eyes as she looked back at me, but I saw the tiniest hint of the sadness that, I'm afraid, was to grow in proportion with my success.

'Of course I'm glad, and don't you forget to leave Oxford behind tonight,' she replied, putting on a cod public-school accent. 'You've got to be as posh as Latters.'

We both laughed as we drove around Hyde Park Corner. We sang our favourite song, 'Be Careful, That's My Heart': 'That's not my watch you're holding – that's my heart.'

A little later I stood in front of a mirror dressed in a jacket that looked like an overcoat. My chest size was 40. Ian was a 48. My waist was 30, Ian's 38.

'Clothes pegs,' said Auders.

'What are they?' said Latters.

'Look in the kitchen drawer,' snuffled Hammers.

Auders folded the extra eight inches of trouser over at the back and did the same with the shirt. Then they pulled the cummerbund really tight, securing it with three large safety pins. At a distance I just about passed muster. Six clothes pegs down the back did the same trick with the jacket.

'Keep the jacket closed, come in sideways and don't show them your back,' Hammers managed to wheeze.

As I looked at the strange sight in the mirror I heard Mr Hyde grumble, 'Maybe we should call it off.'

'You can't,' said Ian. 'We'll be sued for a fortune. We're the top act – we're the Debs' Delights. Just get the smile going like you did in that revue for Princess Margaret at the Scala. Look at every girl in the audience, make them think you're singing just for them. They'll love you.'

And, from the moment we crab-walked on to the stage with a little sideways boxstep we had worked out, they adored us. Mind you, I think that night I wrote more lyrics than Alan Jay Lerner. Cabaret is an *act*. I was to do the show many times later with Mike and learned that, even if you are not going down brilliantly, you tell the audience you *are* and eventually they will believe it. That is because they are there to be entertained, not to sit in judgement – unlike so many theatre audiences, who feel endowed with some superior intellect as soon as they enter the auditorium.

As we picked our way through the patter they loved it. We did some funny walks, told some saucy, very non-PC jokes, poured on lashings of charm, and they adored us!

We did a false exit, came back and gave them our prearranged encore – and they adored us again! Especially the well-endowed debutante sitting with her parents at one of the front tables. Was this her coming-out party? Her breasts obviously thought so because, in her very low-cut dress, they had been struggling to make an appearance all evening.

I had obeyed Ian's instructions and sang as personally as I could to as many young, and not so young, ladies as I could see in that very large club. And I had obviously convinced the very well-proportioned young lady who was sitting so close that I was madly in love with her.

The audience applauded rapturously. 'We've got away with it,' Mike whispered from the corner of his mouth. 'Three bows and off sideways, remember.'

Three bows and then Mike went off.

'More. Please, please, please.' It was my over-ample blonde.

I turned and blew her a kiss and then I bowed a bow that was only to be bettered by Sir Donald Wolfit when I worked with him at the Duchess Theatre. A real theatrical knight of a bow. A Restoration bow, where one hand sweeps down to the ground and your nose nearly touches the floor. A real show-off bow.

I don't know whether I felt the pins holding my trousers up burst before or after I heard the first 'ping' of a clothes peg. I know I looked up to see the peg flying gracefully through the air. It went in a perfect parabola, revolving and spinning, to end up nestling very happily between the two perfect orbs belonging to the beautiful baying blonde who had been trying to tempt me all evening.

The remaining pegs had a more vertical trajectory because as I stood up my enormous trousers fell around my ankles. The trouser legs fell with perfect timing and perfectly spaced, one after the other. The five other pegs rapped me on the head.

The button at the front of the jacket had also come undone and the now voluminous garment slid gracefully to the floor.

It was as though I had finished the act with a Chinese tumbling trick. The audience burst into fits of laughter. My blonde was clapping and screaming, 'Off! Off! Off!'

I stepped out of my trousers and in desperation did a little twirl to see Mike whispering to the band leader.

Almost immediately the trumpeter came to my rescue. The baleful, wailing music of 'The Stripper' started up and the whole audience joined in calling, 'Off! Off! *Off!*'

Now all my RADA movement classes came in handy. I did a few bumps and grinds, then attempted to take my tie off. The problem was that Ian had tied it for me and I had not a clue how it worked. So I sashayed and swayed over to my lovely warm clothes peg, or rather to its new owner. The audience loved it!

After she had removed my tie, to tremendous cheers I removed the clothes peg with my teeth and pulled her out on to the floor, gesticulating for her to undo my shirt buttons.

I hope I've put on clean pants, I thought, as I pretended to swoon at the close proximity of delicious temptation. As she reached the last button, I held up my hand as if to say, 'Desist.' My vanity told me that an Englishman in Y-fronts and black dress shoes and socks is not a pretty sight. I slipped quickly out of socks and shoes and, to the audience's delight, beckoned her to begin again.

She peeled the shirt from my shoulders and I did a few muscle-man poses. But what next?

I got her to hold the shirt in front of me and telling her to look the other way, whipped off my pants and stood in all my glory. Except for a large black shoe covering the most vital part. I'm glad it was a size 11!

$$\boxed{7}$$

A Step Up

WHEN I LOOK back I find that nothing in my career has ever been straightforward. Obviously an actor's life involves a lot of waiting for the phone to ring and it still niggles at the back of my peanut brain that I made the biggest mistake of my career when I auditioned for the Royal Shakespeare Company. It was in 1961, at the Aldwych Theatre, just off the Strand, and I remember doing one of Benedick's great speeches from *Much Ado About Nothing*.

In those days, all actors aspired to go to Stratford-upon-Avon and those auditions were an absolute must. If you were lucky you were offered a year, or if extremely lucky two years, at Stratford 'spear carrying'. What this really meant was being a glorified extra in the battle scenes or suchlike while you were supposed to learn your craft by watching the Greats – Paul Scofield, John Gielgud or even the mighty Olivier performing their Shakespearean kings and princes.

I ended my speech, '...and so indeed it was,' and a voice from the darkened auditorium said, 'Thank you.' I heard a scrabble of paper as he obviously checked my name. 'Patrick … Mower?'

'Yes – would you like to hear my second piece?' I had a rather exciting version of 'To be or not to be' which my Hamlet delivered as he practised his fencing, so allowing me to show off my skill with a foil.

'No, thank you, I have heard quite enough,' replied the voice.

An involuntary 'Oh' popped out of my mouth. 'Are you sure?' I enquired, disappointed.

'Yes, quite. We'd like you to join us at Stratford.'

Beyond my control, the crestfallen young 22-year-old Dr Jekyll, having taken in the potion of these words, suddenly turned into the impetuous Mr Hyde.

My Hamlet metamorphosed into Hotspur.

'What parts would I be playing?' I heard my voice call out into the darkness. I even remembered to put the 'g' at the end of 'playing' and not to say the word as my pre-RADA accent would have dictated.

A laugh came closer out of the gloom and turned into a tall, handsome man with a little goatee beard. It was Peter Hall.

I felt Mr Hyde suddenly disappear. Did I really say that to the mighty Peter Hall?

'Mr Mower, we encourage young actors to come to the Royal Shakespeare Company to watch and learn their craft – how to act.'

'I know how to act.' Mr Hyde had returned. 'I wasted five years in an apprenticeship and I have wasted another two at RADA. I won't learn any more by two years watching other actors.'

'You didn't learn anything at RADA?'

'They taught me how to speak properly. But I knew how to act when I went there.'

Peter Hall looked at me intently. 'You're in a hurry,' he said quietly.

'Not so much a hurry – but I feel ready. Now. I know I only look 20 but I'm really 24,' I exclaimed as if this information by some osmosis now qualified me to play King Lear.

At this period in my life, I was naturally reserved, shy even, when, for example, offering my seat to ladies on buses or the Tube. This I still do today, although the offer is usually completely ignored or the lady in question looks desperately round for a guard, thinking I'm up to no good.

I was unsure at dinner parties and similar gatherings, suffering from a severe inferiority complex when it came to social etiquette and mores. In those days, anyone with a public-school accent was my superior, no question.

But when it came to acting I knew I was good.

On my regular two-hour journeys to and from Oxford I read plays voraciously. Shaw, Ibsen, Brecht. If the carriage was empty, as was often the case on the 7am train to Paddington, I could be heard giving my Shotover from *Heartbreak House* or Elyot from *Private Lives*.

When I was on stage I became the character. Mr Hyde would disappear and I would become 'the Shy Reluctant Hero', 'the Bastard', 'the Poet'. I had learned how to escape my unhappy home. I soon discovered that the faster I could immerse myself in a role the sooner I could leave my real self behind.

I became so fast I could transform myself into a new character almost instantaneously. Nine years later, at the Old Vic, having seven weeks of rehearsal with Eileen Atkins for Shaw's *St Joan*, was purgatory. I was ready the *second* day.

So telling Peter Hall I was ready was not arrogance. I wasn't boasting, I was just being honest. I really was ready.

Hall looked at me with even more intensity. 'Do you have an agent?' he asked.

'Ah … nearly.'

'How do you mean?'

'I haven't made my mind up yet. It's between Philip Pearman and Al Parker.'

A smile lurked at the corner of Hall's mouth as he asked, 'Do you have the choice?'

I nodded. Why did I feel guilty?

His eyebrows rose. These were the two biggest and best agents in London.

'*Julius Caesar* is one of the productions this season. I haven't cast Octavius Caesar yet. When you have decided who the best is, ask Philip to call me.'

As I walked out past the line of actors waiting for their turn to audition, some desperately mumbling through their pieces, others ashen and silent, I tried to keep the 'I'm in' smile off my mouth. But I couldn't.

'A star is born' was written all over my face. Move over, Gielgud. Make way, Olivier. Look out, Stratford, here I come!

Several years later, I had the good fortune to play Peer Gynt in a television production of Ibsen's great play. Three times the Button Moulder (given an incredibly persuasive performance by Kenneth Cranham) tries to ensnare Peer, saying, 'Till the next crossroads, Peer.'

In retrospect, my encounter with Peter Hall and the events of the following three weeks were one of my major crossroads, when I had to make a life-changing choice.

A dream had come true. I was going to Stratford to join the Royal Shakespeare Company.

But it was to remain a dream. A dream, in fact, until today. Because I could feel the shadow of the Button Moulder, that crossroads was getting closer.

Things happened very quickly over the next three weeks. The very next day – I was in regulation black tights, having carefully positioned myself behind Maureen Blott, a gorgeous, slender actress with the most perfect bum, who later married Harry H Corbett – when the most extraordinary thing happened.

It was in a Yat Malmgren class, punching and wringing and flicking and dabbing exercises which, when combined and applied to each word in a speech, were supposed to be the secret key to giving the 'perfect' reading of a line. A load of cobblers, you might think. Many of us also thought that, but dared not say so. This was, after all, the Royal Academy.

'You! What's your name?' The harsh Swedish accent woke me from my affair with the Blott bum.

All eyes turned to see who the mighty Yat was pointing imperiously at.

I looked over my shoulder at Mike Leigh, standing behind me. He's in trouble again, I thought.

'It's you, you pillock,' hissed Mike in his broad Barnsley accent.

I turned back to face Yat. Yes, the finger was directed at me.

After two years, you might have learned my bloody name, I thought, but shouted, 'Mower, Patrick Mower.'

'You nearly have it. You work hard and you will have it.'

The smirks and giggles from the rest of the class were stopped by a stentorian 'Punch... and... press...'

Two years later I was walking down Haverstock Hill in Hampstead when I became aware of Yat Malmgren staring at me from the other side of the road.

He stood stock still, back ramrod straight, holding two Afghan hounds, which were also fixed on me, posing like their master. I felt compelled to cross the road and as I did those foreign eyes never left me.

I stood in front of him, but before I could speak the accent broke the silence, 'You have it.'

'Thank you,' I replied, puffing out my chest, only to have it quickly deflated as Yat continued, 'What was your name?'

What Yat was looking at was not magic. I think he could see a young actor who, in the two years since leaving RADA, had appeared in two West End plays, starred in a musical and was just about to sign a contract with ATV to star in a new television series called *Haunted*.

After Yat's class, we changed into our street clothes and moved on to the next.

It was Restoration! And events became stranger and stranger.

Mike Leigh and another mutinous actor, John Davies, had just taken out their imaginary penises. Madame Phedra sat bolt upright, lips pursed into a thin razor line, her eyes like rivets burning through the two students. She had made the mistake of setting the class an exercise in improvising a piece of Restoration comedy on the manners and mores of the day.

Mike and John's Restoration fops, while elegantly discussing Congreve's *The Way of the World*, had been searching for a pissoir. As the world would later discover from his very successful films *Abigail's Party* and *Vera Drake*, Mike was a master of improvisation.

His very detailed mime of undoing his doublet and hose was a perfect illustration of how difficult it must have been for a 17th-century gentleman to actually have a pee. The class turned scarlet with suppressed laughter. Madame Phedra's face went from its normal lavender to pale ashen.

Having apparently relieved themselves, the two students shook their members elaborately, stowed them away in their imaginary pants and shook hands. Then, with perfect comic timing, each looked at his own hand and, remembering where the other's had been, hastily wiped it on his trousers.

This was too much for we poor students. Involuntary

applause turned into a communal cheer at the way those two had perfectly pricked the pomposity of Madame Phedra's class. She gave an impression that she was several cuts above RADA, especially the students, and her haughty manner would have been suited to a finishing school. But I would add in her defence that some parents who had paid for their children to be tutored through their audition speeches, thus ensuring their successful entrance, saw the Academy as just that.

Madame Phedra's grey face remained stony as the clamour trailed away into silence. You could almost hear the calculation of her brain as she worked out the next move. Should it be rage at being humiliated, or should she allow the stone to crack and pretend she found it amusing?

Her dilemma was solved by a furious pounding on the oak door of the rehearsal room. No one would dare enter one of Madame Phedra's classes without permission.

The urgency of the knocking forced the lips to part and rasp, 'Enter.'

The door was opened by Sergeant, the doorman, who now stood perspiring after making his way up three flights of stairs. Obviously having felt the lash of her tongue before, without speaking he proffered his left hand, which held a small brown envelope.

'What is it, Sergeant?' she demanded.

'A telegram, miss.'

This was the 1960s, long before mobile phones and when even having a phone in your own home was still quite a rarity – my parents *never* had one. So any pressing communication could only be achieved by telegram and, unless it was for a wedding or similarly grand occasion, a telegram out of the blue usually meant very bad news.

This was serious.

An audible gasp escaped from those tight lips. 'For me?'

'No, miss,' croaked the doorman. 'For Patrick Mower.'

The room was silent. My brain raced. Had something happened to Audrey? My mother? I'd had telegrams before, at my wedding, but they were of the 'Hope you keep it up tonight' variety. This was entirely different.

Madame Phedra's eyes turned from Sergeant back to the class. We knew she never bothered to learn any of our names, so I raised my hand.

'All right,' she said almost kindly.

I rose and slowly walked to the door, where Sergeant now stood holding the telegram as if it were about to explode.

'Sorry, sir,' he said. As I reluctantly took the envelope he turned swiftly and left.

I was stunned. I looked at the envelope. Yes, sure enough, it said, 'Patrick Mower. Royal Academy of Dramatic Art, 64 Gower Street, London WC1.'

I looked up at Madame Phedra, who nodded, as if to give me permission to open it. My tongue was dry as I slowly and deliberately poked my finger into the back of the brown envelope. I didn't want to read what it contained.

The tension that had been building in the room from the moment we waited for Madame Phedra's reaction to Mike and John's two-fingered salute had increased with Sergeant's dramatic entry. Now, with my own melodramatic opening of the mysterious envelope, it was almost tangible.

As a result, the broad grin that spread across my face as I read the contents might as well have been an audible gasp. I had enough presence of mind to return my features to what I hoped was a state of shock – I was, after all, a drama student. Then, in my most plaintive voice, I asked, 'May I be excused, miss?'

Once outside the door I took a deep breath. With the sound

of Sergeant's boots echoing up the stairwell as he slowly made his way down to the ground floor, I thought, Did it really say that? I unfolded the telegram and reread the capital letters:

'Have secured you the lead in the film *Night Must Fall* – call me urgently.

'Philip Pearman – 934 4192.'

8

Stage or Screen

THE MESSAGE IN Philip Pearman's telegram was amazing, but not completely unbelievable.

Night Must Fall was a fine play by Emlyn Williams about Danny, a young Welsh psychopath who carried a head around in a box. I had played Danny with the Gladiators company barely three years before and, by all accounts, had been rather good. With a Welsh father, the accent had come naturally.

I flew down the stairs, overtaking Sergeant just as he reached his desk.

'Can you lend me a few coppers for the phone, please?' I asked breathlessly.

'I'm sure it would be OK in the circumstances for you to use this, sir,' he added kindly, indicating the telephone on his counter.

Knowing he would expect to hear a rather tearful conversation, I explained that I would rather be alone to collect my thoughts. The dear man understood and gave me the money.

I then dashed down Gower Street and into the phone box outside Bertolucci's, the students' coffee shop.

Could I see Philip that evening?

Yes.

At his office?

Yes, I could come now.

Now?

Yes.

He would explain later, said Philip Pearman before hanging up.

At his office the agent pointed out that, although the director of *Night Must Fall* was very keen on me, he himself couldn't finalise arrangements because I had not agreed to be represented by him.

I had met Philip once before, after his initial letter congratulating me on my performance in *The Day of the Lion*. He was a tall man, at least six feet two, impeccably dressed in a light-grey suit with waistcoat, pale-blue shirt and yellow tie. He had blond hair turning grey and blue eyes that carried a constant twinkle. This very intelligent, intellectual man was to guide me through a minefield of sexual and theatrical scrapes in my virgin years in the business.

Framed photographs of Albert Finney in *Saturday Night and Sunday Morning* and Alan Bates in *A Kind of Loving* were among many other showbiz luminaries who covered the walls of his spacious office just off Regent Street.

'Alby' Finney was *the* big star at the time, especially for students at RADA, from which he had only recently graduated. Indeed 'Don't let the bastards get you down', a line from *Saturday Night and Sunday Morning*, was the students' *cri de coeur* and could be heard constantly echoing around the corridors at Gower Street – delivered, of course, in a thick Bradford accent.

I think Finney was responsible, along with the character Jimmy Porter in John Osborne's *Look Back in Anger* at the Royal Court, for the change in style and approach of all British actors from that day to this.

'Yes, I represent Finney and Bates,' Philip replied in answer to my enquiry. So, when he reminded me that he couldn't finalise the arrangements to meet with Karel Reisz, the director of *Night Must Fall*, because I wasn't represented by him, I'm afraid Al Parker didn't get a look-in.

There and then I signed a contract with Philip Pearman and Associates that bound me to them for all my 'Theatrical, Television and Motion Picture Productions'. They would receive 10 per cent of all monies I received. A small price for heaven, I thought.

As it turned out, it wasn't exactly heaven, but it was still way up in the clouds, and I did come down with a very gentle bump.

Karel Reisz was a very serious, intense person – a bit scary. I was called back for three meetings with him and other people I assumed were involved in the production. It was my first experience of film casting and I soon learned that the others in the room were trying to visualise me in the role as they asked seemingly banal questions such as 'What food do you like?' and 'Do you have any hobbies?'

What's that got to do with a Welsh psychopath? I asked myself. But I was to discover that what they really wanted was to see your face animated in different moods or attitudes. If you pass these inspections, they ask you to read and then, if you are lucky, you get to do a screen test.

I was lucky. A car was to pick me up at RADA at 3pm one Wednesday afternoon to take me to Pinewood Studios. They gave me two pages of dialogue to learn and asked me to wear a dark-green shirt. No problems with the shirt, and the lines I remembered from my stage production.

But how was I to get the time off? Ian McShane had been refused his scholarship because he missed his last term at RADA to play the starring role in *The Wild and the Willing*. In those days films and the then young medium of television were not considered to be the 'Dramatic Art' the Academy was training us for.

My one saving grace was that, with typical theatrical fear of bad luck, I had kept the contents of the telegram a secret. As I had confided in only my best two buddies at RADA, Mike Latimer and Terry Taplin, I thought I could chance my luck with the Principal, John Fernald.

In my two years at the Academy I had never spoken to the Principal, a figure of authority I had always felt was unapproachable. When I had arrived I had been in such complete awe of 'The Royal Academy' that I had half expected the Queen, or at least one of her equerries, to pop out at any moment. So the head of such an establishment was a figure far removed from the likes of me. John Fernald seemed a very remote man anyway. On the few occasions I had seen him in a corridor he had given no indication that he had the foggiest idea who I was.

So it was with some trepidation that I stood outside his office door, having arranged the meeting with his secretary that morning. A rather thin voice bade me enter and then asked, 'What can I do for you, Patrick?'

'It's about Wednesday afternoon...' I began.

'Ah yes – you had a telegram, didn't you? The funeral, I expect. What do you want – the whole afternoon?'

'Err, yes please,' I stammered.

'That's fine, I'll let the right people know. By the way, good performance in *The Day of the Lion*. I didn't know you were South African.'

'I'm not, sir.'

'What? Well, great accent. Where are you from?'

'Half Welsh, sir.'

'OK. That's fine. You can go.'

That was the first and last time John Fernald spoke to me in the whole time I was at RADA.

From one o'clock on the Wednesday I stood hiding around the corner of Bertolucci's, peeping nervously back down Gower Street at the entrance to the Academy.

Audrey had bought me a dark-green shirt and to this day I don't know why they requested that colour. We had also slicked my hair straight back, as I had done when I had played the part on stage, because in early photographs my father always had his hair greased back. I don't know why, but it made me feel Welsh – and still does.

At exactly two minutes to two o'clock, I saw it. The biggest, blackest, shiniest Rolls Royce I had ever seen purred past me, before gliding to a stop at the entrance to the Academy. Terrified, I had to pull my feet off the ground to get them moving. I knew I had to reach the car before the chauffeur went inside. I ran in the road to the driver's side. 'Have you come for me?' I asked breathlessly.

'If you're Patrick Moaner, I have,' a cockney voice replied.

'Mower. Patrick Mower.'

He examined the slip of paper carefully. 'It looks like "Moaner" to me.'

I looked anxiously at the Academy doors. John Fernald's office was right on the street and if he looked out I would be dead.

'Yes, some people call me "Moaner",' I lied. 'You're taking me to Pinewood Studios, right? Can I get in, please?'

'Allow me, sir.' He stepped carefully out of the Rolls, held his hand up to an approaching car which dutifully stopped and, with a deferential nod, opened the back door.

Embarrassed, I said, 'I'll sit next to you in the front.'

'Oh no, sir. More than my job's worth. In you go. Sorry about the misunderstanding, Mr Moaner,' he added, ushering me into the car.

Inside, the Roller was about the size of the first flat that Audrey and I had rented in Oxford, and until the car pulled silently away I pressed myself deep into the soft leather seat, breathing a sigh of relief.

I noticed the walnut C&D door panels – after five years as an apprentice engineering draughtsman in the car industry I still thought in the technical language we had always used. This was certainly more luxurious than the Austin Princess I had been working on when I left the Pressed Steel Company.

As we passed the Shaftesbury Theatre, I felt, for the first time in my life, part of it all; no longer an outsider.

We turned into Charing Cross Road and the heavy traffic caused our car to slow down and stop. As I sat in the back of the luxury limousine with my own chauffeur, the lights of the Phoenix Theatre seemed to be saying, 'This is where you belong – don't go away.'

I thought of all my ambitions to star in a West End theatre and here I was setting off to be a film star. Being in a film had not entered my mind. In those days film stars literally were stellar. Publicity machines kept them in the public eye, pumping out only enticing seductive titbits of adulatory information about Elizabeth Taylor, Richard Burton, Rock Hudson, Doris Day, with the sole purpose of keeping them inaccessible and immortal.

Little did I know as I looked at the Phoenix's lights that in exactly one year's time those very lights would proclaim, 'Starring Patrick Mower'.

In those days traffic was allowed to turn left into Oxford Street. We passed Marble Arch, Hyde Park and journeyed on through Notting Hill Gate and then Shepherd's Bush, eventually passing the BBC studios. Again I was to come to know the inside of those imposing buildings very well. At the White City road junction a large sign read: 'A40 Oxford 61 miles.' This was the way to Pinewood – but it was also the way home.

I felt uneasy. Was I selling my soul to the money devil – something I had vowed never to do? I had always prided myself that, unlike many students at RADA, I had become an actor simply because I loved acting. I loved the read-throughs, the rehearsals, trying to find the key to the character. Waiting for the feeling when suddenly you've got it and the character's lines become your lines. When you know how he feels and why he says and does things. I love the tensions, the nerves, but most of all the performance. When you get it right there is no comparable feeling in the world.

Being in total control of an audience, when you 'have them'. When they are riveted and hanging on your every word. Whether playing the Duke in *Measure for Measure* or the murderer in *Gaslight*, that feeling of power is the same. Those nights are gold dust. It's not the applause or the praise, nice though they are to receive. They are not a necessary part of the equation for me. I know if I've been good. I know if I've been very good. I've tried never to be less than my very best, even in front of that proverbial one man and his dog.

So as I sat in the make-up room at Pinewood I was not as excited as perhaps I should have been. I wasn't 100 per cent sure this was the right time or the right place.

A charming bespectacled man came in and introduced himself as 'Freddie Francis, the DP', and asked me to come on to the stage when I was ready.

'What's a DP?' I asked the make-up man.

'Director of Photography. You want to keep in with him, he's the one who makes you look good.'

I wasn't to know that Freddie Francis was probably the best in the business.

The screen test was disappointing. Karel Reisz was nowhere to be seen and all I had to do was stand on a cross taped to the floor and look left, straight ahead and then right.

Freddie placed me about eight feet from his camera, made a cross on the floor where I was standing and said, 'Right. Thanks, Patrick.' He then called out, 'Stand in,' and as I stepped aside I watched another young man come in and stand on the taped cross.

I stopped Freddie and, indicating the young man, asked quietly, 'Is he testing for Danny too?'

'Oh no,' he replied, 'he's just being lit to make sure you look your best.'

'Why don't you light me?' I said.

Freddie laughed. 'You go to your dressing room and have a rest.'

'I don't need a rest,' I replied. 'I haven't done anything yet.'

And when they called me back I still didn't do anything. I just stood on my cross looking left, straight ahead and then right, and was then asked a few more of those banal questions about where I was born and what pets I liked.

And that was it. No acting required. My Danny never got a chance to show himself.

In no time I was back in the limo on the way to my little Finchley flat. I asked the chauffeur if he would wait outside as I ran in, collected Audrey and dragged her down the stairs. I persuaded the driver to take us to the French Horn in Haverstock Hill, where a young Ronnie Fraser was leaning against the wall clutching a pint as we allowed the driver to open our door and then tip his cap goodbye with a 'Good luck, Mr Moaner.' Until he died prematurely, Ronnie would always call me 'Moaner Mower'.

I told Audrey about the day's events and we thought things couldn't possibly get any better. Little did we know.

The end-of term-shows at the Vanbrugh Theatre had only four performances each. I'd given my 'Angry Young Man' in *The Day of the Lion*, so on the following Wednesday night my Baron Bruticus made his appearance. It was an original *Cinderella* script written and directed by Michael Ashton, a real maverick, quite unlike any other teacher at the Academy. I loved the way he and the composer Ed Begler worked, always open to suggestions and ready to improvise or experiment. I can't, for the life of me, remember why, but I had a stuffed parrot on my left arm, a strong German accent and a monocle and always carried a long cigarette holder. I did a 'vent' act with the parrot, who would constantly criticise my performance with comments like 'That was terrible', 'Was that supposed to be funny?' and 'Who wrote this rubbish?'

It was courageous of Michael to let me create this performance in the hallowed halls of the Academy, but the audience loved it. So did I. And so did Vida Hope!

My agent – I remember being so proud to use those words in conversation as not every student got one immediately and some never at all – left a message the next morning for me to call him at his office.

Philip asked how the panto had gone and I told him that it was a strange experience but the audience loved it. 'I know they did,' he replied. 'I had someone in to look at you – Vida Hope.'

Vida, I knew, had directed the incredibly successful *The Boyfriend* with its annoyingly memorable tunes like 'Look At

Me, I'm Dancing' that had made their composer, Sandy Wilson, a millionaire.

'Did she like it?' I asked.

'She liked you!'

He then told me Vida wanted me to audition for the lead in a new musical called *House of Cards*. I would need a song prepared and he would let me know the time and place. I knew that my cabaret songs and the two that Begley had written for me in *Cinderella* were completely wrong, so I searched out Curt Dawson, an American student who I knew could pick out a tune on a piano. Curt was a really good friend. A talented actor and singer, we all thought he was destined to become a big musical star. He would have done, too, if he had not been cut down in his prime by those four dreaded letters AIDS.

Curt was very helpful and we spent a couple of hours in one of the rehearsal rooms looking for possible show songs. It soon became clear that, while I knew bits from lots of songs, there wasn't one where I knew either all the words or the whole tune. As Curt reminded me, I was sure to be nervous so I needed to know a song really well. At the time the title song from the West End musical *Standing on the Corner* was constantly being played on the radio and we decided that if I at least knew the tune I could probably get by even if I had to make up most of the words – an ability that has come in handy many times in my career when my mind has wandered during the fourth month of a long run.

At 5.30pm on the following Thursday, I caught a number 6 bus to the Aldwych as I headed for my audition at the Players Theatre at Charing Cross.

The theatre was a bit of a shock as it was situated in one of the arches which supported the railway track serving the major station. Passing through a small foyer covered in old music-hall photographs, I wondered what I had let myself in for and that feeling of unease was not helped as I entered the long, dark, cavernous tunnel that was the auditorium.

Miss Vida Hope was also not what I had expected. It was a rather mumsy, middle-aged woman who turned from the seated pianist to greet me. She seemed to shuffle under her long skirt towards me, saying, 'You must be Patrick Mower,' as she took my hand in a very firm clasp. Her voice was slightly slurred as she spoke from the side of her mouth. Just as I sounded, I thought, when speaking with the pipe in my mouth while playing the Inspector in the Agatha Christie play we were then rehearsing at RADA.

'I enjoyed your pantomime,' she said. 'Your parrot was the best thing in the show.'

'Maybe I should have brought him,' I heard myself saying nervously. 'He's a better singer than me.'

The man at the piano laughed. 'I'm Peter Greenwell, the composer,' he said offering me his hand.

They made small talk about RADA and about panto, mainly, I suspect, to put me at my ease. Then Miss Hope said, 'Right, shall we hear you sing?'

I climbed the four steps up on to the stage and looked out at the auditorium. It must have seated about 400 people and from where I stood it seemed a welcoming space.

'What are you going to give us?' Miss Hope's voice came from the centre of the stalls about six rows back.

'Standing on the Corner Watching All the Girls Go By.'

'Oh, good, I like that,' she said.

I took a couple of deep breaths.

'Patrick!'

I looked down to see Peter holding out his hand. Strange, I thought, we've already shaken hands. Thinking he was wishing me luck, I knelt down and shook his hand. 'Thank you,' I said.

'No, your music,' urged Peter.

'My what?'

'Your sheet music.'

I honestly had no idea what he was talking about, having had no experience of a musical audition for a show before. 'Don't you know it?' I said and innocently proceeded to sing him the tune.

'Yes, I know the tune – but I have to play an accompaniment,' said Peter.

'Oh,' I said, still not understanding the problem.

Peter sat back. 'Well, we'll have to give it a go. What key do you want it in?'

Not wishing to appear any more stupid, I remembered my encounter with the Kenneth Williams impersonator. 'C,' I said boldly.

'Good,' Peter said, his fingers poised over the piano keys. As he played the first notes I tried to join in – not recognising the tune at all. He stopped playing. 'No. Wait. Wait...'

'But that's the wrong tune,' I interrupted. 'It goes...' and I started 'la-la-ing' the song again.

There was a hint of impatience in Peter's voice as he said, 'This is the introduction, Patrick. Wait until I nod my head – I'll bring you in.'

I heard a barely stifled laugh from the stalls. I waited for the nod and luckily it seemed as though C was my key after all and I managed to bluff my way through to the end.

'At least we both finished together, even if we did not start together,' Peter said with a smile. 'You have a very nice voice.'

'Hear! Hear!' said a woman as she strode down the aisle with a broad grin on her face.

'I'm Stella Moray, now you've got to seduce me!'

Unbeknown to me, they had asked Stella to come in and read a scene with me. *House of Cards*, I learned, was based on a novel by the Russian writer Alexander Ostrovsky. It was the story of a young Yegor Glumov's climb from rags to riches, using his wits and charm and eventually marrying the Princess Mischenka. Stella was to play my aunt, whom I, as Yegor, then seduced to get to meet her husband. As it was a musical the seduction was mainly by dialogue and songs but the main scene, which we were about to rehearse, did end with a kiss.

Vida gave me a copy of the scene and said they would have a cup of tea while I looked at it. Luckily I've always been very quick at studying a part and as it was very well written I knew instinctively how it should be played. When they returned we had great fun. Vida became very involved as she directed, her eyes shining with enjoyment. She loved it and her enthusiasm was infectious.

Although Stella was not the most beautiful woman in the world, she was a terrific actress and had the most incredible singing voice. She and Vida were of a similar age, quite a bit older than me, and I think doing this rather naughty scene with a quite handsome 24-year-old buck quite got them going.

I was elated as I walked up to Charing Cross Station. It seemed to have gone very well. Vida said they had more people to see, adding that Yegor was a massive leading role with eight songs so they had to choose carefully. Still, as I walked past the station, I felt pleased that I had done my best.

I bought the *Evening Standard* to read at the bus stop and a little box on the front page immediately caught my eye: 'Finney's New Film Role, see page 7'. Being a great fan, I eagerly turned to see what it was. The article read: 'Albert Finney has just signed up to play the psychopath in Karel Reisz's new film *Night Must Fall*.'

Sitting upstairs on the bus on the way home, I realised that Philip Pearman must have known all along that Finney was to play Danny.

Had he lied to me? Had he used Danny as bait to make sure that I signed up to his agency? Was that why Karel Reisz had not been at the test?

But the chauffeur was real. The limo was real. Maybe they just didn't like what they saw on camera. Maybe there wasn't even any film in the camera.

There are so many games played in our business; so many lies, half-truths, platitudes. Leeches that hang on to you only until they have gorged on you and found another mug to suck dry.

The highs and lows; the elation and dejection; the success and failure. This incident was a glimpse of what was to be repeated throughout my career.

But all was not lost. My Yegor, I was soon to discover, had carried the day after all. Vida loved him – and I was heading for the West End!

9

Short Cut To fame

*H*OUSE OF CARDS was the opportunity I had dreamed of. And, although the gloomy Players Theatre hadn't impressed me at first sight, it was to prove the perfect launch pad for my career. The play lived up to Vida's hopes and from the first sparkling reviews we knew we were going places.

My gamble in turning down Peter Hall's offer of a place with the Royal Shakespeare Company in favour of the musical had paid off. It had been a difficult decision because at RADA it had been drilled into us that if you were to be a 'serious actor' you had to be a Shakespearean actor, but I was sure that *House of Cards* would prove a faster route to fame and fortune. And so it was.

The audiences loved it. In fact, it was so popular that the management decided to take it into the West End proper and put up a notice inviting punters who wished to invest '£100 and upwards' to see the theatre secretary.

I could barely contain my excitement when Philip rang to tell me that the show was to transfer to the West End, although we would have to wait for the theatre to become available.

My initial disappointment at the delay was quickly tempered when Philip told me he had found the perfect 'fill-in' role for me: in Bill Naughton's brilliant new stage play *Alfie*.

'The Naughton play is far too good an opportunity to miss,' he enthused. 'I know you are under contract for the musical but this will give you a lot of experience. I'll arrange for a get-out clause in your *Alfie* contract. As well as playing Perc, they want you to also understudy Alfie.'

I was 24 and needed no further urging, especially when Philip said that, in addition to John Neville, who was to play Alfie, they had also signed Glenda Jackson and Gemma Jones, one of my RADA mates.

Philip was right. *Alfie* was sensational. A triumph from its opening night at the Mermaid Theatre with John as Alfie while I played his mate Perc, it was to become a household name and later an international hit in the 1966 movie starring Michael Caine. Its impact was so unique that it was twice revived as a movie, one of them nearly starring me – but more of that later. The other, later version had Jude Law taking no prisoners in contemporary Manhattan.

In addition, it gave me the opportunity to showcase my talents in yet another West End hit when it transferred to the Duchess Theatre, although unfortunately I could only do a limited run because of my contract with *House of Cards*.

But it was far from plain sailing at the Mermaid. I shared a dressing room with an actor I'll call Steve, and David Battely, my sidekick in the play. It became very clear that Steve was a pretty weird guy. He was a giant of a man whose eccentric behaviour became more and more worrying. He would leave the theatre without his socks and shoes, and return with bloodied feet. Then he started to persecute David, a very shy, quiet young actor. Steve would stand behind David, staring at him in the mirror and icily whispering, 'I'm going to have you. Wait until we're alone.'

David was terrified. He really thought Steve was going to murder him. He became so frightened he would arrive at the theatre early, do his make-up and then wait outside in the street until curtain up to avoid his tormentor.

Ever the white knight, I decided this had to stop.

So the next night, while sitting in the make-up room with its long, horizontal windows overlooking the Thames, I had a word with Steve. 'Leave David alone,' I told him. 'You're making his life a misery and it's got to end now.'

Steve didn't bat an eyelid.

In answer he took his cigar from between his teeth and stubbed it out in the palm of his hand without uttering a sound. I could smell burning flesh but he didn't even wince. Then, looking me straight in the eye, he said quietly, 'I mustn't do that again, must I?'

Without another word he turned his back on me and began switching off the lights one by one.

He's going to kill me, I thought. The hairs on the back of my neck started to prickle. Finally the room was in darkness. Apart from the water of the River Thames lapping outside the open window, there was silence.

In my mirror I could just make out Steve slowly coming closer. I couldn't breathe as he stood threateningly behind me. I prayed for someone to come in. I could feel on my back the warmth from his body. Then he turned abruptly and crossed to the open window and started to climb out.

My God, I thought, what am I going to do now? He's going to kill himself. I sprinted across the room and yanked open the door, screaming, 'John, here, quick!' and then ran back, dived at Steve and grabbed his legs.

He was halfway through the window and I hung on for dear life. By now my yelling had brought the assistant stage manager to the rescue and together we pulled Steve back into the room.

Steve did finish the Mermaid run but he never made it to the West End. David Battely and I did.

House of Cards was due to start in a few weeks, but they asked me to do the opening of *Alfie* at the Duchess, and it was a night to remember. The tension was palpable but from the moment the lights went up we could scent success. Alfie, making comments to the audience as he seduces his string of conquests, went down a storm. We were a hit.

And during my short run with the show – my second experience at the Duchess having been there in *Caesar and Cleopatra* – I even got to play Alfie, standing in for John Neville on two occasions when he was away filming.

John, who later went on to run a theatre in Canada, had been a very big heartthrob at the Old Vic with Richard Burton and, one night, as we gathered for a bracer in the Opera Tavern, just down the road from the Duchess, the word went round that Burton and Elizabeth Taylor were coming to see the show – and they did. This starry couple, who had just become engaged, were the biggest thing in the world since their triumph in the film *Cleopatra*. They were the Posh and Becks of their day, ten times over.

It was a particularly special night for me as I was celebrating my birthday and I had invited the cast back to a party at the two-bedroom flat Audrey and I now had in west London. But first we went back to the Opera Tavern after the show – and Richard and Liz came too. I have never seen so many photographers – paparazzi as they are now called – gathered round the golden couple's gleaming white Rolls-Royce as they were driven the 50 yards down the road to the pub.

The atmosphere was electric. We were all on a high from the play's instant success, and having these two enormous film stars with us was an added adrenalin boost. The pub was warm, noisy and buzzing with excitement as we boisterously ordered drinks. The stars' two bodyguards stood at the door to keep the press and everyone else out. I was downing a pint when John called me over.

I will never forget Liz's amazingly beautiful violet eyes as she looked up at me. As I shook her hand, I thought, You can launch my ship any time.

She was only about five feet two and Richard about five nine. They said how much they'd enjoyed the show, and I told Richard of my Welsh ancestry and how playing Morgan Evans, like him, in Emlyn Williams's *The Corn is Green* had ignited my desire to be an actor. We were getting on famously when John asked me, 'Would it be OK for Richard and Liz to come to your party?'

'Yes, of course,' I said. 'But only on one condition.'

'What's that?' Richard asked.

'If you give me and a couple of the cast a lift it will save us catching the bus.'

'Sure, pile them in,' that wonderful deep voice replied.

I then called Audrey from the phone behind the bar. 'I've got a couple more people coming – Richard Burton and Elizabeth Taylor.'

'Don't be silly,' Audrey laughed.

'Yes they are,' I assured her.

And, God bless them, they did. Eight of us were sardined into the Rolls. I was squeezed between Willy Rushton and his beautiful girlfriend, Wendy Varnals, when the door opened and Burton looked in, saying, 'There's no room for us.'

'I'll sit here,' said the gorgeous Miss Taylor, and plonked herself down on my lap. Twenty years later, I would retell this story to the fabulous Tina Turner as she sat in exactly the same place.

And so we drove to our little flat in Olympia followed by this huge phalanx of reporters and photographers, horns blaring.

In retrospect, one thinks of Princess Diana and Dodi Al-Fayed in that fateful French underpass. Our chauffeur certainly did put his foot down to try to lose our pursuers – to no avail.

As we tumbled out on to the pavement outside the flat, Richard took me by the hand and apologetically said, 'Sorry, dear boy, but I am not going to let you suffer from these bastards. They'll be here all night. It isn't fair, so we will be off. I'm really sorry, but thanks very much… And I loved your performance.'

I like to think that Liz was reluctant to go – in my dreams! But she did wave from the back of the Rolls-Royce as it disappeared down the road, followed by the incredible army of photographers, cars and motorcycles, lights flashing and horns blaring once more. It was a sight to remember.

And Audrey never even got to meet them.

But our paths were to cross again years later when Richard would warn me of the pitfalls of being both famous and Welsh. I had become famous as 'The Man We Love to Hate' in the hit television series *Callan*.

In those days, the only popular television channels were BBC1 and ITV. There was BBC2 but no one ever watched that. The streets would literally empty when *Callan* was on, and over 20 million people would stare at their screens. It was a phenomenon. I played the nasty James Cross, forever poking my Walther PP handgun up Lonely's nose. The brilliant Edward Woodward was Callan, and William Squire played our boss, Hunter.

Bill Squire, a wonderful, very Welsh actor, was a great friend of Burton – they had been in *Camelot* together on Broadway. In those days Bill and I lived near each other in Kensington and became very good friends. One evening he invited me over to his flat in Church Street to meet an old mate of his from the Valleys. I got there and discovered his mate was none other than Richard Burton. I was delighted, of course.

The three of us spent the evening in Bill's flat sipping whisky and wine, longing to go out for a pint but knowing we would be mobbed. Burton had a reputation for mammoth binges, so it was really quite tame by his standards – just three 'boyos' having a drink and a natter about the ways of the world.

I nearly died laughing at Richard's face as Bill told me how one evening Burton and Liz dropped into his dressing room to show him the world's biggest diamond. Burton had just given Liz the famous £5-million ring, and Bill, ever theatrical, kissed Liz's hand with a great flourish, took the diamond in his mouth, pulling it off her finger, and pretended to swallow it.

Not surprisingly, Burton was apoplectic with fury. Today that ring would be worth £40 million. 'I really tested our friendship to the limit that night,' Bill said. 'I told Elizabeth not to worry as I was quite regular and I was sure she could have it back in the morning.'

He went on to explain how he then produced the ring. Richard saw the funny side of it, but I don't think he did at the time.

After a while Bill suggested going to a nearby Chinese restaurant, but Richard said he would rather stay in and that a bit of bread and cheese would do him. So that's what we had. Bill popped out to a delicatessen and came back with bread, cheese, ham and tomatoes. Richard and I ended up in the kitchen making sandwiches.

The more we drank the more frank Burton became. He was about to shoot *Who's Afraid of Virginia Woolf?* with Liz but he said he had become sick of the fame and all that went with it.

'Don't follow me, Patrick. I set out wanting to be a great actor but I've allowed myself to be seduced by it all, the trappings, the bullshit,' he said, adding that, having taken that path, he realised he couldn't go back.

'It's so difficult to refuse because you are offered everything you want. And the drink doesn't really help, but it's my way of solving things, of making the decisions seem right. But even then there is something gnawing away inside you because you have taken the easy option.'

He said he knew the drink relieved his inner anger and that he was often irrational because he had the mother of all hangovers. He said, 'Here I am, as rich as Croesus, married to the most beautiful woman in the world, but what I'd give for a pint and a shag up against the wall in Merthyr.'

Having seen me on TV, he warned me that I had the famous 'Hywll' – the Welsh 'something extra special'. And that I would soon have uncles and aunts, nephews and nieces I never knew existed coming down from the Valleys. Half the people in Wales claimed to be related to him, and the other half claimed to be sired by him, he said. Indeed, later I was to receive many such claims about sisters and cousins and uncles. But most of mine turned out to be true!

It sounds an obvious thing to say, but I have found that, with Kirk Douglas, Trevor Howard and Maggie Smith, among other really famous names with a reputation that precedes them, once you get through the armour they've had to build around themselves, they are all quite normal.

I experienced the downside of fame one night when I went to Tokyo Joe's club in Kensington High Street with my pal Michael Latimer and nearly ended up being stabbed to death.

At that time, I was in *Special Branch* on TV, playing the tough guy Tom Haggerty. My character was very popular, especially with the girls. During the evening many young ladies asked me for a dance and I remember one long-limbed lovely wearing lime-green hot-pants asked me several times. I thought nothing of it at the time. About 1.15pm, while Mike and I, along with others, were waiting outside the club for a cab, some instinct caused me to turn around.

I was just in time, for at that moment a young man smashed a litre gin bottle on the pavement and then thrust the shattered, lethally pointed end of it to within an inch of my nose. It was like a scene from a movie. I had enacted scenes like this many times on TV and knew you were supposed to either keep fixed on the weapon or on the eyes.

I chose the bottle and started to back away. As I retreated, I asked, 'What're you doing?'

He didn't reply but just kept advancing on me.

As I continued to back away we went faster and faster into Kensington High Street. 'What're you doing?' I repeated.

In reply I got another lunge, causing me to speed up.

This is getting really serious, I thought. I was a really fast runner and knew I could easily race away from him. But, having no idea what was going on, I turned in a wide arc back towards the group outside the club. Quite honestly, at that moment it was rather amusing. I had no idea it was suddenly going to get very dangerous indeed. As I neared the others, I turned to look over my shoulder, tripped on the kerb and went flying into the gutter. He fell on top of me and I felt a punch in my stomach. Mike ran over shouting, 'Leave him alone,' at which point the man jumped up and slashed the front of Mike's shirt.

The attacker then strode angrily through the crowd outside the club, cutting another man on the back of his neck before grabbing a girl by the wrist and pulling her after him down the road. From my lowly viewpoint, I couldn't help noticing that the girl had extremely long legs ending in the most perfect buttocks that were encased in – yes, lime-green hot-pants.

As I stood up, I put my hand to my stomach, it felt wet. I looked down. I had been wearing virgin-white trousers, now I had one white leg and one leg that was rapidly turning red. Blood was pouring out over my hand.

'My God, he's stabbed me,' I gasped, and then I lost my temper.

The man had hailed a cab, and with the girl in tow, had started to climb in. I ran to the front of the taxi, lifted up my shirt to reveal my wound and shouted to the driver the immortal words, 'Don't take him, he has just bottled me!'

The cabbie didn't hesitate. I jumped out of the way as he put his foot down and, with the girl inside and the door swinging open, the cab raced away, throwing the bottle man back into the road. I moved forward trailing blood in my wake.

Still clutching the bottle, he turned to face me, yelling, 'You want some more, you bastard?'

When I was in *Callan* I was supposed to be a black belt in judo and I knew quite a lot of the moves, so I raised my hands into a karate pose, but this was real life and I decided to be Patrick and not James Cross after all. I lowered my hands and backed away. He seemed relieved and ran off down the road.

The club bouncers had called the police and an ambulance and I was taken to Accident and Emergency at nearby St Mary Abbot's Hospital.

'You couldn't have been stabbed in a worse place,' said the pretty black nurse who treated me as she carefully pulled my trousers down. 'What have you been doing?' Her eyes widened as she gasped, 'Wow!' I sat up painfully to see what she was looking at, but unfortunately it was only the size of my wound that had surprised her. The inner wall of my stomach lining had pushed its way out of the gash. Staunching the bleeding with a pressure pad, she carefully pushed the lining back into the wound. As I told her what had happened, for the first time she looked at my face, 'Oh my God, it's Patrick Mower!' she cried, and she pulled my trousers up higher to cover my manhood, saying, 'I didn't look, honest.' People do the strangest things when they're embarrassed.

'What about my stomach?' I countered with a smile as she stitched up the wound.

'Well, you are very lucky, that could have been really serious,' she told me, before we were interrupted by a row outside the room. The police had brought the witnesses to the hospital and I heard a policeman say, 'We've got him. Anyone recognise him?'

'Yes, that's the bastard,' said Mike, and the bottle man, who had been caught as he ran up Kensington High Street, shouted, 'I'll get you too.'

Someone else said they would also be a witness and the police wanted to charge the man, with me as the key witness. But I was very reluctant as I knew there might be serious repercussions down the line.

At the time, Audrey and I were living in a basement flat in Addison Crescent, Kensington, and above us lived a very posh lady who always wore big picture hats and was the only miniaturist painter who had done portraits of all the Royal Family. A couple of weeks before the bottle incident, our house, which was owned by the film director Michael Winner, was being painted by cockneys. They were always effing and blinding and there was scaffolding everywhere, so the lady asked them if they would make themselves scarce the following Wednesday as Princess Anne was coming for a sitting.

'Don't worry, ma'am, we'll be very quiet,' they assured her. And, sure enough, when the royal car drew up they were nowhere to be seen. After the police had checked that everything was all right, Princess Anne, wearing a large white hat, stepped through the gate. As she walked up the drive a girder came crashing down, accidentally on purpose, right in her path. The air then turned a right royal blue with their effing and blinding, which included every swearword imaginable. One of the painters then shouted down, 'Sorry, my mates aren't used to dealing with you Royals, not like me. Same time tonight, Annie?'

Princess Anne just smiled, bent to admire a flower and carried on as if nothing had happened.

But those painters taught me a valuable lesson. The next day one of them had a big turban of bandages swathed round his head and I said, 'Hello, John, have you been in a fight?'

'Yes,' he said, explaining that he had been slashed in a brutal payback attack for not providing a villain called Bert with an alibi for a robbery. John said he had refused to help because Bert had been caught red-handed and he would have been done for perjury. As a result Bert had been sent down for two and a half years. The day before, Bert had been released from prison and, after beating his girlfriend to a pulp for having an affair, he had called on John. 'Hello, John,' he said, 'I've just done two and a half years because of you – here's a present!' He then slashed John with a Stanley knife, causing a huge wound and only just missing his eye.

So I was very wary when the police came round to see me after the stabbing. 'You are the luckiest man alive,' the police inspector told me, pointing out that if the shard of glass that cut me had been two inches longer I would have been killed instantly. He said that if I testified that the man had tried to kill me he would be jailed for a very long time as he had a record of violence. The man had told them he had become insanely jealous because his girlfriend – the beauty in the lime-green outfit – had said I was so lovely. He had lost his temper and it was a spur-of-the-moment attack, he said. But all the same it was a very serious attack.

With John's experience in mind, I told the police I didn't want to get involved despite the danger I had been in. I was a television star renowned for my Charlie Charm and didn't want to have to worry about the day someone would tap me on the shoulder and slash my face with a Stanley knife. So I didn't press charges and the man got away with it. But I continued to sleep soundly.

The danger with being a television action man is that you can become a target for yobs, and another time, when I was in *Callan*, I had a broken glass thrust into my face.

Audrey and I had taken our children, Simon, who was then seven, and Claudia, five, on holiday to a very expensive five-star hotel near Benidorm. This was then a new resort, not yet used by British holiday firms, so I was confident I wouldn't be recognised.

After five days of genteel peace, we were continuing to enjoy a nice relaxing time when our tranquillity was shattered by the arrival of a group of Brits who had been given a free holiday at our hotel because the hotel they had been booked into hadn't been built.

They behaved like your worst nightmare – swearing, falling around drunk, dive-bombing into the pool. It was one of those hotels where you had to dress for dinner and one evening we were having a pre-dinner drink with some Swedish friends near the pool when six yobs came back from the beach obviously the worse for wear and using the foulest language.

I told Audrey to keep Simon and Claudia back and went over to the group and said, 'Leave it out, lads.'

'Piss off, you poof,' they shouted back.

'There are children here and these people have paid a lot of money for a quiet, peaceful holiday.'

'Who the fuck do you think you are, just because you're on TV?' shouted a surly Glaswegian climbing out of the pool.

'It's about common decency. You are using foul language. I don't want it in front of my children,' I replied.

'You can fuck off! Do you want a pint or a half?'

'What are you talking about?' I said.

'I'll show you.' He smashed a glass on the poolside. 'That's a pint,' he snarled, and put the shattered glass to my face.

I could feel everyone's eyes upon us as he stared at me. 'Come on, tough guy, let's see if you really are tough.'

I could feel the glass pressing into my skin but not quite puncturing it. I needed all my acting skills to keep my super cool as I heard myself say, 'You can do what you want. You can push that into my face if you want. I'm only asking you not to swear.'

He blinked.

I continued, 'But I think you'll be a bigger man if you don't.'

I didn't wait for another blink. I then turned slowly and walked away. The sweat was running down my back because I knew he would have to do something. He couldn't back down in front of his friends and I feared I was going to get the glass in the back of my head.

Suddenly, the guests and waiters applauded. I never looked back and turned to Audrey saying, 'Come on, let's go in.'

'You're all a load of fucking wankers,' I heard the Scot yell as he threw the broken glass into the pool. 'Come on, let's go and find some real people,' he called to his gang. They left and I'm very happy to say we never saw any of them again for the rest of the holiday.

It was a really nasty moment but I couldn't help it – I had to intervene. I'm like that.

10

Big Screen, Little Screen

SADLY *HOUSE OF Cards* proved to be just that. The initial show was so popular that people invested thousands of pounds and the West End production was massively oversubscribed. And it was that very success that was to lead to its spectacular demise – it collapsed under the weight of its own ambition.

The producers, awash with money, got carried away and the show, instead of being allowed to remain a charming, witty and intimate musical, was blown up into what they hoped would be a big Broadway hit. Instead of a trio of piano, drums and guitar, they employed a 14-piece orchestra. There were ten singers and 12 dancers and I was given two more numbers.

Puffed up by its own importance, it was simply blown away by the critics, who pronounced the opening night at the Phoenix Theatre its 'death knell'. Although I personally received rather good reviews, the show itself was universally panned.

But then one Friday afternoon at the end of a matinee my

dressing-room phone rang and the stage doorman informed me that the great David Ross was downstairs and wished to have a word with me.

The David Ross? A tingle of excitement ran up my spine as I said, 'Send him up.'

Ross was a very powerful producer and director. He owned his own theatre on Broadway and was doing a cycle of Ibsen plays which he wanted to complete with a top British production in the West End before taking it to Broadway.

In response to a powerful thumping on my door, I opened it to be confronted by a scene straight out of Hollywood. A short swarthy gentleman, a large cigar clamped firmly between his teeth and a fur coat draped over his shoulders, raised his Homburg and, through clouds of cigar smoke, said in a guttural Bronx accent, 'Patrick, I thought you were fantastic. I got Sir Donald Wolfit playing your fadda and Dame Flora Robson playing your mudda. I'm going to buy you outta this show... Come out to dinner.'

Bob Hoskins could have based his character in *Who Framed Roger Rabbit?* on Mr Ross, but this was no dream. This was reality.

Before I could reply, a high-pitched American voice said, 'Yeah, please do!' It came from behind the fur coat and belonged to what I can only describe as a 'moll' of the kind that anyone familiar with Sixties gangster movies would recognise.

Long blonde hair was artfully draped over the long false eyelashes of her left eye and a long cigarette holder was held hovering two inches from her bright-red pouting lips. She also had a white-mink coat around her shoulders, carefully draped so as not to obscure the paleness of her neck. Around this hung a sparkling diamond necklace which led my eyes down to a pair of breasts that appeared to be as pleased to see me as I was to see them.

The situation was so outrageous that if it had been happening in 2007 I would expect Jeremy Beadle to poke his head around the door shouting, 'Patrick, you've been had!' So, disbelieving, I made my excuses and gratefully declined the dinner engagement.

The following day Philip Pearman told me that David Ross had been no mirage. The production was to be Ibsen's *John Gabriel Borkman* with Wolfit and Dame Flora and, he stressed, every young actor in England would give their eye teeth to play their son, Erhart. Fortunately, Ross had called him that morning and was still willing to buy me out of *House of Cards*. Not only that, but after the West End run the show was going straight to Broadway. In those days, even more than now, to appear on Broadway was as big as you could get. Talk about a shooting star! My first year out of RADA and I was a rocket. That was the good news.

The bad news was that *House of Cards*, after only a seven-week run, had been given its notice, which meant I had just two more weeks starring in the West End.

I had the Ibsen play to go straight into, but it is always terribly sad when a show closes, especially a musical. So much effort, energy, the hours learning song and dance steps, perfecting routines. All those weeks rehearsing to get to the point where you are ready to let the audience see the finished article. The main thing I miss about being in *Emmerdale* is the rehearsals. Not because I think they would improve my performance, but that's where the heart of the show is created from the intimacies, the jokes, the tall tales, the anguish, the pain. In rehearsals you bare your soul, you experiment, you *dare*, because you can make mistakes. You're with like souls who all have one thing that, for the next few weeks, will dominate their lives above all else – be it lovers, family, friends, food, though maybe not sex. For them 'the play's the thing'!

And so I became Erhart.

Before rehearsals started, we were instructed that Wolfit was not to be spoken to unless he spoke first and then he was to be addressed as 'Sir Donald'.

Dame Flora simply said, 'You can call me what you like.'

Sir Donald and Dame Flora had a vow of silence between them, born of past experience of working together. Throughout the rehearsals at the Vaudeville Theatre in the Strand one ignored the other, speaking to each other only as their characters on the stage. It was to be an entirely different atmosphere after the gaiety and the glamour I had enjoyed in *House of Cards*. It was as though the dour Norwegian Ibsen was himself creating the mood.

On my first day at rehearsals, Sir Donald stepped in front of me in the corridor. Raising himself two inches on his toes, until his eyes were level with mine, he started the following conversation:

'Patrick Mower.'

'Yes, Sir Donald.'

'You have been in a musical.'

'Yes, Sir Donald.'

'I hear you were very good.'

'Thank you, Sir Donald.'

'I hope you are not going to let me down.'

'I won't, Sir Donald.'

'You may go,' he said, but didn't move.

His broad frame, still on tiptoe, stood in the corridor, blocking my path. I hesitated, but decided not to push past him, and returned the way I had come from.

In an echo of his glacial silence with Dame Flora, Sir Donald never said another word to me for four weeks, always referring to me in the third person as 'the Boy'. He would say to Ross, who was directing as well as producing the play, 'Do you think the Boy ought to move there or the Boy should be here?'

One day in rehearsal, Ross asked, in his thick Bronx accent, 'Patrick, how tall are you?'

'About six foot,' I told him.

'What sort of heel do you wear?'

'Oh, an ordinary heel.'

'Maybe we should try it with flat shoes.'

Having recently left RADA and being a 'serious' actor, I thought, Hey, Alec Guinness always works from the feet up. Maybe that's the key to Ibsen.

So I went home and knocked the heels off my shoes.

After three very uncomfortable days one of the stagehands informed me that the only reason Ross had wanted me to remove my heels was because he'd heard Wolfit complaining that I made him look small on the stage.

My heels returned.

After our first night in Brighton, where the play had a run to iron out any creases in the production before going into the West End, I was walking past Wolfit's dressing room when I heard his mellifluous voice call out, 'Goodnight,' then a perfectly timed pause, followed by, 'Patrick.'

Patrick?

I knew that Wolfit had the reputation when he did his famous King Lear of surrounding himself with lesser actors so that he would shine even brighter among the dross.

Patrick?

Did that mean I was now dross or was I being accepted as worthy? Choosing the latter, I cheerfully replied, 'Goodnight' – I paused – 'Sir Donald.'

The following morning the cast were assembled in a semicircle on the stage of the Theatre Royal, Dame Flora knitting; Margaret Rawlings reading *The Times*; Delphi Lawrence, my femme fatale in the show, rearranging her lipstick; Karen Fernald, RADA boss John Fernald's daughter; and myself, along with the director. The only person missing was Sir Donald. But not for long.

The last of the old-fashioned actor-managers in the tradition of Henry Irving and David Garrick, Sir Donald made his usual grand entrance. Black cape swirling, silver cane twirling furiously, he doffed his large-brimmed, black 'Toulouse-Lautrec' hat and greeted us, 'Ladies, gentlemen, Dame Flora...' before launching into the following diatribe.

'Mr Ross, for four weeks I have endeavoured to follow the direction you have sent me on – the path to *John Gabriel Borkman*. As you will have read in this morning's papers, that path, as I informed you, was wrong. I now intend to play Borkman as Henrik Ibsen himself intended him to be played. I have left instructions with the company manager that I wish to have no further communication with you.'

He then turned to the company and said, 'Ladies, gentlemen, Dame Flora, good day,' and with a swirl of his cape he strode from the stage.

The poor befuddled American seemed to diminish even more before our very eyes. Wolfit did attend rehearsals but completely ignored the director. He ranted and raved as Borkman, giving what I shall politely call a very large performance. David Ross directed us to be more modern in our approach, more real, 'more American – remember this show's going to Broadway'.

Sir Donald and I never exchanged another civil word off stage until, in a rage, I charged into his dressing room after the first night at the Duchess.

In rehearsals and at Brighton Sir Donald always turned his

back on me in disgust as I entered with Delphi, my femme fatale, stunning in a bright-red dress.

On the opening night in the West End he remained looking at me. All the critics were there, pencils poised – this was my big moment. As Dame Flora, tears running down her cheeks, spurned me after my heartbreaking speech, the audience sat open-mouthed. The tension was palpable. I could see my reviews: 'A star is born…' I gloried in the silence that filled the theatre.

The resounding crash of brass curtain rings exploding all over the stage shattered the spell. Sir Donald, with an unscripted roar, had ripped open the pair of massive velvet curtains, crashing the brass rings together.

Not only did the audience jump, Dame Flora and I jumped, and the deputy stage manager in the wings jumped so much she dropped the script on to the stage and was now scrabbling on hands and knees to pick up pages.

We all looked round as Wolfit, who only now, slowly and deliberately, turned his back on us. The moment was his, not mine.

In his red dressing room immediately after the show, I was more angry than I had ever been in my life. Pushing open his door, I said, 'You did that on purpose, Sir Donald.'

'Patrick, it was you… You were wonderful,' he replied. Then, turning to a pink, grey-haired man standing in the corner, he said, 'Have you met Binky Beaumont?'

'Don't ever do that again,' I said, still furious.

'You're good, Patrick. Very good,' he smiled, 'I knew you could make it, and you did. Watch and learn, Patrick. Now calm down and have a glass of port. Very good for the voice, you know.'

It was Sir Donald's last production in the West End, but he knew how to win – and hold – an audience. He had an amazing rapport with them and enjoyed engaging with them. If the 'gallery first-nighters' booed him, he would boo them back. He would stop in the middle of a speech and raise his fist to them.

One very hot summer matinee, the sweat dripping from him, Sir Donald stopped in the middle of one of his long speeches, looked at a woman in the front row and shouted, 'That woman's asleep. Wake her up.' At which the wag sitting next to her shouted back, 'You sent her to sleep. You wake her up!'

So it was all the more amazing that, at the first-night party at the Ivy, in those days a dark, smoke-stained restaurant, Wolfit actually said sorry. I saw him talking animatedly to Audrey and afterwards she told me he had apologised for his behaviour on stage. I think that was a first, but he couldn't bring himself to tell me personally.

The critics raved about Sir Donald's bravura performance – it was truly amazing. I used to watch his death scene every night. But the rest of us and the production were uniformly panned – for being too modern. It ran for six months, though sadly we never made it to Broadway because Sir Donald still refused to talk to David Ross. It was such a shame that throughout Wolfit's career he never allowed anyone to peep under the hard exterior in which he had enclosed himself.

Audrey and I were inseparable in those early rock 'n' roll years of RADA and my stabs at West End glory. We were a terrific team and so in June 1964 we were both absolutely delighted when we discovered Audrey was pregnant. Everything in my garden was perfect. No money worries, no career worries and a baby on the way. And later that year our handsome son Simon was born at St Mary Abbot's Hospital in Kensington. We were so thrilled. He was a joy then and he is a joy still. Our happiness was complete two years later, with the birth of our daughter Claudia. I'm happy to say I witnessed one of the most breathtaking moments of my life as I watched her pop out into the world at a convent in Guildford.

It was also the time I had to sacrifice my precious MG. Reluctantly I gave it to a young musician, Mike Leander, who would later enjoy triumphs as writer and producer of a string of hits for Gary Glitter, become a millionaire and form the Mike Leander Orchestra. This connection could have opened another glittering career path for me.

The great British pop breakthrough was in full swing with the Liverpool sound, immortalised by the Beatles, which swept aside Elvis Presley and just about everyone else. Leander was desperately keen for me to cash in on this phenomenon. He'd heard me sing at parties. 'You're a good-looking young man, you'll make a fortune,' he enthused. So he wrote a song for me called 'Lately' and persuaded me to cut a demo in 'Tin Pan Alley', or Denmark Street, off Tottenham Court Road.

As we opened the sound-proofed doors of the recording studio, the smell of marijuana went straight to your brain. Two long-haired musicians, one with a guitar and the other with a drum kit, ignored me as they improvised. It took half an hour to record my little demo. Like a duck to water, I took to the pop world, aided, I'm sure, by the fumes that filled the room.

The next morning Audrey and I listened with Leander to my dulcet tones coming from the record player. 'Patrick, you could be a new Bobby Darren' he beamed. 'We'll make a mint.' I looked at Audrey, and in unison we shook our heads. 'No thanks, Mike, I'm an actor,' I said grandly.

So, convinced that I was well on my way up the ladder to theatrical stardom as the next Olivier, I grandly refused to go down that route to fame and fortune. What a fool!

Television, however, was beckoning. Dodo Watts, the most powerful casting director at ATV, had, unbeknown to me, seen my three varying West End performances and cast me in a massive leading role in a production in the Armchair Theatre series. In a precursor to *Cathy Come Home* with echoes of Joan Littlewood's *A Taste of Honey*, I starred as John Paddington alongside Tony Garnett, who is now a film producer. It was a stark drama about a young girl who becomes pregnant and then loses the baby. The reality was even more dramatic and, while it was a fantastic part for me, it was also a very tragic time as the actress playing the girl committed suicide two days after recording the show. As a result it was never shown.

It wasn't long, though, before I was on television – as council PR man Kenneth Wiley in the BBC's twice-weekly soap *Swizzlewick*, a satire which was way before its time as it poked fun at Mayor Bent and his cronies on a mythical local council. It was taken off after six months following complaints from irate local councillors. Typical BBC! But it led to my being cast in a new major ATV series, *Front Page Story*.

Made at Elstree, it was a follow-up to the hit show *The Plane Makers*, and we made 26 one-hour episodes following the adventures of four news-hungry journalists on a national newspaper called the *Globe*. I played the posh one, John Brownhill, with my best Michael Latimer accent, while the others were played by Derek Godfrey, Harry Towb and Derek Newark.

I was now occasionally recognised in the street. The public reaction to actors never ceases to amaze me. From fan mail to hate mail, adoration, derision, amusement, amazement, very rarely ignored unless deliberately so. I had a really bizarre experience in St Mary Abbot's Hospital.

I was booked in to have my nose cauterised. I had broken it saving a try in one of my heroic rugby tackles in an Old Boys' game five years before and, while it didn't normally cause me any discomfort, when I had a cold my left nostril completely ceased to function. The answer was to stick a hot poker up the nostril and burn a hole through the broken bone. A simple enough procedure, they said. You went in one night, got your nose poked and came out the next day. Except I didn't.

My nose wouldn't stop bleeding. I had to stay in hospital for two weeks with a large white plaster stuck across my nostrils, walking around the wards doing my impersonation of Groucho Marx. One day I noticed in *TV Times* that I was to be on television on Friday at 9pm.

I had recorded an episode of *The Avengers* some weeks earlier in which I played the guest baddie, Eric Duboys. It was a marvellous showy, exhausting part in which, dressed as Robin Hood, I swung from vines, fenced with Diana Rigg and fought manically with Patrick Macnee. It was tongue-in-cheek high-action thrills at their best and I was rather proud of my performance, so I asked the matron if I could go home and watch myself on my own 24-inch TV set – the hospital one was only 18 inches. Black and white, of course; there was no colour yet.

'You might be contagious,' she said guardedly. But as I lived just down the road she eventually agreed that an ambulance would take me home – and bring me straight back after the show.

Although I was far from famous, the word went round that I was on television that night and the whole ward congregated around the television as the ambulance drove me away. At the end of the show I kissed Audrey goodbye and was immediately transported back to the hospital. I entered the ward to find my fellow patients still gathered around the box.

'What did you think?' I asked daringly.

There was silence – until one man, electing himself spokesman, stood up and enquired, 'Patrick, why didn't your nose bleed?'

'What?' I asked in astonishment.

'Why didn't your nose bleed when you took the plaster off?'

I had been in that hospital for two weeks and they thought I had nipped out and, without any rehearsal, had dressed up as Robin Hood, kissed Diana Rigg and fought Pat Macnee. So much for two years' training at RADA.

Throughout my career I have been a very fortunate actor. Although not sometimes making necessarily the right choice of role, I have still been very choosy and even at this early stage I turned down certain television work my friends thought I was mad to reject. Even so, I still did parts in *Z Cars*, *Riviera Police* and the 'Wednesday Thriller' series, and also did three Babycham adverts for director Nick Roeg, but my heart was still set on being a stage actor. Birmingham Rep was the place to go in those days, and when I told Philip Pearman he got me contracted for a season there doing three plays, including playing Mortimer the Younger in Christopher Marlowe's *Edward II* opposite an extremely shapely young actress called Gabrielle Drake. I rented a tiny garret in the backstreets of Brum. An exploding tin of Fray Bentos steak and kidney pie rendered my Baby Belling cooker useless for the rest of my stay. I didn't know you were supposed to open the tin.

Dodo Watts urged Thames TV's Michael Chapman to see my Edward. He did and rang to ask me out for dinner. While I was in Birmingham, Audrey and I moved back to Oxford to live with her parents, so I met Michael at the city's famous Randolph Hotel. In the elegant dining room Michael told me that he was creating at Teddington Studios a new series called *Haunted*, about a university lecturer who investigated the paranormal, poltergeists, telekinesis and things that go bump in the night. His name was to be Michael West and he was considering me for the star role.

'One question,' he said. 'It must be statistically right and by my reckoning he has to be 28 years old. How old are you, Patrick?'

I was 26, but without a pause I, of course, replied, 'I am 28.'

The meeting went well and later Michael introduced me to his executive producer, a man who was to play an immensely important part in my television career.

It was his Head of Drama, Lloyd Shirley. Lloyd was a stocky, red-haired, red goatee'd, no-nonsense, shoot-from-the-hip Canadian. He had the habit of letting his cigarette smoke drift out of his mouth rather than exhaling it, so that the pale-blue eyes seemed to be constantly in a mist. Again the meeting seemed to go well.

I returned to Birmingham to appear in a new play called *A Boston Story*, an adaptation of Henry James's novel *The Bostonians*. I played a cheroot-smoking, cowboy-booted gambler. Adopting a Stetson hat, bootlace tie and a St Louis drawl, I had a ball. I didn't hear anything after the meeting with Lloyd Shirley until the postman dropped a script through my parents-in-law's front door. But it wasn't for *Haunted*.

Instead, it was a script for *Public Eye*, a hugely popular television series of the time starring Alfie Burke as Frank Marker, a pre-*Columbo*, pre-*Shoestring*, down-at-heel detective. It was an enormous guest-starring role and I gladly accepted it.

I duly filmed this at Teddington as soon as I had finished in Birmingham and two weeks later was called in to see Lloyd and Michael. They told me that the part I had just completed had been specially written for me as a screen test for *Haunted*. He said they were delighted with my performance and were happy to offer me the role of Michael West.

Haunted is one of the programmes I am most proud of. It had terrific scripts, directors and great guest stars, and of course a whopping starring role for me. Because of its 'spooky' subject, it didn't go out till 10pm on Saturdays.

Unfortunately for me, something else had a new starring role on television. To a great fanfare, the BBC launched *Match of the Day*. For the first time football matches were to be seen on television, and at what time? Saturday evening at ten o'clock, of course. Even I wanted to watch it.

Haunted gained a cult following but inevitably not the ratings ITV wanted.

Lloyd asked me if I would like to do another series of *Haunted*, to be screened on a Friday this time, or a new series, *Frontier*, a saga of the Indian Empire which he was planning to make in India. He offered me the part of Captain Rifkind, one of the major characters, but I would prefer to do *Haunted*, I said. *Wrong!*

Frontier went ahead but suddenly the company I was working for, Rediffusion, merged with ATV to form Thames Television. In the merger *Haunted* was spirited away into the night.

However, fortune was still smiling on me. I was asked to reprise the role I had created in the Henry James play in the West End, this time with Tony Britton, Dinah Sheridan and the gorgeous Nicola Pagett, and so I found myself back at the Duchess for the third time in four years.

Another Simon was now to appear in my life. I was lucky enough for my first film role to be cast as Simon Aron in the wonderful classic horror movie *The Devil Rides Out*, from the book by Dennis Wheatley. In this I played alongside horror icon Christopher Lee, Paul Eddington, later to be the comedy face of politics in the Thatcher era as the hapless minister in *Yes Minister*, Sarah Lawson, Charles Gray and Leon Greene. My girl in the film, which, under the brilliantly imaginative hand of director Terence Fisher, has achieved must-see cult status, was Nike Arrighi.

Having experienced Wolfit's height obsession, imagine my amazement on my first day's filming to be looking up five inches to not one but three co-stars: Charles Gray, Christopher Lee and Leon Greene. Now I understood just what Wolfit felt.

What was even more striking was the bitter but friendly rivalry between these big men. My dressing room was linked to Greene's and after our first meeting on the studio floor I could hear him muttering, 'I'll show the bugger,' in a high-pitched voice that was at total variance with his massive build.

As I poked my head round the door I was surprised to see that he was cutting folded newspaper and putting it into his shoes.

'What are you doing, Leon?' I asked.

'I am not having that Christopher Lee taller than me,' he piped back. 'I'll show the bugger.'

It was all quite bizarre. In the interests of integrity I didn't run around looking for a box to stand on to boost my height, so my Simon Aron looks about five feet tall in scenes with these giants.

But height isn't everything. In fact, Christopher Lee has long complained that he was not as successful a movie actor as he should have been because he was too tall and made his co-stars look short. I agree with them.

And as for the huge-framed Leon Greene, who later played Little John in the Robin Hood films, moviegoers never heard his real voice. Sarah Lawson was married to lantern-jawed Patrick Allen, the most famous voice-over artist ever, whose strong, deep voice sold, among many other products, Wilkinson Sword razor blades. It was Allen who was called in to re-voice Leon's high, piping pitch with his own dark-chocolate tones.

When we finished filming I was offered a three-year contract by Michael Carreras, the director and producer and son of Sir Michael Carreras, the founder of Hammer Films, the first of which was to be *The Land That Time Forgot*. I desperately wanted to be a film actor but, after consulting my agent, I considered the part they were offering was too small, and turned it down. Was this arrogance? I like to think it was belief in myself.

I must have seemed perfectly at home in the film studios because I soon struck up a firm friendship with Ursula Andress, widely acclaimed as the ultimate Bond girl. We had our own table in the studio restaurant. Well, if it's a choice between Ursula Andress and Christopher Lee...

I remember showing her the picture of my dream girl that I always carried. It was Sophia Loren dripping wet in *Boy on a Dolphin*. I wonder if that's where she got the idea for her spectacular emergence from the ocean in her white bikini as Honey Ryder in the original 007 movie *Dr No*.

Ursula was making the adventure movie *She*, based on Rider Haggard's novel, and we hit it off right away. Girls like to be seen with nice blokes and find me easy to get along with. Some men find themselves overawed and dumbstruck when confronted with such beauty, but I never have. I'm sure this made Ursula feel secure. I was very happily married to Audrey at the time and I never sent out dangerous or provocative signals. I flirted with her, of course, but obviously there was never going to be anything more.

11

'The Name's Mower...
Patrick Mower'

AFTER A LONG illness, my dear friend and agent, Philip Pearman, had sadly died, and now, after being head-hunted, I was managed by top theatrical agent Jean Diamond.

When the Mr Hyde in me comes out, it inevitably ends in tears – for yours truly. And, thinking back, incredible though it now seems, I really believe I actually talked myself out of landing one of the great movie hero parts – that quintessentially British action phenomenon, James Bond.

Back then in the 1960s I was aware of the effect Bond, as portrayed by Sean Connery, was having and how he had taken hold of the public's imagination. And my walk-on role in the saga had all the cloak-and-dagger melodrama of a cheap thriller.

It all began, in the best tradition of thrillers, with a death: Michael Caine's, or, to be more precise, that of his character Harry Palmer, the bespectacled hero spook in the Len Deighton espionage thrillers.

Jean rang to tell me that the famous producing partnership of Harry Saltzman and Cubby Broccoli were planning to make a new Harry Palmer film based on Deighton's best-selling novel *Horse under Water*. The Caine films had been such enormous successes they wanted to continue the role and had asked if I would audition for the new Harry Palmer. Initially, I wasn't even faintly interested, telling Jean, 'You must be joking. There is no way I am going to impersonate Michael Caine with those awful square glasses.'

She laughed, insisting, 'Don't worry, Harry Palmer is just a code name. The part is for a new spy who'll be sent out into the field without the Russians realising there's been a substitution.'

At the time I had built up a reputation as a bit of a dandy, having twice been voted 'Best Dressed Man on Television', and I always wore a flower in my buttonhole – I had a passion for yellow chrysanthemums – and used to get my more fashionable clothes from John Stephen, 'The King of Carnaby Street'. John was always ahead of the trends, and one day, when I dropped into his Wigmore Street shop, I spotted a pink suit with round lapels – really cool, man! He had just two, but one was a perfect fit and I bought it. When I returned to the shop a couple of weeks later John raced over and, with a broad smile, said, 'Patrick, you'll never guess who bought the other suit – Mick Jagger.' Trendy or what?

Now, decades later, Matthew Bose, who plays my son in *Emmerdale*, turned up at the Soap Awards in a pink Prada suit. I couldn't resist telling him, 'You've no idea how far behind the fashion you are, boy.'

Luckily, I overcame the urge to wear the suit at the Harry Palmer audition. Now these are always quite tense moments and I was determined to make an impact. So I dressed very carefully and looked the epitome of 'Mr Elegance' in a black polo neck beneath a beautifully cut suit, plus my trademark yellow chrysanthemum.

It was just as well I had put on my best front, for the room was packed with the aristocracy of English acting – Ian Holm, Ian Richardson, Michael Gambon, Anthony Valentine and every luminary from the theatre and television world, household names to a man. In their hunt for a suitable star to replace Mr Caine the producers were looking at only the best.

I took a chair determined to play it cool as we all sat around looking at one another, as you tend to, until Dyson Lovell, the casting director, called out, 'Patrick, can you come up now?' He knocked gently on the door of the adjoining room and ushered me in.

After announcing my name, Dyson left and I found myself standing in an enormous, 30-foot-long room. Harry Saltzman was sitting at his desk leafing through papers while Broccoli, twiddling a pair of glasses behind his back in his usual fashion, looked out of the window, away from me.

At that moment Mr Hyde took over. You're not intimidating me, I thought, and instead of meekly walking over to the desk I remained standing by the door. There was silence. The only sound, the steady ticking of a rather splendid clock sitting on an equally splendid Regency side table.

At that time, although I say it myself, I was pretty hot property from starring in the West End and being in a TV series. So, instead of being overly impressed and thinking, Gosh, this is exciting, I simply decided, well, they're obviously not interested.

I couldn't have been more wrong. I continued to stand my ground by the door. As the hands of the clock reached 11 its sonorous Westminster chime seemed to concentrate Harry's mind. He looked up from his papers and swept his gaze over me, did a double take, sat up and coughed twice to his partner. As Broccoli turned round, Saltzman nodded towards me at the end of the room as if to say, 'Look.' Putting his glasses back on, Broccoli turned to Saltzman and asked, 'Who is he?'

Looking down at his papers to see who was in the 11-o'clock slot, Saltzman said, 'Patrick Mower?' I nodded, not moving. Then, eyes fixed on me, he said, 'Come closer, please, Patrick.'

Two pairs of eyes were riveted on me and the steady tick of the clock seemed to keep time with me as I approached the desk. I stopped. The tick continued. No one spoke. There was a long silence. They looked at each other and then back at me. Then, out of the blue, Saltzman suddenly blurted, 'What's your body like?'

'I've never had any complaints. Everything's in the right place,' I let Mr Hyde reply.

'Sit down,' Saltzman said at last. He then asked me what I was doing and then we began the usual interview process.

When you go for an audition, you know you have just eight minutes in the room during which to make your mark. If you don't make the right impression in that time, you've lost it and one of the others waiting their turn to shine will clinch the role. But, to my surprise, Saltzman and Broccoli didn't seem a bit bothered about the time as they went on to tell me about *Horse under Water*, explaining that it was to be a different kind of film but they hadn't yet signed a director.

The clock chimed a quarter past.

'I'm not playing Michael Caine,' I said, at which they smiled.

'That's fine,' said Saltzman. 'We're looking for a new actor.'

He explained that the whole point was to have a new special agent in the field who, by using the same code name, would fool the Russians. What a devilish plan!

'Excuse me,' said Saltzman, then picked up the phone and

Target caused great controversy for its violence and I became notorious as tough-guy Detective Chief Superintendent Steve Hackett. A comic even took the name for its title and featured cartoons of me inside. Here, I am pictured with my son Simon, who played my son in the show (*bottom*).

In my pink jacket for the fanclub photo all the girls received. Watch out Mick Jagger!

In the seventies I made the cover of both the *TV* and *Radio Times*, and am pictured picking up my framed souvenir cover at the 1974 *Radio Times* Christmas party for those featured that year (*Bottom left*). A few years later, I won the 1985 Best Dressed Man on TV Award. Glad the suit's not in colour (*bottom right*).

My starring in the West End and in major TV series caused no waves in the Emmerdale green room, but when this *Viz* cartoon appeared the room was green with envy.

Above: With Maggie Smith in *Night and Day* at the Phoenix Theatre.

Below: Me as 'Il Lupo' in *The Devil's Advocate*, with Raf Vallone (*middle*) and Sir John Mills (*right*).

I appeared in Callan as the smooth killer James Cross (*top left*), and looking back now I can see why I was considered to play Bond, though I couldn't believe it at the time. Here I am camping it up as Captain Cook in Peter Pan in St Albans, a panto I also directed. I was also delighted to join the *Carry On* team in *Carry on England*. Here, I'm pictured with Kenneth Connor.

Above: Guest-starring in Minder for the episode 'A Number Of Old Wives' Tales', with Vivienne Ritchie, who played one of my six wives, Dennis Waterman (*left*) and George Cole (*far right*).

Below: Playing Zangler in Gershwin's *Crazy For You* was a real adventure. Anya and Honeybee the horse came on the road with me and all the girls in 1995.

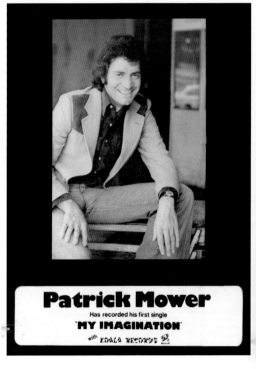

(Clockwise from top left) Elton John's party in Sydney for Bette Midler's birthday was no modest affair. Notice Sydney Opera House shaped cake – some modifications had been made as a nod to Bette's famous onstage boob-flashing! With Suzanne Danielle at the opening night of Stringfellows. I also had my own show on Capital Radio giving away champers and roses. I never played my own single though – some say it wasn't released, it escaped!

dialled a number. 'Can you come up?' He spoke urgently. 'Now... *Now*... OK...'

As Saltzman put the phone down, Dyson put his head round the door and asked, 'Is there a problem?'

Twenty minutes had gone by and the other actors, with appointments to keep, maybe matinees, voice-overs, were getting fidgety. But Saltzman and Broccoli said, 'No, no,' and Dyson left. They kept on chatting and I had run out of questions.

The clock chimed the half-hour.

Eventually, an elderly lady came in laden down with Bond Street shopping bags.

We all stood as she approached us, her eyes never leaving me. 'This is Patrick Mower,' offered Harry.

As a gentleman I'd been taught that you never offer your hand to a lady; she should offer hers to you. I don't know if my attempt at politeness was appreciated. She probably thought I was being terribly rude, but, as an Englishman, I've always been taught that manners are important.

She said simply, 'Hello,' and slowly walked around me, looking me up and down.

The two film men watched intently, obviously waiting for her reaction, then she walked away and stood behind the desk. I felt like a mannequin promoting clothes in a store, or as if I was being sold in a slave market.

Finally she gave the slightest nod.

As if relieved, the clock struck 11.45 and Dyson popped his head round the door and told them, 'Some of the artists have to go.'

Broccoli and Saltzman chorused, 'We've finished,' before turning to me and saying, 'We'll call you in again when we have a director.'

As I reached the door, Saltzman called out to me, 'Patrick, I know you are with Jean Diamond, but can I have your home number?'

Puzzled, I gave it to him. What a strange interview, I thought as I left.

Later I told Jean that they seemed to like me. She was a bit peeved about my giving them our phone number. But it was just as well that I had, for that Sunday afternoon Harry Saltzman rang me at home. He told me that they now had a director and asked if I could go in the next day to meet him.

When I arrived, the following day, at their offices in South Audley Street, I was surprised to find that there wasn't even a receptionist on duty. I felt this was very strange, but pushed the buzzer for Eon Productions and Harry Saltzman answered and opened the door himself. He seemed very pleased to see me and ushered me into the same room, where Broccoli stood in his usual position.

After accepting a coffee, I asked, 'Who is the director?'

'We haven't decided on one yet,' Broccoli replied.

The two of them stood behind the desk. I sat in front of it. Bemused, I said, 'But I thought that was the whole point of me coming in today.'

They both looked down at me. There was another silence. I became aware of the clock again.

'This is for something else,' Broccoli said.

More silence. More ticking.

Then Saltzman asked, 'Have you seen the Bond films?'

'Yes, I should think everyone has seen them,' I replied.

'Do you like them?'

'They're fantastic,' I said. This is really weird, I was thinking as they continued to stare down at me from behind the desk.

Then Broccoli dropped his bombshell. 'This is in the strictest

100 per cent confidence,' he said, 'but Sean isn't going to do another Bond.'

'Why not?' I said. 'He's amazing!' To this day I think Sean Connery was by far the best Bond.

'He believes he has done enough. So we're looking for another Bond.'

Yet another pause.

I looked from one man to the other. Then, in complete innocence, I said, 'Who are you thinking of?'

They didn't reply but just continued staring at me.

The clock ticked on.

It was only then that the penny dropped. It was as if someone had poured a bottle of ice-cold champagne over my head. My jaw dropped to the floor and in disbelief I stammered, 'You're thinking of me!'

They nodded in tandem. I gulped.

'But Sean is a man,' I said. 'I'm... I'm a boy...'

'You're a man, Patrick,' Saltzman replied. 'Believe us. We think you've got it.'

They again asked for my trust. 'Only we three in this room and Sean know of his decision.'

What a burden. I wanted to shout it from the rooftops.

At that time, every man fantasised about being James Bond. Kids played him in the street, men imagined themselves being on a beach with Pussy Galore. He was the ultimate modern hero. But I had never, ever imagined stepping into the role, because Connery *was* Bond. He had made the role so completely his own.

'Did you get it then?' Jean asked when I telephoned her. She still thought I was up for the Harry Palmer role – we had even discussed how I would play him.

'No,' I said. 'They don't want me for Harry Palmer.'

'I'm so sorry, Patrick,' she said.

Mr Hyde wanted me to deliver the punch line, 'They want me to be James Bond!', but Dr Jekyll said, 'Yes, it's a shame, but that's showbiz.'

I headed for the theatre with my sensational secret. At the stage door Tom Stoppard was waiting for me. 'Patrick, I saw the show again last night,' he said, 'and I just wanted to thank you for reminding me what a very funny play I had written.'

What a lovely day!

Over the following weeks I had several meetings at Eon, with Harry and Cubby again insisting upon total secrecy.

But I fear my conceit and sense of humour were beginning to chip away at their confidence in me. Called to meet a writer, I would enter humming the Bond theme and announce, 'The name's Mower... Patrick Mower.'

I would then turn to them and say, 'Now, you mustn't make me laugh because it makes me look too young!' What a fool – sowing seeds of doubt!

I didn't take it seriously and really think I talked myself out of it. But I honestly felt that at 28 I was too young.

Now, looking at myself in old television footage, I can see what they saw and believe I would have made a fantastic Bond. One morning Jean called to tell me they were casting for a new James Bond and she had got me a screen test the next day at Pinewood.

'Is it just me they're testing?'

'Oh no, I think there are ten of you,' she replied.

I was so disappointed I couldn't face the test. I stayed at home and cried. I'd had a part of a lifetime in the palm of my hand, and I had let it slip out. No! – I had thrown it away.

They chose George Lazenby. *Wrong!*

I was, however, to discover that my foot was still holding James Bond's door firmly open.

Having had a taste of the film world, I wanted more. A few television scripts and theatre tours were offered to me, which, once again in the grandest manner, I turned down – only to chalk up another mistake in my life. I worked with a cockney charmer called Robert Hartford-Davies. He was a film director, and I wanted to be a film star.

Hartford-Davies took me to lunch at Pinewood and told me that he had a wonderful script which was not quite finished but which would also star Dennis Waterman, the 50-year-old classical actress Renee Asherson and a hot new discovery called Madeline Hinde. The film, called *The Smashing Bird I Used to Know*, was a typical movie of the time and was to be shot around London in six weeks.

One scene in the film, which was later also released as *School for Unclaimed Girls*, required my character, Harry Spenton, to whack Madeline's character, Nicki Johnson, around the face and pull her dressing gown off, thus exposing her breasts in daring Sixties style. After we had filmed the scene a stills photographer took various shots of arms swinging, gown-pulling and pretend screaming.

The rest of the film was fun. Dennis and I had a laugh. Madeline and I had to simulate sex with me lying on top of her but our bodies separated by a white sheet which she clutched to her chin.

One wet afternoon at the Essoldo a few months later I emerged bleary-eyed into the mini-skirted, white-booted world of the King's Road to spot Dennis creeping out after me. We both held our heads in shame at this farrago of a film that we were involved in and swiftly made our way to the World's End pub, where we got completely inebriated. It was such an unmitigated load of old tripe.

Worse was to come a month later in the shape of the

American scandal paper the *National Enquirer*. Jean Diamond called me into her office and showed me the double-page *Enquirer* spread of pictures of Madeline and myself under the heading 'Actor rapes starlet on set'.

The pictures were of us, although they had changed the names, with 'interviews' allegedly from the actors giving the most horrendous description in sordid, graphic detail of how the actor got carried away with his seduction and, although the director was yelling, 'Cut, cut,' he wouldn't stop and eventually penetrated the actress. This was dynamite.

We immediately consulted Oscar Beuselinck, the famous show-business libel lawyer and father of the actor Paul Nicholas, as we wished to sue to clear my name. But he advised that it was impossible as the litigation laws in England did not apply in the United States and it would be ruinously expensive. Obviously I was not only devastated but extremely angry and thought long and hard about this course of action. In the end, however, Oscar having made it clear that the legal difficulties were such that I could end up causing more bad publicity and heartache for myself, I accepted his advice and dropped the case.

This was not to be the only time I was to be the victim of a fabricated story. Did I learn a lesson? No. And did working with Robert Hartford-Davies teach me anything? No. I was to do it again a couple of years later.

James Bond may have eluded me but I nearly metamorphosed into an entirely different kind of suave hero.

I was doing an episode of *Department S* for Monty Berman at the ATV studios when I got a call asking if I had a dark-blue suit and a white shirt. 'Yes,' I said, and I was then instructed to go down to Stage B after I'd had finished shooting. When I arrived I discovered it was a test for a new series, *Jason King*, and I was being considered for the lead role. In the end the part went to Peter Wyngarde. Just think, I might have been famous as a moustachioed, frilly-shirted dandy. A lucky escape.

But I was far from finished with Bond.

When the 'Chocolate Man' melted away in the blistering heat of the Secret Service scene, handing in his 007 credentials after just one outing, Saltzman and Broccoli sent for me again.

This time they said, would I please do a screen test? I was whisked down to Pinewood and did a scene with Lois Maxwell, who played Miss Moneypenny.

I thought I did rather well. They didn't. As it turned out, once again I missed out as they gave the part to Roger Moore.

The same year another script was sent to my agent which might have become a major turning point in my career.

At the time I was concentrating on film work and turning down television and theatre roles, so I needed no urging to join Vincent Price and the rest of the cast for American International Pictures' Gothic horror thriller *Cry of the Banshee*, directed by Gordon Hessler, whom I knew already. I played Roderick, the evil spirit exacting revenge on Price's witch-burning magistrate in not-so-jolly 16th-century England.

It was exciting stuff. Roderick, after making love to a girl, would suddenly start up in bed when the Banshee howled. They would then find another of the magistrate's sons with his throat ripped out. The old crone who summoned Roderick from the darkness was Elisabeth Bergner, who had been such a major Hollywood star in the 1930s that she had only just been pipped by Greta Garbo for the title role in *Queen Christina*.

I was always called to make-up one and a half hours after Elisabeth and when I asked the reason the make-up man explained that poor Elisabeth, like Marlene Dietrich, had had, throughout her Hollywood career, the skin of her face pulled tight behind her ears with bulldog clips. As a result, her face was horrendously falling down in dewlaps on her chin and so it took an hour and a half in make-up to get her looking like an ordinary 85-year-old lady. Off set I never saw her without a scarf around her neck, poor woman.

One day I got an unexpected call to the office of the AIP producer Emile Zarkoff. I feared I was in for a wigging as that was normally the only reason actors were summoned in this fashion. So I was surprised to find a limo waiting to pick me up. I was even more surprised when, facing the American over his desk, he asked me in his high-pitched voice, 'Patrick, have you ever read *Wuthering Heights?*'

'Yes,' I replied.

'Have you seen Olivier's Heathcliff?'

'Yes. Fantastic!'

'We're planning a remake of *Wuthering Heights*. We've been looking at you in the rushes of *The Banshee*. We think you'll make a fantastic Heathcliff. Are you interested?'

Of course I told him I most certainly was.

'But we have a problem,' he warned me. 'You're unknown in America.'

Let's change that, I thought.

He paid for Crispian Woodgate to shoot a series of photographs of me as Heathcliff in breeches and a *Hamlet*-style shirt, looking very dark and brooding. Then he told me he needed my press cuttings, 'So we can sell you to Hollywood.'

This posed a problem as English actors tend not to keep their cuttings unless they're terribly vain. I wasn't! You don't want to keep the ones that say you are wonderful and you try to ignore the others. I managed to cobble a few together but there was a more serious problem. They were due to start shooting in six weeks and I couldn't get to the States to see their production team as I was still filming *The Cry of the Banshee*.

They dithered and dithered – until finally the part went to a young actor who had just finished *A Lion in Winter* with Peter O'Toole and Katherine Hepburn. He was Timothy Dalton, who, later in my career, was to pip me for another iconic figure.

I became very friendly with Vincent Price, in my opinion a very underrated actor, and a man with a tremendous sense of humour. I was in his room on the final day of shooting when the producer gave me the bad news that they were going to go with Dalton. Vincent said, 'Patrick, you would have been fantastic.'

'I know,' said Zarkoff. He then asked me to leave as he wanted to have a word with Vincent.

The wrap party was in full flow when, in real showbiz style, they wheeled in on a trolley an enormous celebration cake, four feet high and four feet wide. Given a huge knife with which to cut it, Vincent drawled, 'This looks like the one I have just found in my back. I would like to thank AIP, who have just terminated my contract after 20 years.'

He then plunged the knife into the cake with a vengeance – and to tremendous cheers, out popped a gorgeous naked girl with her arms outstretched. Ta-ra, ta-ra...

Vincent, completely ignoring the posing beauty, launched into a half-hour diatribe against the producer and AIP. He had the cast and crew in fits of laughter as he insulted the bosses, saying their films had all been a pile of crap which he alone had turned into the successes they were. As he ranted on, the girl's smile and her outstretched arms slowly sank lower and lower as she realised that no one was going to tell her to stand down.

I was so sorry for her that later I felt it only decent to help get rid of her goosebumps – always the gentleman!

On the film I also became very friendly with Hugh Griffiths. He had won an Oscar for his role in *Lawrence of Arabia* and not only was he a sensational actor but he had a sensational presence too. With his eyebrows bursting out above his fiery Celtic eyes, he reminded me of my father.

As he was an alcoholic, his wife used to chaperone him on the set in an attempt to keep him off the bottle. When Hugh discovered I was Welsh, he entrusted me with one of his most sacred possessions. Every morning a half-bottle of malt whisky appeared in my dressing room.

I learned to keep the Scotch hidden in my Banshee fur skin. We worked out a code so that Hugh could give his wife the slip and join me for a dram. 'How is the Banshee today?' he would boom, to check if he could drop in for a drink. If I said, 'Fine,' his eyes would light up and we'd celebrate, but I was very careful not to let him have too much – except on one occasion, when he was too smart for me.

Hugh was playing the gravedigger and, having just completed his last scene on the film, remained six feet down in a newly dug grave. As the crew dispersed to shoot the next scene he whispered to me, 'How's the Banshee today?' The coast being clear, I tossed down a half-bottle of malt. Hugh caressed it lovingly and sat down in the grave. He looked up at me, winked and said, 'Tell the witch I've gone to my caravan.'

Half an hour later we looked down at his prostrate figure. He had the crew in fits of laughter as, empty bottle by his side, he called up, 'Fill the hole in, boys – I'm ready to go!'

Mrs Griffiths was *not* pleased.

Hugh wasn't the only actor on the set who liked to party. One of my brothers was Michael Elphick, then a very powerful and handsome actor. He too was more than partial to the odd drink – a compulsion which, sadly, would eventually ruin his career and kill him.

Years after we worked together on *The Banshee*, when he found fame as the urban cowboy star of the hugely successful television series *Boon*, they had to stop filming at one o'clock because he couldn't stand up.

Late one afternoon Elphick came into my dressing room and said, 'I'd like you to meet my mate Ollie.' And there, handsome smile flashing, was Oliver Reed, clutching an enormous two-litre bottle of whisky.

'Fancy a drink?' he said, proffering the bottle in one massive fist.

As I looked for a glass, Ollie said, 'You don't need that.' Effortlessly swinging the giant bottle up to his lips, he swallowed deeply. That was the start. When filming finished for the day the three of us descended to the crypt for what Ollie described as a 'serious drink'.

As I had a starring role, I had a driver waiting for me – and that was to prove my salvation. After an hour of the three of us sitting in that extremely dark dungeon swapping horny and hairy stories between swigs, a voice echoed down the stairs, 'Mr Mower... Mr Mower...' It was Charlie, my driver.

'Tell him to sod off,' said Ollie, but, knowing that I had a lot of lines to learn and an early start in the morning, I made my excuses and managed to escape.

The next morning, as I opened my dressing-room door at 6.30, I heard a voice shouting, 'Mower, come and finish your drink.'

Oliver Reed and Michael Elphick were still in the cellar, Ollie clutching the bottle with the remaining dregs of whisky in his giant hand. Laughing, I couldn't resist – and had a quick small double.

Many years later, I was to run into Elphick in another cellar – in the Buxton, a famous actors' club off Shaftesbury Avenue. I was appearing opposite Susan George in *The Golden Girl* at the Globe Theatre and was enjoying a pre-matinee drink when Michael walked in.

'What are you doing in London?' I asked, knowing he should be in Nottingham filming *Boon*.

'They sent me down to see a specialist. I've been spitting blood,' he told me casually.

When I asked what was the doctor's prognosis, Mike replied, 'He said if I don't stop drinking and smoking I'm going to die. I'll have a pint, please – and 20 fags. What's yours, Pat?'

He had cirrhosis of the liver and had to stop drinking, but he wouldn't. Every time I met Mike after that, I would try to get him to stop, but to no avail. The last time I saw him was at a television awards ceremony at the Albert Hall when he was appearing in *EastEnders*.

He greeted me in his usual slurred voice, 'Oh no, Pat, don't tell me off again. You always tell me that I'm a fantastic actor and that I'm going to kill myself.'

'Believe me,' I said, 'they're both true.'

And sadly they were.

I was reminded of my lovely early-morning whisky bracer with Michael and Ollie some years later when, coincidentally, I was again starring with Susan George, in the Hammer film *Czech Mate*.

At 6.30 on the first morning of filming in Prague, I noticed the technicians gathered in a tight huddle around a table. When I asked what was going on, they made it clear in their broken English that they were having a sip of vodka.

Ever the perfect Englishman abroad, I looked down my nose and thought, How unseemly at this hour of the day.

But the next morning I wasn't so snooty. Having downed one glass of wine too many at dinner with Susan the previous night, at 6am I was feeling decidedly fragile. I allowed myself a nip of their real Polish vodka and, boy, was it rough! But 20 seconds after it hit the back of my throat it exploded in my brain. I felt wonderful.

I knew from my chats with Richard Burton that early-morning vodka bracers were the start of the road to alcoholism. But, I'm ashamed to say, every morning before we started filming on *Czech Mate* I had a shot. It doesn't half make you feel better at the crack of dawn.

Strangely enough, when Susan was making the notorious Sam Peckinpah film *Straw Dogs* with Dustin Hoffman, I was going out with her body double. Whether they thought my girl's body was better or Susan refused to do the scenes, I don't know. But my girl certainly made Susan look good, and me feel good.

12

Icons

AND SO DID the beauty who out-manoeuvred me with a cunning that left me breathless.

It was 100 degrees outside the villa and inside I was feeling twice as hot as the most perfect pair of 36 Double Ds rolled themselves around on my bare chest.

I'd sworn never to work with Robert Hartford-Davies again after the awful *Smashing Bird*. He, however, had other ideas. I think he saw dollar signs. He bombarded me with scripts, all of which I rejected until *Doctors Wear Scarlet* landed on my mat. A steamy take on vampirism, it was adapted by Simon Raven from his novel. So, two months in Cyprus; lots of money; and a good script for a film co-starring Patrick Macnee, Edward Woodward and Peter Cushing: *The Flesh Is Weak*. And mine certainly was as I lay beneath that dusky beauty. The owner of those two magnificent orbs – whose hand had now slipped inside my pants – was the incredibly sexy, sultry actress Imogen Hassall.

Apart from the camera crew and the director, the sweltering room was packed full with sparks, chippies, plasterers, hairdressers, make-up artists – in fact, the whole film unit seemed jammed in. All, I thought, to catch a glimpse of Imogen's famous bazookas!

The sex scene we were shooting was, as they say, an integral part of the plot. Which usually means it has been inserted to help the producer raise the finance.

The director – who after this picture went to America and, calling himself Lord Hartford-Davis, did rather well – had told me that after the initial few lines of dialogue Imo, or 'Aphrodite' as her character was called, would start to seduce me.

'We'll just have a few minutes rolling around and the camera will pan off you on to the beach with waves crashing in and out.'

Original, I thought.

'How will I know when you've panned off us?' I asked.

'I'll wiggle your big toe,' said Bob.

Then, turning to the crew, he ordered, 'All right, let's get ready for a take.'

As Imo stood with her back to me, having her make-up checked, I couldn't help noticing how beautiful her little purple knickers looked contrasting with the glowing golden brown of her dark skin. They were those quick-action pants which undo at the sides and they now stretched tightly over the shining cheeks of her firm rounded bum.

She slipped under the sheet next to me and pulled it tightly up to her neck before removing the towel that she had been clutching to her ample bosom to preserve her modesty. Mine was also preserved in a natty little pair of black pants. Bad luck, boys, you didn't see anything!

The first assistant yelled in his best sergeant-major voice, 'Right, now this is a very sensitive scene, so let's not have a squeak.' Then, turning round to the packed room, he roared, 'And I thought this was supposed to be a closed set. It looks to me like bleeding Wimbledon!

'Right, turn over. Sound.'

'Yes.'

'Camera.'

'Rolling.'

'Action!'

On that instruction, before I had a chance to say my first line, Imo let out a little moan and rolled her left leg over on top of mine. Now, underneath my rather flippant, nonchalant exterior, I'm actually a rather serious actor – RADA and all that, remember – and I quite admired this move of Imo's. Yes, I thought, that's exactly how we should be lying.

As we did the dialogue, Imo interspersed each of her words with a little kiss on my lips and then on my neck. Good, I thought, this is really acting. She then eased herself up, to enable her left breast – which, as I've pointed out, was not on the small side – to settle gently on to my chest. The little patch of purple knickers between her legs had now started to rub itself against my leg.

While I had been saying my last line of dialogue, Imo's tongue had been exploring the inside of my left ear, making little slurping sounds so very suggestive that I feared the sound man might call, 'Cut', especially as now, with no more words to say, 'Aphrodite' had seriously started to moan again.

The character I was playing, Richard Dane, was a rather repressed Englishman, but, not wanting to let the Old Country down, I thought, Come on, Dickie Boy, keep your end up! And I did a bit of improvisation of my own.

With my free right hand – Imo was lying on my left – I took her face and kissed her gently on the lips. Talk about hitting the

G spot! I thought I'd hit H, I, J, K, L and M as well. Her tongue must have discovered that at the age of 32 I still had my tonsils as it shot in and out of my mouth. At the same time she had taken my right hand and placed it firmly on her left breast. Still holding it, she moved it around in a circular motion twice and then squeezed her nipple with my thumb and forefinger.

Having made sure that I'd got the message, the nails on her own hand started doing some serious damage to my back.

Meanwhile, her purple patch had stopped rubbing. It was now writhing – only it was writhing sideways, moving over my thigh until it found what it was looking for, hidden snugly inside my little black pants. A little too snugly at that moment because, Method actor though I am, a block of ice I am not. And Richard the prig was becoming Bruce Banner – only it wasn't the Hulk that was growing larger!

All this action had taken place under the sheet and, not knowing where the camera was, I kept my eyes firmly closed. But any second now, I thought, I'm going to get my toe tweaked, so I'll give the crew a peek of what they want to see.

I rolled over on top of Imo with the intention of sliding the sheet back so that the boys could get their money's worth. Mistake! I must have hit the O spot, for in one movement Imo's legs spread wide and then clamped themselves firmly round mine. Her hand slid down into the back of my pants and grabbed my buttocks, one in each hand.

The writhing now became a grinding. The Hulk was starting to burst out of his little black costume and, with a flip she must have learned in a circus, Imo now was on top of me, forcing one of her breasts into my mouth. Was I still filming?

I felt something soft and silky caress my face, like a butterfly's wing, but the delicious, hot, musky smell told me that this particular butterfly was a Purple Empress. How on earth did she manage that? I was thinking, when her hand reached down into my pants and released my now rampant monster from its bondage.

'Yes! Yes! Yes!' she screamed.

I had just time to think what a great lover I must be to give her such an orgasm, when she suddenly whipped the sheet back, exposing me in all my glory, and cried, 'He's got one! That's a tenner each, you bastards.'

Imo had bet every one of the crew £10 that she could make me get an erection.

Realising that I had been well and truly stitched up, the one-eyed snake very rapidly decided the time had come to collapse and return to the safety of his little black pants – especially after Colin Corby, the camera operator, called out, 'Call that a stiffy? I've seen more meat in a potato pie! I'm only paying a fiver.'

Not one of my greatest moments, on or off screen, but compensation was just the sensuous sway of a beauty's hips away.

Within days of Imogen's sensational, but rather enjoyable, put-down, I found that being called Patrick can have magnetic qualities – and a case of mistaken identity lead to the most exotic delights.

I'd been having dinner with Patrick Macnee and some crew in the nightclub attached to our hotel, relaxing after a hot day on the set, when the gorgeous Turkish belly dancer who had been entertaining the residents swayed across the dancefloor towards our table with little silver bells dancing on every moving part of her body.

To applause she sat on the laps of most of the crew until she ended up on mine. She put her lips to my ear and breathed into it, then, thrusting her boobs in my face, said, 'Patrick, I love you. I have to talk to you.' And, taking my hand, she pulled me out on to a veranda and started covering my face with kisses and, as I discovered later, bright-red lipstick.

'I want to be your lover,' she said urgently.

Not wanting to be ungrateful, I replied, 'I think we can arrange that,' to which she instantly asked, 'What is your room number?' I told her 316, and rubbing her body against me, she said, 'Patrick, I have to do another show, but I will come to you.'

Surprised that she knew my name, I assumed they got English TV there. What's going on? I thought. I looked around for Jeremy Beadle. Had the crew set me up with a Belly-Dancer-A-Gram?

Back at my chair, the boys started to rib me mercilessly. Pointing out that I was covered in lipstick, Pat Macnee laughed as he said, 'Ah, you old bugger, Patrick. I don't know what you've got but could I have a dozen jars?'

As I wiped my face, I thought, This is ridiculous. There's something not right here. I must be dreaming. But the dream continued.

Later the strangest of sounds, tiny bell sounds, p...shing ... p...shing, awoke me from my slumber and, staring into the half-light of early dawn, I saw the girl twirling her tassels and making the little silver bells undulate all around her waist.

I could barely believe my eyes as she started to do the most amazing of stripteases, never losing her rhythm or stilling the gentle tinkle of the bells as she slowly peeled off her scanty costume.

The bells p...shinged as the last item of clothing dropped to the floor and, still without uttering a single word, she slipped under the sheets and gave me one of the best nights of sex of my life. I'm no slouch at coming forward, but with her I never had a chance. She didn't make love, she used me – completely and wonderfully.

As I lay there completely exhausted, she breathed into my ear, 'When they are filming here, I am always the lover of the star of the movie.'

More than a little taken aback, I replied, 'Well, that's nice.'

Then she murmured, 'I will come to you tomorrow night.'

And next night I was awakened by my 3.30am alarm call going sensuously p...shing ... p...shing ..., and I certainly p...shinged her. And she, from the sounds coming from deep inside her throat, obviously loved being p...shinged!

She told me she was so proud of me and she had some friends she wanted me to meet. So that evening I went along as arranged to the pool and there she was, turning heads in the teeniest of bikinis. Proudly she presented me to her two beautiful friends, saying, 'This is the star of the film – Patrick Macnee.'

'Mower,' I said.

'What?'

'Mower. I am Patrick Mower.'

Looking confused, she said, 'No, you are Patrick Macnee, the star of the film.'

'No,' I said, 'that's Patrick Macnee', and pointed to where he sat reading his script with his usual ice bucket and champagne.

Her face looked like thunder. 'You have deceived me!' she cried, and gave me the most tremendous whack around the ear, causing more bells to p...shing.

The crew loved it.

'I'll make it up to you tonight,' I ventured.

'Oh no you won't!' She turned on her heel and flounced off, shouting back over her shoulder, 'I only make love to the star of the film!'

Pat Macnee looked up from his script, smiled and said, 'Did somebody call?'

She had obviously chosen the wrong Patrick, although I could tell from the way she looked him up and down at the pool that she knew she had really chosen the right one.

On the set the next day, I asked Pat Macnee if the bells had rung for him that night.

'No such luck,' he laughed.

Doctors Wear Scarlet would later be released as *Incense for the Damned* and also as *Bloodsuckers* – something I should have seen coming. This being a Bob Hartford-Davies movie, more breasts were involved of course.

As we shot the closing scenes of the film, fatally bitten – in more ways than one – by the vampiric Imogen, I, as the hero Richard Fountain, in turn swept the gorgeous Madeline Hinde off in my red cloak and, responding to her pleas to make love to her, bit her neck, thus bringing vampire hunters Macnee and Cushing bearing down on us to drive stakes through our hearts.

A fairly standard horror-film ending faced us as we lay in movie coffins about to be gorily dispatched. They shot my death first, using a cut-off stake with rubber on the end which, when struck, spurted blood as it appeared to enter my chest. Having been bloodily disposed of, I climbed out of my coffin and glanced over at the blonde Madeline as she lay in hers revealing her nice but tiny boobs as she waited for her turn to be staked.

As we'd all been together for over three months I thought I knew everyone. However, standing by my shoulder in this closing scene, was a most attractive raven-haired beauty in full make-up, holding a dressing gown around her.

'Hello,' I said. 'Who are you?'

'I play Peter Cushing's daughter. I've been bitten by a vampire and now they have to drive a stake though my heart,' she replied. She artfully let her dressing gown slip open. Alarm bells rang but I didn't listen.

Meanwhile, Bob waited for Madeline to leave the set, then

turned to the dark-haired beauty and, pointing at the coffin, said, 'OK, love, in you get.' The girl dropped her dressing gown and, stark naked, climbed in and lay down with her enormous breasts pointing proudly to high heaven.

'Don't worry about the mush – just get the tits!' ordered Bob. That just about summed up his artistic direction.

Her dark hair was pushed out of sight, Hartford-Davis called, 'Action,' and the stake was placed on her left nipple. They then simulated the stake being driven in.

It all worked out very well, with the finished film showing Madeline's face above these beautiful boobs. To Bob's salivating satisfaction, the scene was shot seven times until the blood slowly and sensuously made its way over the impressive contours. He, of course, insisted upon personally wiping the poor girl's breasts clean between every take.

The movie career upon which I had set my heart was now really taking off. It was 1971 and within weeks of finishing *Doctors Wear Scarlet* I found myself starring alongside Hollywood icon Kirk Douglas and the highly acclaimed Trevor Howard in the Cold War comedy thriller written by Dick Clement and Ian La Frenais. There was certainly plenty of comedy in *Catch Me a Spy* – and not always in front of the cameras.

The making of this film in Scotland had received a lot of publicity. On the first Sunday morning, the whole crew watched as Kirk Douglas teetered down the path to sign the autograph books of the 50 or so girl fans. They had been sitting patiently on the wall surrounding our hotel for about two hours. The 'lifts' that he wore in his shoes made him lean forward, giving him that slightly aggressive posture that had become his trademark.

We were in Oban, on the Firth of Lorne in western Scotland, and even on that sunny Sunday morning, five-foot-nine Kirk felt he needed his 'elevators'. Some of the girls turned to see who was approaching but none of them got up as he reached the gate. He took a sip of his pint of beer and looked back at the hotel. He then turned and stomped all the way back up the path.

Pushing open the swing doors, he stood for a moment in the foyer, took another swig of his beer and, through his famously clenched teeth, rasped, 'Patrick Mower, get your ass out there!'

A load of the girls were waiting for *me*!

This was greeted by a huge cheer from the crew because 'Mr Douglas', as the director had asked us to address him (it wasn't Kirk's idea), had only arrived on the film three days earlier and, after watching Trevor Howard and I do a scene together, he had said in a loud voice, 'I've heard of Trevor Howard, but who the hell is the boy?'

He had, of course, known full well, because Kirk and I had clashed the moment he arrived at the location with his huge retinue five days after we had began shooting. He had been flown by private plane to a tiny airport near by before being driven to the cliff top above the jetty on Loch Etive, where we were all waiting to greet him.

Catch Me a Spy was about intrigues in the world of British versus Russian espionage, and the Norwegian Army greatcoats we were wearing were very welcome as we stood watching for our first sight of our star on that bitterly cold quay at seven in the morning.

He didn't disappoint. Followed by a great phalanx of people – his personal assistant, make-up artist, dialogue coach, secretary and at least four others – he came stomping down the long winding cliff side, his breath white on the freezing air erupting from between his clenched teeth, his jaw jutting forward.

The whole crew, about 40 of us, were crowded on the jetty looking up to see this big Hollywood star proceeding in his stomping rhythm, and as he approached I started trumpeting the theme from his hit Fifties film *The Vikings*, 'Da ... da ... DA.'

The closer he came the louder I went, 'Ta ... ta ... da ... da ... da ... do ... da...'

Kirk Douglas had a fearsome reputation and all the crew hissed at me, 'Shut up, Patrick, shut up!' until he was standing right in front of us.

Glaring, he rasped out, 'OK, who's the joker?'

Now, I have always been famous for having a dimple in my chin and as a joke I had got the make-up girls to put white all around it with a big black spot in the middle – to mimic 'Mr Douglas's' renowned cleft.

I leaned forward and held out my hand. 'Mr Douglas, that's me. I am Patrick Mower and I'm playing John. We're in the first scene together.'

Kirk went to shake my hand, but as he reached forward he suddenly saw the mickey-taking artwork on my chin. Fixing me with an old-fashioned look, he snorted, 'OK, who else we got on this picture?' and everyone burst out laughing.

I don't know whether he intended it as a joke, but it broke the ice. We would get on well together.

Funnily enough, it was Dick Clement, who was also directing, who unintentionally made dealing with Kirk far more difficult than it should have been.

I was doing a bedroom scene with the French star Marlene Jobert, the mother of Eva Green, one of the latest Bond girls. It was the first night of our honeymoon, she was looking absolutely stunning in a negligee and I was just about to do the dirty deed, when Kirk, impersonating a waiter, came into our room behind us. Surprised to see us, he was to say, 'Just come to turn down the bed.' This extremely rude waiter and his aggressive manner, in no way servile, caused me to respond in the same tone, 'Well, hurry up about it, and then get out.'

'Cut!' shouted Clement. He then turned to me and said, 'I don't think you'd talk to Mr Douglas like that.'

'I don't know he is Mr Douglas,' I said. 'He's supposed to be a waiter. If a waiter spoke to me like that, I would punch him.'

The next time we did the scene, Kirk was more polite.

I got on quite well with Trevor Howard, who was playing my father-in-law, although he was dangerously unpredictable.

We had been filming for a couple of days when Trevor joined us. I was sitting with a group having dinner when I saw him arrive in the foyer. One of our party was Robin Parkinson, who had a small character part and was, I knew, a great fan of Trevor's and familiar with all his work.

Turning to Robin, I said, 'Why don't you ask Trevor to join us?'

'Oh, I couldn't, he's too big a star,' said Robin.

'Go on,' I urged. 'He has been travelling and it will make him feel more at home.'

Reluctantly, Robin went and spoke to Trevor, who came over to join us. I introduced him to the others and he was terribly polite. He said he had been delayed as he had met some Royal Air Force boys who had recognised him. They had persuaded him to have a couple of glasses with them, which had been fun. He was perfectly sober and said that, while he didn't want anything to eat, a glass of wine would be nice. He was delightful company. His hell-raising reputation was obviously unjust.

Eventually, Trevor, Robin and I went over to the bar. I asked Trevor if he would like a drink. 'A Scotch, if I may,' he said.

I ordered a large Scotch for Trevor, a small one for myself, as I was filming at 6.30 the next morning, and Robin had a beer. We carried on chatting, Robin talking about *Separate Tables* and all the other films Trevor had made.

Robin was very knowledgeable about the films and I could see that Trevor was quite impressed. Robin then bought a round, the same again.

Trevor then said we should have one for the road and, insisting we have doubles, he knocked his back in one. All still very polite and civilised – the calm before... Then, as Robin began again, 'When you were...' Trevor exploded. Bending his knees, he turned on him and snarled, 'You've been up my fucking arse since you met me, you fucking little squinty cunt!'

Robin tried to speak. Trevor staggered back and then screamed at Robin, 'I don't want you anywhere near me, you little weasel.'

I've never seen anything like it. He just snapped. The last whisky had taken him over the brink and, from being absolutely sober and nice as pie, he suddenly turned into an abusive, alcoholic drunk. The legend was true.

Robin recoiled as though he had been shot and hastily retreated to the other end of the bar. At that moment, two ladies, who had been sitting on the other side of the room, finally plucked up the courage to come over to us. They asked if they could have my autograph and foolishly I said, 'Would you like Trevor Howard's autograph as well?'

Turning to Trevor, who, with his back to the bar, was staring at the women, I said, 'These two young ladies' – actually they were rather old biddies – 'would like your autograph.'

'Well, they can fuck off,' he snapped.

Startled, the women backed off. Trevor was so vitriolic, with fire in his eyes as if some demon had taken over his soul.

As he stood there swaying, I thought, I'm clearing off, and while Trevor wasn't looking I slipped my drink to the barman, telling him to get rid of it.

Trevor then straightened up and, completely ignoring me,

went over to the women, sat down at their table and said in the most polite voice, 'What are you doing here, ladies?'

He had completely changed. And I talk about Jekyll and Hyde!

I walked over to Robin, who had tears streaming down his face because his hero had turned on him so viciously, and said, 'Don't worry, he won't remember a thing in the morning.' And he didn't.

After that I treated Trevor with absolute respect – and a bit of distance.

He was absolutely fine during the day and we got on very well in the scenes we did together. He was very charming, but there was always this element of danger, for you never knew if, in the privacy of his trailer, he was knocking back a bottle of something.

We met again some years later when Trevor was doing a lunatic film called *Sir Henry at Rawlinson End*. Suzanne Danielle, my lady at the time – more about her later – had a great part as Candice Rawlinson to Trevor's Sir Henry and when I went up to see her Trevor and I enjoyed more than a few drinks. But I was always wary because you never knew quite how the night might end.

One day when we were setting out from the hotel Trevor leaned over to the chauffeur and said, 'Make sure we are back at the hotel by seven o'clock.'

'This evening?' the chauffeur queried.

'No, you cunt. In the morning.' That was Trevor.

There was also genuine excitement that was never in the script. A stunt went spectacularly wrong, resulting in everyone patting me on the back, telling me how brave I was and generally treating me like a hero. Their praise couldn't have been more misplaced, for it wasn't so much bravery on my part as pure panic and self-preservation. But if it had been on camera it would have looked pretty good.

We were shooting a sequence in which Kirk was chasing me across the very deep Loch Etive in 12-foot rubber dinghies with powerful outboard motors. Frank the cameraman, a big guy, had the camera perched on his shoulder and was standing in the front of my dinghy so that he could shoot my face and also the pursuing Kirk over my shoulder. In the sequence I had to do a U-turn and head my dinghy straight back at Kirk's and bump him in an indirect collision.

We did this half a dozen times until the director decided I should bump Kirk's craft a lot harder to make it more exciting. As there was an element of risk involved, Kirk's stuntman, Alf Joint, took over from him and we lined up to shoot the scene once more.

Clutching the camera over his shoulder, Frank urged, 'Let's go,' and, as Dick Clement yelled, 'Action,' I revved the outboard and we sped towards Alf's dinghy.

But, instead of nudging Alf's dinghy as planned, we hit in a head-on collision with such force that Frank, still clutching his camera, was thrown eight feet in the air. In terrifying slow motion he was catapulted over me while the camera whizzed past my head, brushing my right ear.

The dinghy turned turtle and I was hurled into the water beneath it. Instinctively, as the craft folded over on top of me, I kicked out with my feet and it bounced back over on to its right side. It was full of sea water and the engine had cut out, but I clambered back on board and looked for Frank.

He emerged spluttering from beneath the icy water and I paddled with my hands towards him. As I drew alongside he disappeared.

Seconds later he again forced his way to the surface and I threw the painter at the prow of the dinghy towards him. Grasping the rope, he pulled himself towards the dinghy, which was precarious and threatening to again turn over. As I grasped Frank's shoulder, yelling to him to hang on to the painter, I could see he was in serious trouble. Between mouthfuls of water, he explained that his waist-high waders were filling with water and were pulling him down.

He went under the water. Grabbing him by his beard and hair, I shouted, 'Breathe,' then let his head back under, using the sea's buoyancy to stop him from drowning. With another heave I pulled him back up, screaming, 'Breathe.' He gulped in air before I allowed him down to boost his buoyancy. By now, with his waders full of water, he was an enormous weight and I thought my arms would be wrenched from their sockets as I continued to hold and pull him up. We must have repeated this process ten times before Alf Joint came to our aid.

Alf had immediately sized up the situation and, after diving in, managed to give Frank more support. Eventually, after several minutes of my pulling and Alf pushing, we got Frank onboard. But it was a near thing. I saved his life.

Divers went out the next day looking for the camera and the precious film, but although they dived to 300 feet they couldn't find the bottom of the loch, let alone find the camera.

I met Kirk Douglas a few years later in LA at an awards ceremony. *Escape from El Diablo* – yet another straight-to-video movie of mine – had been nominated for best screenplay, which was strange because we had made up most of the dialogue as we went along. I went over and said hello to Kirk and he still didn't know who I was. Mind you, he was talking to a very beautiful young brunette at the time.

13

The Callan Cult

M Y TASTE FOR adventure truly whetted, the pace was to get even more explosive as a certain James Cross entered my life.

Cross was the ultimate hardman secret agent as Edward Woodward's ruthless accomplice in *Callan*, a show that transformed Britain's viewing habits. The streets emptied as everyone went home to switch on *Callan*, described by the respected television correspondent Philip Purser as 'what Ian Fleming set out to make Bond – a blunt instrument'.

Cross was even blunter. As the brutal Cross I used to intimidate fellow character Lonely, played by Russell Hunter, by sticking the barrel of my pistol in his nostril – and then lifting him up! No wonder Cross became universally known as 'The Man We Love to Hate'. While *Callan* had a conscience, Cross enjoyed killing, on one occasion callously throwing a woman to her death on a railway line. It was strong stuff but the nation was riveted to the screen – and my popularity soared.

The brilliant Teddy Woodward was always ferociously protective of his creation, Mr Callan, but Cross became a bit of a heartthrob with the ladies and was the foundation for the Patrick Mower fan club. But it wasn't only the ladies who noticed that Cross, being younger, had a different kind of appeal from Teddy's. The producers and writers did too, and my part became increasingly prominent.

Indeed, after our usual first-day rehearsal for a new episode, Teddy, sailor's cap firmly on his head, teased Reg Collin, the producer, declaring, 'The show should be called *Cross*, not *Callan*!'

Not for the first time in my career there was a bit of friction between me and a fellow leading man. Obviously, the producers wanted to sell the show. And, as now with *Emmerdale*, where they are bringing in younger girls with larger breasts because that is what sells soap at present, in *Callan* the Cross character was presumably selling their product.

My relationship with Teddy was always professional. We were both aiming at the same target – to make the show the finely honed piece of quality television it was.

But eventually, to the bitter disappointment of the fans and not by my choice, Cross was killed off. This was television dynamite. I was aware of the hold Cross had on the country, but I was never prepared for the sensational impact his death was to cause when it was screened three months later.

I was playing one of my favourite roles on stage, Jack Tanner in Shaw's *Man and Superman* at Birmingham Rep, the night the episode showing Cross falling to his death went out.

Was Cross shot, or did he jump? The nation was in thrall and Thames Television's switchboard was jammed.

Callan went out at 9pm and at 10pm I was in the middle of a speech when the stage-door keeper appeared in the wings.

'Pssst,' he whispered loudly, motioning me over.

Pausing, I moved towards the wings to be told, 'You're wanted on the phone.'

I carried on acting.

Three minutes later, 'Pssst, you're wanted on the phone.'

Giving the door keeper a piercing look, I continued my performance.

This must have happened six more times until, at the curtain call, he told me that every newspaper in England had been phoning to ask if Cross was really dead. They couldn't believe that such a popular television character had been killed.

There was such a furore that the next day *The Eamonn Andrews Show* flew me to Heathrow in a specially chartered plane to record an interview – to prove that Patrick Mower was alive.

Jack Tanner had been described by Shaw as having a full beard and, being a dedicated actor, I had grown one. But that didn't suit Eamonn, who, when I arrived in the studio, went into a huddle with the producer. Eamonn then came over and said, 'Patrick, would you mind shaving your beard off?'

'Why?' I asked in surprise.

'Because last night on television you didn't have a beard and we think it will confuse the viewers.'

Dumbfounded, I refused, telling him, 'This is a GBS beard and it's staying.'

I did the interview hirsute.

But Cross continued to haunt me, with even my car becoming a victim of the *Callan* cult.

One day I stepped out of my Kensington flat to find that the words 'Cross lives' had been scrawled on the bonnet of my 2.4-litre Jaguar in the sticky muck that had fallen from the elm trees lining the street.

Audrey and I found it very amusing – until we went to give the car a wash and found the words had scratched the paint. But those scratches turned out to have a silver lining. When I sold the car a couple of months later for the then princely sum of £300, the dealer, beaming from ear to ear, said, 'Here you are, Patrick,' as he thrust another £50 into my hand. 'You have given me the proof that this is James Cross's car, and I can sell it for £1,000!'

I also learned an invaluable lesson in life making *Callan*. In those days a couple of hundred people would stop in the street and watch as we filmed in Twickenham and Teddy Woodward was probably the best-known actor in England at the time – or rather his character was. Teddy must have been asked for his autograph hundreds of time and, as he was always asked as Mr Callan, he used to bemoan the fact that no one knew his real name.

For the umpteenth time Teddy was approached by a fan. The boy asked him the same question he must have been asked a hundred times that day: 'Can I have your autograph, Mr Callan?' Understandably frustrated, Teddy snapped, 'No, you can't have Mr Callan's autograph, you can have mine – I'm Edward bloody Woodward!'

Taken aback, the shocked boy turned tail and ran off.

That was a salutary experience for me and I have made a point throughout my entire career, whether playing nasty James Cross, tough Tom Haggerty, the hated Steve Hackett or any other long-running character, to ensure I have always done enough publicity to ensure that Patrick Mower is bigger than the character.

So I only did two seasons of Tom Haggerty and two of Steve Hackett, but I had no intention of finishing with Cross and, to this day, my exit from *Callan* remains rather similar to my character's departure. Was I pushed from behind the scenes, or did I deserve to jump?

Well, I certainly jumped – to America, in a bid to kickstart a major movie career.

If Teddy had a lot of power at Thames, I was to experience something far more powerful and sinister one night at Sands casino in Las Vegas. I was in Hollywood doing a test to play an Englishman in a Burt Reynolds film when my friend Brian Brown rang me from Las Vegas inviting me to join him for dinner. An inveterate gambler, Brian was staying in one of the high-rollers' suites at Sands. Elvis Presley was performing – I needed no urging.

Brian was an international salesman in small tools and when I joined him in one of the suites he introduced me to, among others in the same line, Bert Klinksman. Small and bespectacled, Bert was witty and unassuming. He also travelled the world selling. 'But my tools are bigger than Brian's,' he joked.

We were chatting over a drink when, after tapping at the door, a hotel manager told us that Elvis would be shortly starting his act. 'OK,' said Klinksman, 'we'll be there.' But he didn't move when we carried on talking.

After a while I said to Brian, 'Shouldn't we go down?'

Klinksman said, 'It's OK, finish your drink – there's no rush.'

Another tap at the door. 'Elvis is about to begin.'

Klinksman smiled, saying, 'We'll be there.' But again he didn't move.

Itching to go and desperate to see the 'King', I said, 'I don't want to miss him.'

Klinksman stood and replied, 'You won't. I'm just going to the bathroom.'

It must have been 15 minutes later when we went down and as we were sitting in our seats a face peeped out from beside the stage curtain and looked towards our table.

I turned to see who he was looking at and was just in time to catch Klinksman give the briefest of nods, as if to say, 'OK, you can go.' The head disappeared and immediately a voice boomed out, 'Ladies and gentlemen, Mr Elvis Presley…'

The hairs on the back of my neck stood up. Klinksman had the power to keep Elvis, the biggest entertainer in the world, waiting…

I later discovered from Brian that Bert Klinksman was absolute top brass in the American Air Force. But it was all rather mysterious. Was he posing as a small-tools salesman? Was he CIA? Whoever he was, he was a very powerful man and I have been keeping my eye on the American elections ever since for a President Klinksman, or whatever his name really was.

Needless to say, I may have seen Elvis, but I didn't get the part. My agent said I was too good-looking!

I've always been deeply sceptical of people's claims to have been touched by the supernatural, but one hot summer's afternoon in the world-famous Harry's Bar in Paris I discovered that sometimes fact can be stranger than fiction.

My brush with the paranormal began when I went to France to make a commercial for Dunhill cigarettes with the actress Anouska Hempel.

I was living in Kensington at the time and Anouska, who as Lady Weinberg later became one of the richest women in Britain, renowned as a designer, hotelier and hostess, lived up the road. A very beautiful woman, Anouska was talented, delightful company and one of my great chums.

We worked together on the television game show *Whodunnit?* as the resident panellists, solving mysteries enacted by actors. Such was my skill, the presenter Jon Pertwee gave me the nickname 'Bloodhound Mower'. It also led to our being cast to make Dunhill's most opulent of commercials for their Saudi Arabian and Arab Emirates market. No expense spared.

The Dunhill ad really was special. It was directed by John Burrows, who, as the creator of the famous Martini commercials, was in a class of his own, and we had an absolutely wonderful week in France. Anouska and I swept around in a Rolls-Royce, which had been sprayed Dunhill's dark red, smoking cigarettes and looking expensive. I was in my element driving the Rolls down the Champs Elysees and round the Arc de Triomphe before rolling down to our magnificent chateau set amid the stunning beauty of the Loire Valley.

At the end of the shoot we had gathered in Harry's Bar for the wrap party. There were 14 of us and it was a lovely afternoon as we sat around in a big circle drinking champagne.

Now when are you likely to meet a ghost? At four-thirty in the afternoon during a noisy film-unit party in Harry's Bar? In the middle of Paris? I swear to God it happened.

Anouska was on my right and everyone was chatting away when someone tapped me on the shoulder and said, 'Don't worry … everything will be all right.'

I looked around but there was no one there. In fact, the space between me and the bar was completely empty as we had moved all the tables around to form our party.

That's very strange, I thought. Who can have said that?

As a Virgo I tend to be analytical and critical and I was working out that the mystery person must have somehow slipped away to another part of the bar when the chap sitting opposite me said, 'Pat, are you all right? You've gone green.'

'What?' I said.

Anouska looked at me in alarm, and taking my hand, also asked, 'Are you all right, Patrick?'

I wasn't. Sweat was pouring off me, but I said, 'Yes, I'm OK,' as I didn't want to spoil the party.

Even as I spoke I felt a terrible icy chill stealing through my body. Deathly cold, I was freezing from tip to toe.

Anouska, the concern mounting in her voice, repeated, 'Are you all right?'

'Yes,' I replied, visibly shaking. Realising I had to explain my sudden distress, I told her about the mystery voice. 'Someone just spoke to me.'

'What do you mean?'

'I don't really know, but someone just spoke to me and then seemed to vanish.'

'Which ear was it in?'

'What?' I asked incredulously, feeling the whole situation was slipping beyond bizarre.

'Which ear did they speak in?'

'My left ear.'

'That's Costa.'

'Who?'

'That's my late husband, Constantine. What did he say to you?'

'He said, "Don't worry, it's going to be all right."'

'Are you worried about anything?'

'No.'

'You will be. But he is telling you that everything will be all right.'

Even more perplexed now, I asked, 'What do you mean?'

Anouska just said, 'It's Costa, don't worry…'

And as she spoke warmth surged through my body, the chill vanished and everything went back to normal.

Later, Anouska told me that Constantine had been killed driving down the King's Road when his open-topped Porsche had flipped over and he was impaled on railings. Anouska believed in spirits and said that since his death he was constantly with her. 'He is always behind me like a guide,' she said. Costa also looked after her friends, she maintained, adding, 'If the message is in the left ear it is a friendly warning, but if it is in the right ear it's a bad sign.'

Four months later, Audrey and I noticed that our son Simon, who was eight at the time, was having problems reading. We took him to the local optician for some glasses, but the optician was worried and told us we ought to take him to see an eye specialist. Naturally very concerned, we took Simon to one of the best specialists in Harley Street, where we had a devastating setback.

'I have some very serious news for you,' he said. 'Simon's eyes are very bad and they are going to get worse. We think there is a possibility he could go blind.'

As he said that, I heard another voice – the voice from Harry's Bar – saying, 'Don't worry, everything is going to be all right.'

Squeezing Audrey's hand, I comforted her, 'Don't worry, everything will be all right.'

And I believed it.

I told her I didn't believe Simon had been diagnosed correctly and we would get a second opinion. We saw two more specialists and, to our delight, they agreed. They said Simon had been misdiagnosed, and while they agreed his eyes were bad they assured us that he didn't have an eye disease and insisted that they could treat his problem.

If you wanted to be fantastical, you would believe that the first diagnosis was correct and Costa put it right. Or it could simply have been a question of faith. My belief and hope for my son and a simple case of a top specialist getting it wrong.

But it's a true story.

Simon later had laser treatment and, although his eyes are not perfect, they are better than mine. But more of that later.

Not being short of money – I had just completed a highly lucrative deal in which I had been flown to Los Angeles to film three commercials for Top Shop – I was able to be rather choosy about the television and theatrical offers I was receiving as I relaxed with Audrey and the children in our home in Pembroke Gardens in Kensington.

One evening I was sitting down having just sung Simon and Claudia to bed when the telephone rang. Audrey answered it and, putting her hand over the mouthpiece, said in hushed tones, 'It's Lloyd Shirley.' Lloyd was now the executive producer of the newly created Euston Films and a phone call from him at 9pm had to be as important as Audrey's hushed tones implied.

He asked me if I could meet him immediately in the Bulldog Bar in the Royal Kensington Hotel on the corner of Hyde Park. Luckily, this was just five minutes down the road from our house. Sensing the urgency in Lloyd's voice, I kissed Audrey goodbye, jumped into the Alfa Romeo I had recently bought from Anouska and zipped along to the hotel.

In the bar Lloyd fixed me with his piercing pale-blue eyes. I averted my gaze and watched as the last of the smoke escaped from his half-open mouth. It played around the beard and moustache before finally drifting away. The next time I was to see hair as ginger as that was when I was given a freebie by a hooker in Sydney.

She had pulled me – literally pulled me – up to her room at the Sebel Town House Hotel, saying, 'Cor! You must be the sexiest ten inches of muscle on television.' She was a little disappointed – not a lot! But once in the room she threw herself back on the bed, lifted up her skirt, opened her legs and said: Now, is that a genuine redhead or not? The little Japanese buggers pay me $400 a night just to look at it.'

But that's another story...

Lloyd introduced me to a fellow producer who started waffling about how their new series, *Special Branch*, was not going according to plan. After about three minutes of George trying to explain the reason for my presence, Lloyd could contain himself no longer. He interrupted, saying, 'George, let's cut the crap. Patrick, we have got a leading man who is a good actor but he is not a star.'

He then uttered the words that have been etched into my brain ever since: 'Patrick, I want you to go in, grab the show by the balls and give it a kick up the arse!'

That was how I got to play Tom Haggerty in *Special Branch*.

I was a little reluctant to take the part as I had been hoping to break into movies in a really big way. I was being seen by visiting American producers and was being considered for several leading roles, so I was not too keen on being tied to what could be a long-running series. To clinch the deal, Euston Films agreed in my contract that when I wanted to leave they would take my character out of *Special Branch* and guaranteed he would star in his own show.

What actor could refuse such terms, especially as two brilliant writers, Tom Brennan and Roy Bottomley, were assigned to write specifically for my role?

Special Branch was a ground-breaking show as it was the first television series to be filmed completely outside the studios. It was a huge success as a show and gave a tremendous boost to my TV image and public appeal. I now had an official fan club with 15,000 members who had their own badges and held meetings to sing my praises and occasionally requested my attendance.

At one meeting organised by the fan club in Hammersmith I found myself facing 3,000 exuberant girls. But that didn't really work out. When I was on stage talking to them, I felt they didn't want me in that situation. They would rather admire me from afar or take me to bed. Every one of them wanted an individual relationship with me as a fan and not a mass appreciation of Patrick Mower.

I felt they deserved something more personal and that is something you cannot give all of them. I didn't like treating girls the same because I have always been a chameleon. It depended entirely on the girl because I never behaved with one exactly the way I would behave with another. With one I would use my English cool and for another my Latin heat.

I also got a lot of sexual aggression from some of the girls. My phone number was always being discovered by fans who seemed to treat me like a pop personality. The calls came thick and fast and I was always changing my number. They would also sit outside the house and wait for hours. It was almost a cult following of young and not-so-young girls. A lot of them suggested meeting me at the same place – under the Coca-Cola clock in Piccadilly Circus. They would write saying things like, 'I have a 36in bust, a 24in waist and the most terrific body. If you don't believe me come and see!'

My appeal was sexually orientated and one of the pictures the girls most wanted was of me showing my chest. One magazine wanted to do a full nude of me. I declined.

In that period I was really hot and was once again urged to become a pop star. I was doing a lot of voice-overs – 'They came in search of paradise … and found the Bounty Bar …' was one of mine – and while I was in one of the studios singing 'Moonlight Becomes You' a guy said, 'Have you ever thought of cutting a record?'

So I made a single entitled 'My Imagination', writing the 'B' side myself.

In my Top Shop contract, I was opening stores for them all round Britain – Birmingham, Manchester, Leeds, Glasgow – and I found out the names of the music shops that took part in compiling the record charts and visited them. I made sure my record was playing for two solid hours in the Top Shop stores while I was signing autographs, and handed out cards giving the record's name and the number of the record company, along with the details of where it could be bought. And the fans loved it.

But after a few weeks the manager of one of the chart shops got hold of my number, phoned me and, to my horror, asked, 'Where's your record? We can't get hold of it.' To make matters worse, he said that girls had even paid in advance for the single, having heard it at my store openings.

The record company printed only 30,000 records, which were sold overnight. It was played on Radios 1 and 2 and Luxembourg, and if they had printed another 100,000 it would have made the charts. But the producer did a runner with the money – and I never received a penny. That was the end of my pop career. It was a complete rip-off.

People love a bastard and I played Haggerty with a short, flat, Northern accent to separate him from Cross. As this was still the hippy era, I had rather long hair and I allowed the hairdressers to put it into slight curls. Although this sounds rather feminine, it was to prove a great trendsetter, as Kevin Keegan revealed to me one afternoon when we were playing golf together. Kevin said that all the footballers watched *Special Branch* and my permed locks had sparked the fashion for the tightly permed curls that adorned soccer pitches in the Seventies.

Funnily enough, Kevin took years to forgive me for that craze. For while I simply achieved the bouffant effect with big rollers and a light perm, the soccer stars started having the curls set tighter and tighter until they ended up with a frizzy effect – and Kevin blamed me!

There was, though, a downside to all this success. For the second time in my career, through no fault of my own, the Haggerty character was becoming more popular than my co-star George Sewell was as Craven. Although we worked well together and socialised together, I could feel a slight resentment and, behind the scenes, I knew George was expressing dissatisfaction.

This resulted in one whole episode that had been specially written for Haggerty being totally changed. The episode, which was the precursor for the huge movie hit *The Bodyguard* with Kevin Costner and Whitney Houston, was originally planned to have the gorgeous Stephanie Beecham as a film star falling for Haggerty when he is assigned as her bodyguard. Instead, the script was changed, with Haggerty's lines being given to Craven, so I ended up as the poor cop standing outside in the rain while Stephanie was supposed to fall in love with Craven. The episode was a disaster. Situations like this did not help me, or George, or the show.

Haggerty was proving so popular with the ladies that in more and more of my stories I was involved with very attractive actresses and, I am not proud to say, around this period of my life I did occasionally stray from the straight and narrow. Although I was very happy at home, I defy any red-blooded young man not to succumb when having to play intimate scenes as I did with a well-endowed blonde or sexy brunette who was obviously equally attracted to me or my character, or maybe both. Sometimes the tantalising Christmas presents were so tempting I had to unwrap them.

With *Special Branch* being such a creative and popular series, Lloyd and Euston Films were desperate to take advantage of this success by selling it around the world. They asked me to go to America and Canada as an ambassador for the show. I attended a great many conferences in LA and met some very influential people before the junket moved on to Toronto. Everywhere it was the same story: the show is terrific and we love you, Patrick.

But they all wanted the show to be faster, more violent and to have a teaser at the beginning of each episode before the credits started running. In the States in the Seventies, as has now happened in Britain with our multi-channel choice, viewers were very quick on the change-over button. So all American series opened with an exciting piece of action to hook the audience from the very first frame. They then ran the credits and carried on with the story. Back in London, in their wisdom, Euston decided not to change *Special Branch* but to create a new series which was faster, more violent and had a teaser. It was called *The Sweeney*. But, like us, it still didn't sell to America.

After two years in *Special Branch*, despite my high television profile, I wasn't carried away by the glamour and adulation and still regarded myself as a serious actor. So I linked up again with my best friend, Michael Latimer, and we took over the lease on the Act Inn, a fringe theatre above the Marquis of Granby pub in Windmill Street, and started our own theatre group in Soho. It was a stone's throw from the famous Windmill Theatre and surrounded by 'erotic' review bars, most of them run by my friend Paul Raymond. Needless to say, we got to know many of the girl performers behind the beaded-curtained doorways of the Soho strip joints and enjoyed many a show, never once paying for it.

I told Michael that I wanted to try my hand at directing. So we hired four actors and the delectable Kirsty Pooley, and, with our own writer, Tim Rose Price, writing specifically for the cast, launched a series of new plays which proved very successful and which I found tremendously satisfying.

So much so that, when Euston Films approached me about honouring their contract to give Haggerty a series of his own, I turned it down. Tom Brennan and Roy Bottomley had written a terrific script in which Haggerty, having left the police, was a freelance motorbike-riding journalist. It was a major television chance and very tempting, but I wanted to do more with the theatre group and took another of my many gambles.

A gamble it most certainly was, because, although we were doing good business and the plays were well received, the theatre seated only 80 people and at £3.50 a ticket I soon found that my bank balance was going into the red.

As I was living off my earnings from my last year in *Special Branch*, I was delighted to receive a film script for a new version of *Alfie* called *Alfie Darling*. The director, Ken Hughes, had seen me on stage in the original theatre version at the Duchess, and invited me to his house in Hampstead for dinner. We were having pre-dinner drinks when Ken jokingly sold me two old sixpenny pieces for a 10p coin so that I could play his Fifties fruit machine.

I dutifully did so and, after inserting my first sixpence, pulled the lever. The symbols spun... and matched... and 700 old sixpenny pieces spewed out from the machine, cascading over our shoes.

'Oh, bollocks!' cried Ken. 'It's taken me eight years to fill that machine.'

This was not a good omen.

Nonetheless, we had a great dinner. Ken agreed to changes that I suggested and it was all systems go for me to be the new Alfie.

The 12-year-old daughter of the film's producer had seen

Alan Price perform the song on *Top of the Pops* and was captivated. More importantly for me (and whether it was true or not I don't know) I was told later on that she told the producer that Alan would be the perfect Alfie. And he would be – Alfie, that is. Not perfect!

Alan Price was a wonderful musician but not a trained actor. His Geordie accent probably didn't help and, instead of reigniting the original magic, the finished product was written up by one critic as looking 'increasingly like an advert with no product to sell'. That's showbiz.

Having spent all my money and with tax bills to pay, I was lucky enough to have Euston Films once again come to my rescue. I was asked to guest-star in *The Sweeney* as Australian con man Colin McGruder, with his sidekick, Ray, played by George Layton. With a brilliant script and George and I working well together, the characters proved to be very funny and it was such a success that they wrote another episode, in which Ray and Col, sporting his cork-fringed bush hat, returned.

This second episode was a real cliff-hanger. As it drew to a close, Ray was killed in a shoot-out. The camera then panned in on the cornered Col, clutching a hand grenade and looking up at the police standing above him.

'One of you called Regan?' Col yelled defiantly, throwing the grenade into the air as the closing credits flashed across the screen. It was wonderfully funny and they left Col alive because they wanted to bring him back yet again with his beautiful blonde Australian sister. The sister was to be played by genuine Australian Anouska Hempel, but John Thaw thought differently.

We were told that John was not too pleased by the success of Col and told Ted Childs, the new producer, 'If you do any more Australians, I am leaving the show.'

So Col never returned. I really enjoyed working with David Wickes, the director of the Aussie 'Sweeneys', and he tried to persuade me to make a series about the Australian con man and his sexy sister Shane but I said no. *Wrong!*

Determined to further my classical ambitions, I did two prestigious television productions. I played Edmund to Patrick Magee's King Lear and was engaged to play the Button Moulder opposite Leo McKern's Peer Gynt but ended up playing Peer himself. Leo dropped out of the show because of a family crisis in Australia, so I had this marvellous opportunity to play a role in which I aged from 15 to 80, and I still regard it as one of the best things I have ever done.

I was also once again caught in Bond's web.

After Roger Moore had twice slipped into 007's shoes, I got another call from Eon. I was told they were looking for a replacement. I was again in the frame and once more I had to go through the cloak-and-dagger routine I had experienced on my first excursion into the world of Bond.

When I arrived at the office I again found no one else had been called and, as Harry Saltzman had died, this time it was only Cubby Broccoli sitting behind the desk. With him was his daughter, Barbara, and her husband, Michael G. Wilson. Again it was all very hush-hush, with a degree of secrecy that would have impressed the Kremlin at its most formidable.

Each time I had been called back as a replacement for 007, I had always dressed to be Bond and for this meeting I had even gone along to Roger's tailor in Savile Row to get a similar suit.

Roger had this immaculate, debonair image. But, even togged up in Turnbull and Asser shirts and the right shoes, along with the 'Bond' suit, I still didn't get it.

In the end they stayed with Roger.

[14]

Hot Days, Hot Nights

E VER SINCE I grew out of short trousers I have loved the company of girls and over the years, I'm happy to say, I've had more than my fair share. At one stage, at the height of my carefree bachelor days, I was dating 11 different women at the same time.

I've often found that being abroad can add an extra dimension to any affair and I encountered two of the more amazing girls I have known when I signed up to shoot a high-adventure film in South Africa called *One Away*. In the movie Bradford Dillman and Dean Stockwell, two very fine Hollywood actors, played my brothers and the delicious Elke Sommer was the sexy girl to help guarantee the box office.

But, like so many of my more exciting escapades, it all began in London.

Willie Rushton had become a very good friend of mine since playing, or rather attempting to play, cricket for the Lords Taverners. A brilliant cartoonist and the sharpest of wits, he was tremendous company. We found ourselves together at a charity fashion show at Harrods where all we had to do was strut up and down the catwalk wearing some way-out clothes, which we regarded as a bit of a lark.

Afterwards, Susannah York came over and introduced us to one of the organisers, a beautiful girl who was an aristocrat. She was wearing the most amazing silk dress of blue sheathes cascading down her very shapely figure. She was a stunning little blonde of about 26 or 27 and terribly posh.

'Thanks awfully for coming over to do this, it is very nice of you,' she gushed, shaking hands with Willie. She then turned to me and, as I kissed her outstretched hand, she said, 'You're Patrick Mower. I like you on the TV.'

'Oh, do you?' I smiled.

'You should see him on the cricket pitch,' quipped Willie and then, peering at her frock, said, 'Oh, hello, nice to see you,' as he pointed at an erect baby-pink nipple peeping through one of the sheathes of her dress.

Without losing her composure, she smacked it and said in a teasing voice, 'Oh, you naughty thing.' Then, turning directly towards me with a wicked glint in her eye, she said, 'It always does that when I'm excited.'

'Oh, oh, oh,' said Willie, catching her drift, 'I think I'd better be going, Patrick. See you later.' And he left us alone.

We carried on making small talk for a bit and she asked me what work I was doing next. I said I was going to Johannesburg the next day to make *One Away*, which was about a convict on the run, and she told me, 'We have very good friends in South Africa.'

I told her what a lovely evening it had been, adding, 'I hope to see you again.'

'I hope so too,' she replied.

The plop of a puff adder falling off the jacaranda tree outside the window of my Winnebago was to become one of the strange and wonderful sounds and sights I was to encounter in the incredible country that is South Africa.

But it wasn't the only surprise for me and Tom Haggerty's long curly locks.

As I came out of make-up looking, I thought, rather spectacular, the director, Londoner Sydney Hayers, puffing on his ever-present cigar, called to me, 'Pat, I've got the South African police outside and they're having a go about your barnet.'

'What do you mean?' I asked.

'They reckon that if you are in a South African prison you have to have a short back and sides.'

'But that's my image – Patrick Mower, long-haired lover from Oxford.'

'Yes, I know,' called Sydney through clouds of smoke, 'that's why I employed you.'

'But I'm only in prison for the first four minutes. For the rest of the film I'm being chased across the veldt by horses, helicopters, the whole damn shooting works,' I protested. 'And it's only a film. It isn't real life.'

The police, however, were adamant. It was a short back and sides or the film would be cancelled.

'Don't worry,' said Sydney, 'I'll have another word.'

And as I looked out of my window I saw him chatting to two really tough-looking Afrikaners.

It was no use. They were using real policemen and real police dogs for the film and the coppers insisted that I have my hair cut. So I told the make-up man to trim a bit off. He did and I went and stood in the doorway for the policemen to have a look. They simply shook their heads. I went back and had some more trimmed off. Again the heads shook. This went on until finally, thoroughly exasperated, I said to the make-up artist, 'Right, cut it all off.'

'What?' he said, aghast. 'I can't do that.'

'Yes, you can,' I retorted. 'Cut it off. Go for it.' So he did, and my curls ended up all over the floor.

I then went to the door to show the policemen. They finally nodded.

Sydney, who had his back to me, seeing their smiles of approval, said, 'Thank God for that.'

He then turned round, saw my shaven head and was so shocked he bit the end off his cigar. 'Fucking hell, Pat, what have you done?' he choked. 'Oh no. Look at you. Oh Lord, I've hired fucking Yul Brynner!'

But, as it turned out, in the heat of South Africa and running at 8,000 feet, amid the vastness of that beautiful wild continent, it was the best thing I could have done.

Since my arrival in Johannesburg I had done 15 press interviews and as I relaxed in my luxurious penthouse suite on top of the Tolman Towers the phone rang yet again.

'There's a woman on the phone for you,' the receptionist informed me in a guttural South African accent.

None the wiser, I told him to put her on and after a lot more initial confusion she said, 'Patrick, it's me, the Countess.'

'Oh, good God, sorry,' I blustered. 'They said it was someone entirely different and... How are you? It's good to hear from you.'

We carried on chatting for about 20 minutes until she finally said, 'Well, aren't you going to invite me for a drink?'

Totally confused, I said, 'Where are you?'

'In the hotel, you bloody fool,' she laughed.

She was a Polish Countess and I thought she was ringing from Poland, but I hurried down to the lobby to meet her. She was looking gorgeous and I couldn't get over the fact that this classy, very rich and very beautiful woman had followed me out to South Africa.

I had the most wonderful platonic affair with this Countess, but she had to keep it totally secret as she was married to a very rich and powerful man. She said he was much older than her and he never made love to her. We had a great time. She was really nice, but, because she was with her friends, we only met in the evenings for a drink and then dinner.

After ten days she had still not let me have my wicked way, so I hatched a plan. That weekend I decided to take her to Tchobi Lodge, the Botswanan safari hideaway where Richard Burton and Elizabeth Taylor had stayed, confident that it would prove the perfect setting to consummate our relationship.

That Saturday we set off in a tiny little push-pull plane which, as The Countess and I smilingly held hands, bucked alarmingly in the turbulence while the pilot warned, 'We are going into clouds.' The next moment the world blanked out. It was an eerie sensation, but after a short while we flew clear and the pilot took a sharp turn to the left. 'How do you know where you are going?' I asked, and he replied, 'I have got to go higher to avoid the clouds.'

I then asked why he didn't fly beneath them. 'Because there is a great big rock in our way,' he said, pointing to a massive rock escarpment which suddenly filled our vision, stretching impressively away on both sides. And we were heading straight for it.

As there was no Air Traffic Control in Botswana, other aeroplanes were far more of a danger than the rock face.

The pilot explained that it was 1,000 feet high, but said that if we went up to 1,200 feet he knew we could clear it.

But, instead of climbing, he flew towards the looming rock

face, and then, to my consternation, we started to run along beside it.

This was rather more of an adventure than I had bargained for. Flying off into the middle of nowhere for a special date was one thing; playing a perilous kind of dare was quite another.

Starting to get just a little edgy, I asked him what on earth he was doing.

'I'm looking for the gap,' he said. 'It will be a lot easier if we fly through it.' But, disconcertingly, the cloud kept closing in on us, and each time the pilot would have to pull away from the range and then fly alongside it again, constantly glancing to his right, looking for the gap as we flew in and out of small clouds.

The Countess was starting to get really worried but at last we flew round a bend in the rock range and there, sure enough, was the huge gap. It was about 200 feet wide and the pilot flew straight through. When we came out the other side of the range we were in Botswana.

A short while later we landed at Tchobi Lodge, in a setting so beautiful it took my breath away. This was the African veldt of the great adventure movies – a magnificent panorama famous for its prides of lions and every other big African beast. We lost no time in jumping aboard a Jeep to speed out into the bush in search of the elusive big game. But although we went with the head honcho, an impressive rock of a man in his big White Hunter's hat, the animals had gone to ground. It was too hot and we didn't see a thing.

But any disappointment was dispelled that evening as we dined in the black-velvet light on beautiful little impala steaks, washed down with fine wines. In the distance we could hear the lions. It was perfect. Paradise.

We had our own thatched round hut with the most wonderful round honeymoon bed. It was enormous, with beautiful lace and gauze curtains. It was designed for love, and after dinner we intended to use it suitably.

The Countess had filled the little plane with her bags and while I stood in the doorway looking out at the African night, she went into the bathroom, which although open-topped was equally exquisite.

The soft scent of the veldt filled the air: jacaranda, lime and orange. As I took a final deep breath, a tiny pain stabbed in my stomach. As I turned back to the room the apparition on the bed in her pale-blue baby-doll nightie smiled up at me, arms outstretched.

Drinking in this vision, I started to slowly walk towards her, when suddenly I heard this terrible groaning noise, *uurrhhmm*, coming from my tummy.

I took another step forward and my stomach gurgled again. I was now within reach of that the beckoning bed and as I started to lift my leg to climb aboard, my innards wrenched again. My dream of a night of bliss vanished with a chilling finality as I felt this terrible spasm surge through me. In mid-stride I frantically spun on my heel and fled to the bathroom. My hand was fearfully clutching my bottom because I knew any minute I would lose control of my anal muscles.

Never have I had such an appalling attack of dysentery. It felt as though my stomach was dissolving. To make a dreadful situation even worse, the bout went on and on.

It was one of the most embarrassing moments of my life. There, on this huge bed, surrounded by a sea of flowers, lay this beautiful Countess waiting just for me. It was the perfect scenario, with lions roaring in the distance and crickets chattering. And there was I, trapped in the lavatory with this dreadful smell as my body continued to shake and convulse.

I was so ashamed I couldn't bear to come out of the loo. I

must have stayed there for an hour, hoping the terrible effects of severe food poisoning would finally subside.

Obviously I had eaten something that had, almost instantaneously, gone right through my stomach. Groaning, I called out, 'I'm so sorry... I hope it doesn't smell as bad over there as here.'

'Well, I'm going outside,' she gently replied.

Four hours later I finally managed to get myself together and, in my case, through sheer will power, we did make love, but I didn't have a lot of strength to consummate what I had managed to start.

At the safari park the following day I felt as weak as a kitten. But I rallied sufficiently to go out at crack of dawn in a bid to see the animals. We ran across impalas and wildebeest, but again drew a blank with the lions, elephants and other big game.

We were due to fly out at midday and I was still feeling worse for wear when the head honcho told us that one of his 'boys' had just seen a herd of angry elephants. They were about two miles away, having just trampled through one of the villages, and we just had time to catch them if we jumped into his Jeep right away.

The Countess went in the front with the White Hunter while I clambered into the back with one of the Africans, who was purposefully holding a very powerful rifle. As we roared away, with yours truly clinging on for dear life while the Jeep bounced across the bush, I realised that in my haste I had forgotten to take my bush hat. But I didn't give it a second thought when, within minutes, we rolled up downwind of the elephants so that they wouldn't detect us and come charging our way.

It was very exciting as, trunks raised, they found us with their amazing sense of smell.

All too soon we were on the little plane heading back to the film unit.

When I got to my hotel my face felt a bit odd, but before I could see what the problem was I ran into the director. As I asked him how the filming was going, Sydney, clamping down furiously on his cigar, looked at me aghast and said, 'Patrick, what the bleedin' hell have you been doing? Look at the state of your face!'

Of course, I'd been hatless, and my face had swollen up like a balloon from being roasted by the 120-degree midday sun. I had the most terrible sunburn.

The unit doctor took one look at my face and immediately covered it in some thick goo. The next day he peeled off four layers of skin, before covering my face in a special cream. Luckily I had three days before I was required to film.

At least I had the consolation of knowing that I still had a very special date to look forward to.

One day The Countess came on the set and Elke asked, 'Who is that beautiful girl?' I told Elke she was with me and that really boosted my standing with the equally stunning actress. She too was knocked over by the fact that such a beautiful girl had followed me all the way from Poland. And that, I am convinced, is when Elke may have started to find me rather attractive.

Now, this was in the days of Apartheid and we were being sponsored by a South African furniture company. But it meant that we had to go to various parties and be nice to the sponsors.

I took it as all part of a day's work. But Dean Stockwell found these occasions particularly trying, especially when it meant dressing up for a black-tie event. He habitually wore a cowboy hat and boots in the style of James Dean.

When we were lined up for yet another posh dinner, Dean

said to me, 'Patrick, do you want to have a smoke before we go so we can get through this goddamn awful do?'

I said, 'Yes, OK,' and he told me, 'I've got this new stuff called Durban Gold, and hell, it's good.'

After I had changed into the dinner suit that the film company had provided for me, I went along to Dean's room a few minutes before the limousine was due to pick us up at six o'clock. We sat on the edge of the bed he rolled the joint and took a deep drag.

'Holy shit!' he roared, 'oh shit, *oh shiiiiit!*'

He passed it to me, I took a drag and it burned all the way down the back of my throat.

'*Wow!*' I shook my head and returned the joint to him.

He took another drag – '*Wow!*' – and handed it back to me.

The next thing I recall was the phone ringing. I picked it up and the receptionist asked, 'Is Mr Stockwell there?' I passed the phone to Dean, who mumbled, 'Yeah, yeah, yeah ... we're here. Whaddya mean? No, we've been here all the time. No, no one called.'

As he was speaking, I looked down and saw the joint lying on the carpet. It had gone out and as I picked it up I realised it was stone cold.

Dean put the phone down, turned to me and said, 'You'll never believe this, but it's seven o'clock!'

And, Gospel truth, we'd been sitting on that bed not moving for an hour. The joint was so powerful that we never heard the hotel staff banging on the door, or the phone ringing almost continuously. We had been completely zonked out. Durban Gold really lived up to its reputation.

In one sequence in the film Dean, Bradford Dillman and I had to ride motorbikes as we were being chased across the veldt and so we were issued with these little scrambling bikes, really noisy little beasts that roared away at a deafeningly high pitch – *eeyyee-eeyyeee-eeyyeeee*. In between scenes I had been teaching one of the assistants to ride one and after lunch one afternoon, not having any more scenes till the end of the day, we got permission to take two of the bikes off into the countryside and up into the mountains.

It was baking hot, so when we were out of sight I took my shirt off and tied it round my waist, and she did the same. We were like naughty teenagers. As I rode alongside her she took delight in going over bumps on purpose, making her beautiful breasts bounce with the terrain. The bikes roared out their own screeching approval. Eventually we stopped and I got out my flask, but it contained a fine chilled Stellenbosch Chardonnay instead of water.

Sharing the flask, we stood in the wild emptiness, wearing only shorts and without another human around for miles. It was one of those golden, once-in-a-lifetime moments that is made for love. It was such a sexy situation, one no healthy young man could possibly pass up.

And she felt it too. Inevitably we kissed and then, almost by accident, our passion took over with the sun beating down on our bodies. A glorious interlude of three quarters of an hour that still lingers.

Finally we rode back down to the film unit. As we parked the bikes the first assistant director came over to me and said, 'Patrick, I hope you've got a good story. You held up filming all afternoon.'

Startled, I asked why and he replied, 'Because the noise from those bloody bikes was echoing right down the valley and we couldn't shoot a damn thing – except for one little window. And what we are all wondering is why you stopped for three quarters of an hour. That was the only time we were able to do any work.'

Putting on my best nonchalant air, I replied, 'We just stopped for a breather...'

Grinning, he shot back, 'I wish you'd taken longer, Patrick, we're now half a day behind.'

And all this time I was also having an affair with a top South African model called Sue Kiel, who was the first girl I knew to have a butterfly tattooed on her tummy.

Yes, South Africa was certainly good to me. Well, most of the time, at least. But on two occasions the director's thirst for authenticity could have proved the undoing of yours truly.

During the scenes across the vast rolling veldt in which I was pursued by helicopters and police dogs, I had to fall into quicksand and swim across a river. To create the quicksand into which I was to slowly sink, they dug a huge hole beside the river which they then filled with muddy sand and water. This was then covered with grass so that when I ran across it I would sink up to my waist as though in a real quicksand.

To make the scene more exciting, as the dogs and a helicopter closed in I had to sink right down into this stinking hole until the muddy water completely covered my head so that I was genuinely hidden from view while they all passed by.

When I finally came up for air, wiping the muddy mess from my eyes and nose, Sydney called, 'Cut. Well done, Pat,' and bellowed, 'That's a wrap.' Trailing clouds of cigar smoke and dust, he and the whole unit packed into Jeeps and lorries and sped off – leaving me soaking wet and covered in stinking mud. The make-up girl, who had remained, along with my driver and car, held aloft a tiny two-foot-square towel and suggested the best way I could clean up was to jump into the river.

It didn't look very inviting, and I asked nervously, 'What about crocodiles?'

'No, you'll be OK,' she assured me, so I jumped in and splashed about as I tried to remove the clinging mud. I wasn't that successful, but after I had got rid of the worst I dried myself off with the scrap of towel, the blazing sun doing the rest.

On the way back to Johannesburg we stopped at a little roadside antiques place, where I bought a couple of pieces the owner assured me were not the usual tourist junk. He then asked, 'Why are you so muddy?' and I told him we had been making a film. With a worried expression, he said, 'You didn't go in the river?'

'Yes.'

'But that's balotsia.'

'What's that?'

It was the local name for sleeping sickness, he explained, adding, 'No one goes in that river because of the tiny snails in the water. If they get into the pores of your skin they cause sleeping sickness. The river is also full of crocodiles and hippos. It's very dangerous. There are puff adders all over that area and it's the last place I would have chosen to take a bath.'

That really made my day.

I didn't get sleeping sickness after all, but now, every time I feel sleepy, I say, 'I think I've got balotsia.'

At the time I was more worried by the ferocious Alsatians they used in the film.

It was while the doctor was treating my sunburn after I returned from my disastrous trip to Tchobi Lodge with Lesley that I realised just how risky acting with animals can be. As he slapped the thick goo on my face, he asked me what I was doing the next day. I explained that we were shooting a scene where I had to kill a very big dog.

'How are they going to do that?' he asked.

I explained that, for the scenes where I wrestle with the dog before strangling it, the animal would be injected with a knockout dose and I would simply pretend to kill it.

'You have to be so very careful when the dog comes round,' the doctor warned.

When I asked why, he said, 'The police dogs they use out here are very nearly wild animals and they only behave for their handlers. The danger period is when they regain consciousness after being given any kind of anaesthetic. In the first few seconds they will forget all their master's control and become wild, vicious animals again. You must be very, very careful, Patrick.'

The next day, with this warning still ringing in my brain, I went on the set and met the dog I was to 'kill'. He was a massive, long-haired, seven-stone brute of an Alsatian, aptly called Dragon. In South Africa in those days of Apartheid, the police used Dragon and his chums as attack dogs against the blacks. Dogs like him were hated. It didn't take much imagination to see why he was five feet long and mean, like his police handler.

For the opening shots they had to set the dog on me and so, with one policeman holding Dragon back by his chain, his handler urged the dog on in Afrikaans, 'See him, see him, see him.' By the third command the dog was snarling at me with evil intent. And when Sydney Hayers called, 'Action,' the snarling dog bounded towards me, but at the very last moment his handler gave the command, 'Yep,' and the dog jumped past me towards the policeman.

For the next shot, where Dragon was to appear to be leaping straight at me, I was very relieved when they knocked him out with the injection. The unconscious animal was then to be thrown through the air by four sturdy electricians, each clutching a spread-eagled leg, as they swung him back before hurling him in my direction. We were to do the shot twice, so that Sydney could capture the dog 'leaping' from two different angles – directly towards to me as I stood facing him and also from behind the dog. Unfortunately on hearing 'Action' the sparks slung the dog at me with such force that I was knocked flat on my back beneath his crushing weight, unable to move. I was pinned there completely helpless.

It was like being hit by a sack of potatoes and I just wasn't up to handling such a massive weight, especially after losing a stone and a half through my agonising attack of dysentery.

The whole unit fell around in hysterics at the sight of me pinned beneath this huge dog. The film's macho hero knocked out of action by an unconscious dog. I couldn't help it – I burst out laughing with the rest of them. But the laughter was short-lived.

With me urging, 'Steady now, boys,' it took four of them to pull the brute off me – and *they* weren't feeling washed out.

Sydney and I then worked out how we could make the scene look realistic without me being knocked for six. Eventually, I was able to face the 'leaping' dog, catch him and then roll him over and put my thumbs to his throat.

For the close-ups, they used a hand-held camera over my shoulder and Sydney said, 'Right, Patrick, now I want you to keep moving the dog as though he is still alive. We'll dub on some growls, and then, with a lot of effort, roll him off you.'

So the dog was laid on top of me, his long tongue dangling less than an inch from my face. As I put my thumbs back to his throat the hairs on the back of my neck stood to attention.

I could feel Dragon starting to growl. An icy chill swept through me as I rolled him off me, shouting, 'He's coming round.' I leaped up and ran clear.

There was a deathly quiet on the set until an anxious Sydney shattered the silence by bawling for the unit doctor to inspect the still-prone Dragon. Gingerly, the doctor walked over to the dog, and listened to him through his stethoscope. Eventually, he looked up and called out, 'He's still unconscious.'

'I promise you, I felt his throat growling,' I said nervously.

'No, no, no, you can't have,' the doctor replied.

I then repeated the danger I had been told about the night before. Sydney asked the doctor if he could give Dragon another shot, but the doctor said that was impossible as he had already had to give him two injections because of his size. Another, he insisted, would kill the beast.

Oh, God, I thought as Sydney, waving his cigar in agitation, shouted, 'Set up for a take.' He turned to me and said, 'Patrick, what's the matter with you? You turning into one of those puffy actors? I thought you were a TV tough guy.'

The crew, revelling in every second of the drama, loved it.

I looked at the dog. It lay motionless. Perhaps I'd been mistaken. There was no way I could back out, so to cheers I said, 'OK, but let's get it done as quickly as possible.'

They lifted Dragon back on top of me. Sydney said, through clouds of smoke, 'When you've "killed" him I want you to lie back exhausted with the dog still lying across you. We'll then zoom in with the camera to your face for a BCU.'

'Come on then,' I said reluctantly. 'I'm only going to do this once.'

Sydney shouted, 'Action,' and the dog and I started our grapple of death.

I rocked his head backwards and forwards, trying to simulate him attacking me.

With my hands again at Dragon's throat I felt that growl again. Maybe it was wind. I knew there was no point in protesting any further. They're just going to make you do it anyway, I thought, and pretended to squeeze his throat with all my strength. His eyelids were closed but then, to my horror, inches from my face, the lids started to rise.

Then his eyes were glaring into mine...

At the same time I could feel his throat going and the other doctor's warning of the night before hammered in my brain.

Sydney had now got the camera positioned right up to my face and the sheer terror in my eyes was genuine. The thoughts, Have they got it? and, Can I get away in time? flashed through my brain.

Dragon's tongue started to slide back into his mouth. The little eyes were now boring into me. I prayed for Sydney to shout, 'Cut.'

I then did the best acting I've ever done as I looked relieved that at last the dog was dead. I let go of his throat and lay back exhausted for the camera.

Then Dragon let out a growl the whole unit heard.

'Cut,' roared Sydney and I moved faster than at any time in my life. Rolling clear of the dog, I jumped up and ran like mad, leaping at the branches of a nearby jacaranda tree, then hauling myself up.

Dragon's handler walked over to pick him up, but as he clipped a chain to his collar, the dog, with a snarling 'Aarrgghhhh', sank his teeth into the policeman's ankle, ripping right through to the bone, and then threw the burly guy head over heels into a sprawling cartwheel. He then sank his teeth into the handler's right leg.

The other policeman desperately tried to control the dog, shouting at it in Afrikaans and beating it with chains. Dragon went wild. With another 'Aarrgghhhh', he grabbed his assailant's arm and tossed him like a rag doll back over his head. There was a sickening crack as the man's arm snapped.

The crew ran like hell. It was an incredible sight as the maddened, slathering dog raced in all directions until he was eventually subdued.

As I looked at all that ripped flesh I was really shaken at the thought of how close my face had been to those teeth.

I really shouldn't be here today. If the scene had lasted another few seconds I would certainly have been killed.

But that was not my first run-in with a police Alsatian on a film set. Years before, when I was starting out, I played a villain nicked by one while doing a drug deal in an old black-and-white television episode of *Dixon of Dock Green*. They had chosen a retired policeman and his former police dog to play the scene, which opened very artistically with a shot of the pair of them approaching me, seen through the reflection in the dark glasses I was wearing.

But then it all started to go wrong. The dog was supposed to pin me against a barbed-wire fence, at which point I was to utter, 'It's a fair cop, guv,' before his handler called him off. But the dog just wasn't interested.

Realising that he had to get the dog moving, the retired policeman turned to me and asked, 'Is it all right if I tell him to "See you", Patrick?'

'Sure, that's fine,' I replied, so he ordered the dog, 'See him!' But the dog didn't move.

'See him!' repeated the handler more urgently. 'See him!'

The dog continued to just stand there panting.

'You'll have to do something to annoy him,' the handler told me. 'Give him a prod or something.'

So I prodded the dog and he began to growl.

Now, being a Method actor, I thought, I'll do this properly, and as I prodded the dog I too began to growl, '*Ggrrrrrr… ggrrrrr… ggrrrrr…*'

And that worked. The dog probably wondered, what's this guy about? But then he began pulling at his chain and growling properly. So we did the scene and the dog sprang into action, pinning me against the fence. It worked very well and was impressive on screen.

An hour later, I fancied a pee and, after telling the first assistant director, I went around to the back of the warehouse where we were filming. Unbeknown to me, the dog handler had had the same idea but had gone around the other side. As I was standing there peeing I heard a low growl: '*Ggrrrrrrr...*'

Looking down, I saw the Alsatian coming towards me with his head lowered. He was on all fours, coming up sideways like a cartoon dog – and he had me fixed.

Only an hour before he had been told to 'see' me, and he was still going to!

I stood there rigid – through fear I had immediately stopped weeing but was still holding my most precious possession in my hand. The Alsatian was ten yards away.

I know with mad dogs you are supposed to stay still, but with my heart pounding and fingers fumbling I desperately stowed my hero away, thinking, I don't want that bitten off! I tried to calm the dog I had so successfully baited earlier.

'Hello, hello, good boy, good boy,' I soothed, but the dog kept coming forward menacingly. '*Ggrrrrrr... ggrrrrr...*'

He was within three yards of me when his minder came round the corner looking for him. Luckily for me, he immediately sized up my predicament and called the animal off.

If he hadn't come around the corner when he did I don't know what the dog might have done. I might have lost my best friend.

There's a lot of truth in the old adage 'Never act with animals and children'.

Africa was truly a wonderful and mystic place, but in those days there was also a dark side to this paradise.

Blacks and whites couldn't mix and the oppressive conditions under which the black people lived were forcibly brought home to me one night when my old friend from London, Ian Hamilton, whose place I had taken in cabaret, took us to a club. Ian had moved to South Africa and become a famous radio DJ, but that didn't cut any ice with the police.

Ian was a very liberated Englishman, unlike the Afrikaners, and while, like all the other whites, he had an African maid, he treated her as an equal and had invited her to join us for the trip to the club.

We were setting out after the curfew for black people, but Ian had insisted the girl would be all right. Five of us were jammed into Ian's little car and I was in the front with the black maid sitting on my knees when the police – one white, the other black – pounced on us while we were waiting at traffic lights.

The girl and I were ordered out of the car and the black policeman began shouting at her in an African dialect, pointing down the road. At this, suddenly looking very frightened, she took to her heels and fled into the night.

I couldn't believe my eyes and started to protest, 'What's going on here?'

The white policeman copped his gun.

'Don't say another word,' Ian hissed. 'Get back in the car. Don't worry, she'll be all right. She'll make it to one of the African settlements, because she's not allowed on the road after the five-o'clock curfew.'

I was deeply upset by the whole business, especially when Ian told me that the girl hadn't reported for work the next day. I was worried something awful might have happened to her, but eventually she turned up for work.

The Afrikaners could be very horrible and I had many heated discussions with them about the way they treated the black people. Having run a youth club for three years as well as a theatre in Soho, I have always been passionate about people's rights, and while I was in South Africa I regularly went to a black actors' club in a mixed area to discuss their situation. But I couldn't get through to the Afrikaners. They would dismiss my arguments, declaring, 'You don't understand: the black is an animal.' I just couldn't get any reason into them.

It was a great shame. Such a beautiful country.

Fortunately Sue Kiel was quite different from so many of the whites out there at the time. We met at a club in a mixed area, where she was the only white blonde girl. She was a wonderful, very liberated girl, without any of those negative attitudes, and we had a wonderful time together. But she found some aspects of life in South Africa too repressive and eventually moved to America, where we would meet again.

15

Demons

M Y RETURN FROM South Africa was to herald a
major turning point in my life. But it didn't start off
auspiciously.

While I was away, an enormous amount of fan mail had
arrived and it had been tipped in a pile on the dining-room
table. It was lying there, like a small mountain, when a woman
journalist called to see me. When she saw the pile she asked why
I got so much fan mail. With a twinkle in my eye, I foolishly
joked, 'Probably because I am tall, dark and handsome.' In her
interview she quoted me as saying, 'I get thousands of fan letters
every week because I am six-foot tall, tanned and incredibly
good-looking.' That quote was used again and again.

But, fortunately, among the letters was a surprise: a script for
the latest *Carry On* film, a Second World War romp called
Carry On England.

I had done many comedy productions in the theatre and, by
good fortune, Gerald Thomas, the *Carry On* director, had been

suitably impressed when he had seen me performing at the Theatre Royal in Windsor. I was very flattered by the script, in which there were three sergeants, Ready, Willing and Able, and I was, of course, offered the part of the handsome Sergeant Len Able, with Judy Geeson cast as my Auxiliary Territorial Service (ATS) girlfriend.

I readily accepted and left for five wonderful weeks of laughter with the rest of the *Carry On* gang as we filmed in the back lot at Pinewood.

There was one truly memorable scene where Kenneth Connor, as the captain of a mixed-sex anti-aircraft battery, gave the order for the girls to stop wearing skirts, saying, 'Trousers only will be worn.' The ATS girls decided to take the order literally and for the first time, although cinemagoers may find it hard to believe, there was the sight of a bare breast in the bawdy comedy series.

This was ground-breaking stuff, earning the series its first AA certificate. In the past there had only been the briefest glimpse of Barbara Windsor's half-exposed mammary in *Carry On Nurse*. This time there was multiple full frontal, with the girls parading in all their topless splendour.

But there was a problem. One girl wasn't prepared to show off her best points. On the morning of the nude shoot Gerald Thomas took me aside, saying, 'Patrick, Judy Geeson has refused to do the topless shot.'

He told me that her contract specifically stated that she would bare her assets. And he said he was more than a little surprised as she had already shown us what a fine figure she had when she took off her top in the Rod Steiger film *One for the Road*.

Because of my close working relationship with Judy, Gerald asked if I could persuade her to honour her contract.

I told him, 'I can't persuade her, but I will ask her for you.'

I went to her dressing room, where I found a sobbing Judy

cradling the miniature pooch which had been her constant companion during shooting.

'I can't do it,' she whispered. 'I just can't, it's too embarrassing.'

'It's in your contract. They can possibly sue you when the film is finished,' I warned her.

'I'll take the consequences. I just can't do it. It's just gratuitous. If you and I were doing a scene in another kind of film and it was integral to the plot I'd be completely naked, no problem. I'm proud of my body. The other girls are showing their boobs, that's enough. I don't care what they do.'

I reported back to Gerald Thomas that Judy had told me that she wouldn't take her top off in this film, but if he wanted to shoot *Lady Chatterley's Lover* she'd strip naked for him. I told him that she had then said that in a *Carry On* film it would make her feel a right tit. He roared with laughter, saying, 'That's a great line – I'll use it in the film.'

And Judy didn't do it. So, when all the other girls paraded topless, she was missing from that sexsational line-up.

Among the many productions being filmed at Pinewood was *The New Avengers*, with my old mates Pat Macnee and Gareth Hunt, and the lovely Joanna Lumley as martial-arts queen Purdey. Throughout the five weeks I was there we had a great time together, dining in the restaurant every lunchtime and evening and drinking in the bar.

More importantly, as it was to turn out, they were filming *The Prince and the Pauper* with another old chum, Ollie Reed, Rex Harrison and the pneumatic beauty Raquel Welch. Yet it wasn't Miss Welch who caught my eye, attractive though she was, but a tall, gorgeous brunette with the most amazing smile and figure who stood out among the many dancers in the Rex Harrison movie.

Her name was Suzanne Danielle.

By now I was becoming the epitome of one of the roles that had earned me my part as Sergeant Able. Gerald Thomas had seen me in Shaw's *The Philanderer* – and I was now that man.

Suzanne was indeed a very tempting dish, and I hadn't lost my appetite.

Just before the end of shooting *Carry On England*, I began an affair that was to change my life.

Although Suzanne was not the reason that I felt that I had to leave Audrey, she was the catalyst. It is difficult to understand even now, but I was ashamed, and sometimes disgusted, by my own behaviour, the way I was treating Audrey and my children.

Although while at home I could be a loving husband and father, when I shut the front door of our house in Pembroke Gardens, Mr Hyde took over completely – and watch out any young maiden crossing my path.

In a way Suzanne was cathartic. I left Audrey because I knew if I stayed I would carry on leading this double life. And, while it is a very selfish thing to say, it was causing me great pain – although by now, I am sure, it was causing Audrey even more. Strangely enough, I couldn't seem to stop myself. Because of my image, girls – from Page Three beauties to dancers – were offering themselves to me. It seemed that I was the current main attraction. I was every pretty London girl's must-have accessory.

There are many opportunities to stray when you're an actor. A glamorous profession attracts glamorous people and in those days I found the temptations becoming irresistible. Very dangerous for a marriage – or any kind of relationship. It was a world where pretty girls were making themselves prettier just for me.

People scoffed at Michael Douglas for seeing a therapist about his 'sex addiction', but I was not far off that point.

Although Audrey had been a part of me from when we were

teenagers and I knew I still loved her, and desperately loved Simon and Claudia, I knew I had to stop my behaviour.

As I said, Suzanne was a catalyst, but I didn't separate from Audrey because of her. It was a culmination of my struggle with the many demons and devils that were in my mind. Audrey was – and still is – the sweetest person imaginable and was entirely blameless. I was on some sort of roller-coaster of self-idolatry. I suppose I was starting to believe all the praise of the fans and the flattery of sycophants telling me how wonderful I was.

And then, one cocaine-assisted night, I left – intending, I'm sure, sometime to return to Audrey, if welcome.

As ever, my best friend Michael Latimer and his wife, Sheena, took me in and gave me good counsel and true friendship. I stopped my philandering overnight. But I began to see more and more of Suzanne. It wasn't just a physical relationship: I experienced a kind of freedom about my whole being and found that Suzanne really was the 'all things to all men' girl she appeared to be – young, witty, talented, showbiz, sexy. And what began as a naughty dalliance blossomed from that stolen rosebud into a full-blown rose.

But it was hardly smooth sailing. The press subjected me to a feverish character assassination while casting Suzanne in the role of femme fatale. It was not the happiest of times as, naturally, we were both feeling guilty, but we tried our best not to read the most vitriolic pieces that were being written. In a way the attacks gave us an extra bond and the more we were together the more we realised we should be together – and we fell in love.

Fortunately, a film came to the rescue, enabling us to go abroad and escape from the clamour. The director, Guy Green, asked me to play Il Lupo, the Wolf, the leader of the Italian Resistance in an adaptation of Morris West's *The Devil's Advocate*, in which I aged from 28 to 50 years old. We were due to start shooting in an out-of-season ski resort in the Italian Alps, but disaster nearly overtook me before I had filmed a single shot.

I was in Rome for a costume fitting when, forgetting that the Italians drive on the other side of the road, I stepped off the pavement – and was nearly killed. With a screech of brakes a Ferrari clipped my knee and sent me flying backwards, badly spraining my left ankle. Hardly the handiest of developments as my character had to leap fearlessly from rock to rock 6,000 feet up in the Alps.

However, turning on all my charm, I was able to persuade the very camp costume designer that Il Lupo needed boots that laced firmly above the ankle – and I was able to film my scenes. Even with the boots it was fairly exacting as we moved to various locations throughout Italy, but for the final scenes we ended up in studios in Berlin and I was given a four-day break.

With Suzanne, who had accompanied me throughout the shoot, I seized the opportunity to catch a coach to the idyllic Italian resort of Sorrento, where one afternoon we hired a rowing boat. It was a beautiful, crystal-clear day with a duck-egg-blue sky and the sea a shimmering emerald green. I noticed that one of the boat's rowlocks was missing but the proprietor simply shrugged and smilingly assured me, 'No problema.'

We paddled out into the little inlet and 50 yards offshore Suzanne took off her top and let the sun play gratefully on her wonderful breasts. Then we dived overboard and had a delightful, naughty time for ten minutes or so around and under the boat as I changed places with the sun.

But we had obviously done something to upset that fiery orb, for suddenly darkness descended upon the scene. We looked up to see a purple cloud blotting out the rays. It was like a science-fiction movie with the cloud moving very quickly.

We clambered back into the boat and, rowing furiously, tried to head for the shore and away from the three-foot-high waves that had materialised as if by magic. Within five minutes we were in the most horrendous electrical storm I have ever been in. The waves were now five feet high and visibility was like night.

It was then, as we tried to row towards the jetty, that we discovered it is impossible to row a boat in those conditions with only one rowlock. Suzanne was not only extremely fit, she was also very strong and, as she was using the rowlock, her mighty strength was overpowering me and we were going round in circles.

The waves were now mountainous, pushing us remorselessly towards the rocks that lined the inlet. As we got close all we could do to stop the boat being smashed to smithereens was to try to anticipate each wave and then use the oars to ward the boat off the rocks. Slowly we managed to edge our way round the rocks until we came to a tiny bay, where we let the sea drive us up on to the beach. We then pulled the boat up the shingle and gratefully sank down on it, ignoring the rain that was still lashing down.

High cliffs towered above the little beach, which appeared to have no exit, but as we set off to explore in the pouring rain we found a little door with an iron grille set into the sheer rock face. Beside the door there was a chain which looked like it was connected to a bell. We pulled it and, as if by magic, the rain stopped. In the distance we could hear a loud clanging and eventually the grille was pushed up and we were confronted by a nun peering through the gap.

In my best pigeon Italian I explained our dilemma and she reluctantly opened the creaking door and, lowering her gaze, pointed to a path that was obviously the direction from which she had come. She never uttered a word and Suzanne and I set off up the pathway, which was lined on either side by a neatly trimmed three-foot-high box hedge. As we hurried along we both became aware that Suzanne had left her top in the boat. Later we discovered that the place was a closed, silent order. Maybe they thought we had been sent by the devil, for with the hedge hiding our bodies from the waist down, the startled nuns looking at us must have thought a naked man and a naked woman were walking through their convent. Or maybe they thought we were Adam and Eve!

The beach door was obviously never normally used and we exited through a small gate in a high wall, right into one of Sorrento's narrow streets. With Suzanne using her hands to cover her modesty, we jogged rather briskly back to our hotel.

The Devil's Advocate featured many European film stars, among them that fine French actress Stephane Audran and Timothy West. I became firm friends with Sir John Mills and many years later I was to become one of his neighbours when my wife Anya and I moved into Denham Village, just west of London.

We also grew very close to John's wife, Mary Hayley Bell, and when Anya and I took our young son Maxim to Noel Coward's old hill-top home in Jamaica, Firefly, we made a film especially for the pair of them. At the house is a framed poem that Mary wrote about it for 'The Master' and Anya filmed me reading the poem as she panned the camera around the beautiful location. We took the film back to England and presented it to Mary. John, who by then was very nearly blind, told us that she really treasured it.

After returning to England, Suzanne and I rented a flat in a little road in Putney, ten doors away from my old sparring partner Imogen Hassall. We had been firm friends once, but Imo was always volatile and, sadly, one day she took her own life.

I realised that in my hedonistic life I had alienated many

people. In my search for pleasure I had ignored two important ingredients of myself: my humanity and my talent. So I stopped doing personal appearances and garish television personality spots and resolved to re-establish myself as a serious actor.

My career certainly appeared to be heading in the right direction when I was asked to appear alongside one of our greatest stage actresses, the redoubtable Maggie Smith, in Tom Stoppard's *Night and Day* at the Phoenix Theatre. I had been warned that Maggie would chew me up and spit me out, but, strangely enough, my thoughts were not of being in awe of her. Instead, they went right back to *House of Cards*, when, just out of RADA, I had starred on that same stage singing eight songs – and wondering how I had had the nerve to do it.

The rehearsals went well and Maggie and I got on like a house on fire. There was no chewing, let alone spitting. All the stories of her being a dragon were untrue. If you respect another actor's abilities and you can match their high standards, then you have a show. And we certainly had a show.

Suzanne also won a warm place in Maggie's heart when, on the opening night, she lived up to her reputation for putting her foot in it. She brightly gushed to a nervous Maggie, 'Don't worry, I'm sure it will all fall to pieces on the night.'

Maggie, turning those magnificent luminous round orbs on her, said in that Kenneth Williams voice, 'I hope she's not psychic.' We all burst out laughing. The ice was broken.

My role in *Night and Day* as an Australian reporter in Africa was a massive male lead and during the many months I was in the production I tried to reinvent him every night to make it that little bit different and challenging. The director, Peter Wood, saw the character as dour and depressed and directed me as such. During the run I wheedled lines that I thought were funny and played it that way – to the delight of Tom Stoppard.

One day I was sitting in my dressing room when I got a call from Stoppard. 'I'm ringing to thank you for reminding me what a funny play I've written,' he said. He went on to say that his wife, Miriam, had seen the show and had told him it was a complete revelation, and he agreed with me that the director had not quite exploited the comedy in the play.

Praise indeed, and more good news appeared on the horizon when, yet again, I got a call from Eon Productions. Bond had re-entered my life.

As before, they asked to see me at their South Audley Street offices. Once more it was on a funny day and my agent Jean Diamond remarked, 'It's not a proper casting, Patrick, you are the only one going up.'

Sod it, I thought, I'm not going to turn up as Bond in a Savile Row suit again. I'll go as Patrick Mower, successful actor.'

While Audrey and the children had remained in the house in Kensington, I was now living with Suzanne in a house I had bought in leafy Gerrards Cross, and I went into the garden, where there were some big yellow daisies. Perfect, I thought as I picked one and popped it into the buttonhole of the bright, checky jacket which I then wore, along with a vibrant tie, to the audition. As I said earlier, a yellow chrysanthemum had been my usual choice and once, before a performance in the theatre, the stage manager had had to ask the audience not to send me any more flowers because my dressing room was full.

When I got to the Eon offices I was again ushered into the board room. Cubby Broccoli, his legs crossed, sat on my left at the table, twiddling his glasses. On my right was the other producer, Michael G. Wilson, with his wife, Barbara Broccoli, sitting beside him.

These two kept looking at me and then back to Cubby as if

The Royals.

Above: I met the Queen again at Emmerdale's 30th Birthday party. We like to think she's a closet fan!

Below: In the film *Monella* playing Andre with his mistress, played by Serena Grande. Indeed, her boobs were enormously grande.

My family.

Above: Backstage celebrating another successful panto with one of my best friends, Richard Calkin, and my mother.

Below left: A favourite picture of my mother with my daughter Claudia.

Below right: A family snap of me standing proudly with Claudia and my son Simon.

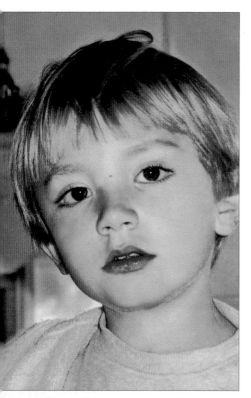

Watching Maxim grow and develop, or just playing football and cricket with him, are the things that mean the most to me now. He is such a wonderful child. These are some of my favourite photos of him.

At home in Lincolnshire with two of our miniature Palomino horses (*top*). Sponsored for the last two years by Tunnocks Biscuits, Anya is one of the best carriage drivers in the country. One of my favourite pictures of Anya and I together at the *Emmerdale* golf classic (I won of course!) and me at home – one man and his beloved dog, Poppy the Great Dane.

The writers can do anything in *Emmerdale* land. They can write you in; they can write you out. They can make you gay; they can make you straight. Luckily, at the moment Rodney is in and is straight. He has been in the village now for over five very happy years. My mother would have been proud, she was an avid fan. I am pictured here as Rodney with Adele Silva. Rodney had the good fortune for her character, Kelly, to fall in love with him! We're pictured with Rodney's son Paul, played by the too handsome Mathew Bose.

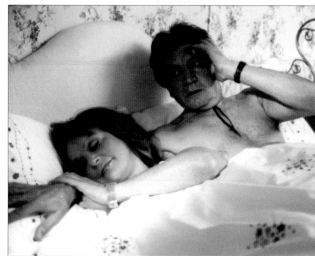

'Hot Rod' practises his technique with the ladies. I wonder what they saw in Rodney, the millionaire!

to say, 'Hey, look.' Cubby kept on twiddling his glasses and rubbing his eyes until finally he said, 'You have done mainly theatre, Patrick, not many films.'

Cubby then asked me a few more questions, interspersed with a lot of aahs and umms, as if trying to make a decision.

Wilson then trotted out their usual line about keeping it all in the strictest confidence.

They then said they thought Roger was getting too old and, while he could do one more Bond, they thought that was his limit. But, they explained, they had a problem. Roger was refusing to sign his contract for just one more film. He was insisting on a three-picture deal.

To put pressure on him they had produced a cardboard cut-out of Bond at the Cannes Film Festival – with the face missing. They wanted to have another Bond ready to go if Roger wouldn't sign for just a year – and they wanted to give it to me.

Suzanne was waiting for me outside the offices, turning heads in South Audley Street, as she sat, with the hood down, in the Triumph Stag I had bought for her. Despite being sworn to secrecy, I couldn't resist telling her of the latest development.

The White Elephant Club, where all the top actors used to go, was opposite Eon's offices and Suzanne was so excited she said, 'We must have a bottle of champagne.'

I said I couldn't as I was going to the theatre, but she insisted that I should at least have a glass.

Then the most amazing coincidence happened. As we crossed the street Sean Connery himself came out of the club. We had never met him in our lives, but he said, 'Hello.'

We said 'Hello' back and, as we watched him walk away down Curzon Street, Suzanne said, 'Out with the old, in with the new. Let's get that champagne.'

On stage that night, in the deep Australian drawl of the

character I was playing, I said to Maggie, 'How do you fancy kissing James Bond?'

With a twinkle in her eye, she drawled, 'Now that's too good an opportunity to turn down.'

As it turned out, Roger did sign and when Roger finally handed in his licence to kill they went for Timothy Dalton.

While Dalton was playing 007 I got another phone call from Eon asking to see me, but I refused to go in for yet more talks. I had tested for the role three times and I said, 'They know my work and they know who I am.'

Whether that was the right or the wrong thing to do, I don't know, but they then went with Pierce Brosnan, who I thought was really good, although I was never impressed by Dalton.

I really think I talked myself out of it the first time round. Looking back at it now, and recalling how I appeared in *Callan* as the smooth killer James Cross, I can see what they were after. I looked pretty James Bondy then and I'm sure I would have made a really good 007. In fact, I was offered another stab at Bond when they made a 007 parody, but I turned it down.

I turned down a lot of things.

I have always been a lucky actor and quite a good one, as well as being commercial. And you need to have that edge to carry a stage show and keep the audience interested for two and a half hours. You have to be witty and funny and tough and strong and exciting and charming. And you have to do all those things night after night to be a theatre star. And that's where stars are created.

But repeating a performance on stage seven times a week month after month can eventually be soul-destroying. I think six months is as much as one's brain and body can take, but at the end of my six-month contract the producer, Michael Codron, asked me to carry on for another three months with Susan

Hampshire, who had taken over from Maggie. And because the show was so successful I agreed. Susan was very good in her role but the last three months playing the same repetitive role was purgatory. My body and brain really had had enough.

Whether it was to expurgate my demons, I'm still not sure, but I became very involved with the Variety Club and the Lords Taverners, both organisations being dedicated to helping disadvantaged children, an aim which had always been close to my heart since my early experience with St John's Boys' Club. Through acting I have been able to indulge my other love.

Apart from acting and sex, my other passion was sport – doing it, not watching. I have been so lucky in my life, for being 'famous' has allowed me to play football with George Best and Rodney Marsh at Molineux in Les Barrett's Testimonial in front of 15,000 people. To 'nutmeg' Bobby Charlton while winning the *Sun* five-aside tournament. To score a hat-trick at Wembley with the crowd cheering, 'Mower, Mower...' – I have to admit it was a ten-a-side match, played *across* the pitch. Rod Stewart and Elton John were in my team – the opposition's goalkeeper was David Frost in cricket pads. I also played at White City in front of 10,000 against Bobby Moore, Geoff Hurst, Jack and Bobby Charlton – the whole World Cup-winners' team. For this match I was in the TV showbiz team, which included the likes of Dennis Waterman, Robert Lindsay and Richard O'Sullivan.

I've also won a yacht race, taking a 20-foot sloop around Marmarus Harbour in Turkey.

My tennis partner against Ian Botham and Peter Cook was newscaster Trevor McDonald, who remains a firm friend. Through the Lords Taverners, I have been fortunate to play cricket with Dennis Compton, Fred Truman, the Bedser twins, Bill Edrich and the brilliant Colin Milburn. I have played golf with Kevin Keegan, Nick Faldo and so on. I have been blessed.

Suzanne and I became friends of the showbiz rich and famous, including Bruce and Anthea Forsyth and Eric Morecambe and Ernie Wise. Suzanne was becoming well known in her own right and not just as my partner, guest-starring in many TV shows, including her famous 'All That Jazz' sequence with Eric and Ernie.

I was to work with Ernie in Ray Cooney's *Run for Your Wife* at the Criterion Theatre in the West End, and he and his wife, Doreen, became firm friends, as did Eric and Joan. Eric could never resist fooling about and cracking gags, even at the most inappropriate moment. On one Variety Club trip to Jersey, the elite of British showbiz and sport – the two Ronnies, Barker and Corbett; Eric and Ernie; Brucie; Ted Dexter, et al – were in danger of being wiped out as our pilot struggled to land in thick fog.

After the pilot, with a thunderous roar of the engine, had desperately pulled the nose of the plane back up, having just missed a rock on our third abortive attempt to land, Eric called out, 'I have to see my surgeon for my second by-pass. Shall I tell him not to bother?'

There were many such freebies around in a happy, carefree celebration of celebrity, and on another occasion we were invited to join Concorde on its first trip to Malaga, where the assembled stars were to play cricket. Having flown down the Bristol Channel so the aircraft could reach Mach 2, we landed at Malaga in a huge flurry of publicity.

People came from all over Spain to see this wonderful aircraft and after we had wined and dined – and played cricket – to the cheers of thousands of watching Spaniards we re-embarked.

The pilot pressed the starter button and, with a sound that reminded me of my old 2.4 Jaguar on a cold and frosty morning, the engines did a couple of turns, wheezed and groaned. The lights dimmed – and then, with a final hiss, the plane slowly descended into darkness.

On board, the embarrassed silence was in eerie contrast to the near-hysterical cheering, swiftly switching into jeering, of the assembled multitude of Spaniards at this example of Anglo-French engineering.

Jimmy Tarbuck encapsulated the whole debacle as his disembodied voice floated through the darkness, 'Anybody got a shilling?'

We all disembarked and drank champagne as British Airways hurriedly recharged the batteries that had caused this PR disaster.

The Bond saga had merely further whetted my appetite to be a movie actor and I met a variety of visiting American producers who urged me to go to Hollywood where all the film action was. At that time, however, I was being offered too much interesting work in the UK to want to take the gamble by accepting their invitations.

In a business where at any time 90 per cent of actors are out of work, I was always in the other 10 per cent and because of this I found myself at loggerheads with Vanessa Redgrave's Workers' Revolutionary Party. One afternoon I was sitting in my dressing room at Thames TV when I was visited by a member of her party who told me I should turn down work so that it would leave roles free for other actors to take. I said this suggestion was absolute rubbish as most of the roles I was offered were being created for me and indeed sometimes a television series wouldn't happen if I said, 'No.' So by working I was actually creating work for others.

As if to prove my point, I got a phone call from David Wickes the producer saying he was sending me the script for a new police series for the BBC. The series had yet to be named but it was a revolutionary concept for the Corporation as it would be their first shot at filming a whole series outdoors.

Four years after Euston Films had paved the way, the BBC were finally waking up. But I'm afraid *Target*, as the series was finally named, was doomed from the word go.

Philip Hinchcliffe, a very nice, intelligent and affable BBC man, was the producer. But they couldn't even get the show's name right. David, its creator, wanted it to be called *Hackett*, the name of my character, in line with contemporary top American shows like *Kojak* and *Columbo*. But the BBC refused, arguing, 'That will give Patrick Mower too much power if he wants to leave the show and we still want to carry on with it.'

They insisted on calling it *Target*, which was an awful title as it made it sound like a nice children's show instead of the hard-hitting cop drama it was to be. That was bad enough, but the BBC, bless 'em, just hadn't a clue about shooting film. With a film you have a director assisted by a first assistant director, then a second, then a third and possibly a fourth assistant, with the orders being passed down the line from the director. Not at the BBC! Being an egalitarian organisation, the BBC insisted on a director and five equally responsible assistant directors.

How many electricians does it take to change a lightbulb?

This was the same ludicrous system.

David Wickes directed the first episode, which involved numerous screeching car chases which left the BBC trailing in their wake. Ken Westbury, the camera operator, tried his best to catch all the action of a car racing at 60 miles per hour into a handbrake turn, and then followed Hackett leaping from the moving car, diving over a hedge and rolling over to reveal his gun. But it wasn't what he was used to.

He complained to me that I was running and diving too fast, explaining that for the past four days he had been quietly sitting on top of a 'cherry-picker' sedately following the flight of a golf ball in a ladies' match at Wentworth.

A problem was that no BBC employee was allowed to request which programme they worked on. Everybody was delegated. And that didn't make for a happy ship. The make-up artist admitted she would prefer to have been on *Jackanory* rather than finding, to her disdain, that she had to apply bruises and bloodstains to battered bodies.

With my experience in *Special Branch* and other outside-broadcast productions, like *The Sweeney*, I was horrified as I watched Wickes going hoarse screaming at these amateurs as he battled to shoot the first episode in ten days. This process continued throughout filming, with most people complaining bitterly that it was impossible to shoot, ignoring the fact that Euston had already filmed 26 hours of *Special Branch*, each episode shot in ten days, and then had done the same with *The Sweeney*.

In fact, two years later, when Trevor Eve was asked to repeat our exercise of shooting an hour of *Shoestring* in ten days he found it impossible. The first episode of *Shoestring* stretched into three weeks, the second episode was cancelled, the third was almost three weeks. The BBC were profligate. The Corporation used to be very high-handed, thinking they were the Almighty, but they were incredibly disorganised. As *Target* was on film, we had no rehearsal rooms. This caused mayhem.

When Douglas Camfield, the director for the third episode, rang up the BBC to ask where I was filming, he was told there was no such programme as *Target*. Persevering, he got through to BBC drama publicity to be told, 'Patrick Mower is an ITV contract artist and does not work for the BBC!'

We used to make one programme in Bristol and the next in Southampton and used those studios' facilities. The rest of the time our headquarters were in Ealing. The BBC were so insular that the crew were told not to watch or talk about ITV.

I wanted to make Detective Chief Superintendent Steve Hackett different from Cross and Haggerty. So, with the producer's support, I based the character more on Clint Eastwood's *Dirty Harry*-style policeman. If he was punched, he punched back. He was tough – and he meant it. He was aggressive and I hid my charm under a bushel.

We shot some terrific episodes and a measure of its authenticity and success was painfully rammed home to me one chilly afternoon when I was playing in Dennis Waterman's Soccer Xl against a Sussex police team in Greenwich. The police had two enormous sergeants playing in their defence and, as I lifted my arms while leaping to head a Waterman cross from a corner, one of them elbowed me in the ribs. As I lay in a crumpled heap, the sergeant stepped over me, looked down and said, 'Sorry, Pat, but I've always wanted to do that to a bleeding superintendent.'

The referee awarded a penalty – and I got up and scored it.

But the sergeant really left his mark on me. He had broken two of my ribs, which, apart from my nose, are the only broken bones I have ever sustained in all my years of high activity whether in sport or leaping, diving, kicking, fencing, judo – you name it – as an actor.

As we began filming the second series of *Target*, I could feel the edge was gradually being taken off the show. I had script approval and director approval but not, it seems, Mary Whitehouse's approval. She had mounted a campaign against the programme with a vengeance, declaring in a letter circulated to members of her National Viewers' and Listeners' Association, 'On Thursday night Patrick Mower, playing Det Supt Hackett, was insubordinate to a superior officer, punched a fellow officer, said the word "bloody" three times and was seen in bed with a drug addict (female). I am sure you will agree that we do not want this sort of programme on our beloved BBC TV. Please send a copy of the above comments to Alasdair Milne, Director General.'

At the BBC, and indeed at my home and my agent's office, we were getting letters by the hundred saying thank goodness the BBC is at last competing with ITV. Possibly few of those letters found their way to Alasdair Milne. But he heard from Mrs Whitehouse & Co.

We were told he received 5,000 letters from her League of Light and he made a statement declaring that he felt it was his bounden duty to stand up and say it was a mistake to make *Target* – and he would take it off immediately.

As if that wasn't bad enough, an influential report on violence from America came out. Its author, Dr William Belson, declared that 'there is too much gratuitous violence, whether verbal or physical, on TV and note what a harming effect it can have on children'.

Critics, policy makers, features editors all looked round for someone to blame and as the only show in town was *Target* we took all the flak. They were looking for violence on television and in *Target* they found it. It was lucky for all the other cop shows that they were not being screened at the time.

But *Target* was not meant to be a programme for children. The police themselves loved its tough style, saying it had far more veritas than *The Sweeney* or *The Professionals*. The show was successful but was a victim of circumstance.

The atmosphere and collective vibes were that it was doomed, and my sense of foreboding at the start proved right.

The BBC killed it off and it has never been repeated, despite constant requests, because of Milne's statement.

16

Golden Days

WHEN I WAS with Suzanne I was a changed person. I never deliberately attempted to eradicate the glint in my eye and still admired a well-turned calf and a well-formed breast, but the lust had gone and we were a very happy couple.

Suzanne's career was going very well and she was being accepted for leading roles. She had star quality and was a superb performer as she proved playing the show-stopping lead made famous by Shirley MacLaine in the hit musical *Sweet Charity* at Sheffield's prestigious Crucible Theatre.

She was also a top-billing solo cabaret artist who could rise above any disaster. One night at an Oslo nightclub the mike cut out in the middle of one of her numbers. Completely unfazed, Suzanne simply broke into a little dance routine and then, using the skills she had perfected as a champion gymnast, did a back flip. As the audience rose to give her a standing ovation, she did another! That was the kind of girl she was. She didn't stand there looking perplexed, she improvised, and when one back flip went down rather well she nonchalantly did another.

She was always the life and soul of any party and was not embarrassed to talk to anyone. Suzanne also had great determination. When she couldn't get an audition for one of the Bond films she found out where the director was staying in Park Lane and went and knocked on his door. That was the kind of dynamic person she was.

We were a golden couple – the Posh and Becks of our day. We opened Peter Stringfellow's London club and were invited to all the premieres and grand events. Through no design or desire of our own, we were the Big Couple. It was just that the press liked us and we were the flavour of the month.

We were seen as a bit of a team and did chat shows together but, understandably, Suzanne did not want to be thought of as getting jobs off my back. She was a particular favourite with the viewers in *Star Games* for Thames Sport, in which sporting personalities and entertainers like Dennis Waterman, Lewis Collins and Gareth Hunt were competing. Suzanne was in my team and with her athletic skills did extremely well – and looked extremely good in a tight T-shirt.

We also acted together and were signed up for a major tour in New Zealand of *Monkey Walk*, a two-hander stage comedy that could once again have changed my life.

Long before the *Lord of the Rings* trilogy, there were only two entertainment high spots in New Zealand – the All Blacks rugby team and two gay cooks, Hudson and Hall. The cooks hosted the nation's top television show, and while Suzanne and I were doing *Monkey Walk* in Auckland we were invited to appear on it. This was obviously a very good plug for our production, but the boys were also tremendous fun and we became very good friends.

Roly-poly funny man Dick Emery, complete with tweeds and monocle, was also in Auckland, and when Suzanne and I were leaving the city I told him I wanted to take Hudson and Hall for dinner. It was our way of saying 'Thank you' because they had been so kind to us, and I invited Dick along too.

'My show finishes after yours, so is it OK if I come along later and can I bring someone else?' he asked.

'Of course,' I said.

I asked Hudson and Hall to choose the restaurant, the food and the wine, insisting that I was paying and assuring them that money was no object. They chose Restaurant 42, which was very posh, very discreet and very tiny. It was more like dining in someone's house and only catered for about eight covers.

It was a magnificent gourmet meal with a different wine – the very finest from all over Australasia – to complement each course. We were tucking into this delicate feast the boys had arranged, when Dick turned up with his date. She had a very strong Australian accent and was of dubious age, possibly 35. Heavily made up and quite stocky, she could have been one of Dick's creations from his own TV show.

As they sat down the maitre d' asked what they would like to drink. We were enjoying a particularly fine Australian Sauternes, having just cleaned our pallets with a blueberry sorbet, but, ignoring our wine, Dick turned to his companion and asked her what she would like.

'Champagne,' she shot back.

So Dick also said, 'Champagne.'

The maitre d' looked at me and I nodded.

Dick then said, 'Dom Perignon, of course.'

The maitre d' looked at me again and Hudson, who was sitting next to me, clamped his hand on my knee.

I again nodded to the maitre d' and said, 'OK.'

Clamping his hand even tighter on my knee, Hudson pulled me closer, whispering, 'Remember you're in New Zealand. Dom

Perignon is French. Do you know how much that is going to be here?'

It was in fact £180 a bottle because the restaurant only kept a rare vintage for very special treats, but I whispered back, 'No, that's all right. I invited them and he's my guest.'

The conversation was witty and Dick was very amusing.

We had now gone on to an exceptionally fine four-star Penfold's Grange Hermitage and I asked Dick if he would like to try some, but he said, 'No. We'll have another bottle of DP, please.'

I again felt Hudson's hand clamping my knee as the maitre d' looked across at me for my consent. Again I nodded and another bottle was served.

Meanwhile, Suzanne and the girl had gone off to the ladies and for some reason swapped dresses. We all had a good laugh and Dick suggested he and I should do the same. We didn't but it was a great evening and a good ending to our New Zealand trip – although, I must admit, a rather expensive one.

While we had been in New Zealand, Suzanne and I were asked to do a poster ad for Levi Jeans, to be seen only in Australasia. Because it was quite a lot of money they asked if we would mind waiting for three weeks for the new financial cycle. I told them I didn't want to wait in New Zealand but was happy to wait in Australia. So they arranged for us to stay at the best hotel in Sydney, the famous Sebel Town House in Kensington, which was used by every star visiting the city.

Our fellow guests included Elton John, Tina Turner, Bette Midler, the pop group Kiss and George Benson, and we soon became very friendly with Elton. His parents, who turned out to be very big fans of mine, were also there and we became really good pals.

One day a bearded Peter Elliot introduced himself to me as

Dick Emery's manager. He had arrived from England to prepare for his client's arrival in Sydney. I told him the story of the champagne.

'That sounds just like Dick,' he said.

'He was my guest and I invited him to dinner,' I replied. 'If he wants to behave like that, it's my bad luck. I just won't invite him again.'

Our paid holiday at the Sebel Town House was one long party. Suzanne and I were part of the pack recovering by the exclusive rooftop pool in the daytime after heavy après-show celebrations every night. Bette Midler, like a little suburban lady without her make-up; Tina wigless – Elton also; George Benson in a shower cap; the primeval Kiss boys without their lurid make-up. We were in fantasy land.

A few days later, on an evening when Elton wasn't working, he invited us to go out on the town with him. And Elton certainly knew how to do it in style.

It was Bette's birthday. So of course Elton hired a steamer. After watching Tina's concert we all sailed round Sydney Harbour with a band playing, fireworks – the lot. It was a fantastic, memorable evening. There was much wine and I'm sure more than a few drugs consumed.

Elton had a birthday cake made with the Sydney Opera House shaped into boobs to celebrate Bet's notorious flashing on stage. We rolled back to the Sebel Town House about midnight and I was first into the bar.

I was just about to order when a bottle of Dom Perignon in a silver bucket appeared at my elbow. The barman explained that it was from the man in the corner and looking over I saw Peter Elliot.

'That's from Dick,' he smiled.

'Cheers,' I called back, and was just about to pour the wine when Elton came in. 'Would you like a glass of this?' I asked with the bottle poised over a glass.

'That would be nice,' he said, and we had just started to sip when Tina Turner and the rest of the group came in.

Pointing at the Dom Perignon, Elton turned to the barman and said, 'Another one of these.'

After that we had another. And another... We got through 15 bottles of Dom Perignon at the bar that night.

It was a great party but it was all too much for Suzanne. At some unearthly hour in the morning, I had Tina Turner sitting on my lap, Suzanne on the chair on my left and Tina's wig on the chair on my right. Suzanne finally crashed out. Lolling over sideways, she fell face down into Tina Turner's lap.

'Oh, I'm terribly sorry,' I said to Tina.

'Hey, it's OK,' she laughed, adding with her famously sexy wiggle, 'I got the best of both worlds, I rather like it.'

And, with Suzanne fast asleep on Tina's lap, we just carried on talking – and drinking. It was that sort of atmosphere where everyone is accepted and has a good time.

I didn't feel so great the next morning when I opened a bleary eye and the thought flashed through my befuddled brain, Did all that champagne go on my bill – or Elton's? Luckily, it wasn't on mine.

We had been in the Sebel Town House for a month when we were told the South-East Asia account for Levi was being delayed for six months. They wanted to fly us back to Britain and then bring us back to Australia later in the year. This was bad news as I didn't want to go back.

Fortunately, the next morning Suzanne and I had just returned to the hotel after appearing on the television programme *Good Morning Sydney* when the phone in reception started to ring. Calling over to us, the receptionist said, 'Mr Mower, it's for you.'

A voice on the other end of the phone said, 'Mr Mower, this is Ian Crawford of the Crawford Organisation.'

My heart skipped a beat because Crawford TV was huge in Australia. Among the hit programmes it made was the massively successful *Cell Block H*.

I then had the most bizarre one-sided conversation which must have lasted all of two minutes.

'I have just seen you on *Good Morning Sydney*,' Ian Crawford continued. 'How long are you out here?'

'As long as I like,' I replied.

'Do you fancy some work? Have you seen *Airways*, the twice-weekly series we shoot in Melbourne?'

'No,' I said.

He then asked, 'What do you look like in a moustache? Like Douglas Fairbanks?'

Before I could answer, he said he would send some tapes of *Airways* to the hotel, adding, 'You will have some scripts within three days.' He was thinking on his feet. 'You can play a British pilot who lives on a yacht in Sydney Harbour, so you don't have to come to Melbourne,' he added.

'Your name will be, er, Rock. That's a good name. You fancy that? And he'll be a bit of a ladies' man, like yourself. We'll find something for Suzanne as well. Have a nice day.'

And that was that.

That night we went to see Tina Turner perform and, when we got back to our room at 2am, sure enough we found a pile of *Airways* tapes waiting for us. Drunkenly, we giggled our way through the lot, one of which featured Kylie Minogue when she was 10 or 11, and thought no more about it.

At the time in Sydney, I was mixing with directors like Bruce Beresford, who later became enormously successful in Hollywood, as well as having many writer friends. When they heard that I had been offered a soap, they all, to a man, declared, 'No way, Patrick. Don't touch it. You should be in movies.'

Suzanne and I were both very tanned and leading a brilliant sporty life, and leaving television behind and aiming for a film career seemed the right idea. The next day three scripts arrived in my room and, while idling by the pool on top of the Sebel Town House – with George Benson lying on one side of me and Tina Turner on the other – I flipped through the scripts. To my dismay they were terrific.

My Captain Rock Trent would make his first appearance emerging from below decks with a bikini-clad blonde on one side of him and a bikini-clad brunette on the other. In the plot the girl star of the series is sent to Sydney to pick up Captain Rock, the new English pilot, and after making enquiries she finds he has a yacht in Sydney Harbour called Lothario. Spotting the bikini-clad blonde she asks if this is Trent's boat. 'Yes,' says the girl, and re-emerges draped on one side of the good Captain Trent with the brunette on the other. Trent drawls, 'Hello Sheila,' to the show's star, who, looking up at Trent, says, 'Oh my God, Rock, I should have known it was you.'

Trent was Clark Gable, Douglas Fairbanks and Errol Flynn all rolled into one – and it was set in paradise.

I was represented Down Under by a top Sydney agent called Christine, who strutted around with a silver-topped cane in her palatial offices overlooking the Blue Mountains. Macaws and koala bears played in the surrounding palm trees as she told me Crawford were offering me $A100,000 for one year's work.

I phoned Jean Diamond in London, who said, 'Don't take it, Patrick. You are very much in demand in London. I think it will be a backwards step.'

I asked the advice of my showbiz pals at the Sebel Town House. They said, 'Don't do it. It's going backwards,'

I went back to see Christine, who dropped her silver-topped cane at the shock of my counter-offer. As the cane clattered on the floor, I told her I would do the show for twice the money and for half the time.

'Two hundred thousand dollars for six months' work! They'll never accept it.'

'Tell them,' I said.

She did and they said, 'Yes,' and agreed to my arrangement.

I phoned Jean Diamond, who said, 'Don't do it.'

I asked Suzanne. She said, 'Do it.'

I asked my showbiz friends. They said, 'Don't do it.'

No, I thought, I want to be a film star.

I turned it down.

We flew back to a dreary, drizzly, grey November London, leaving behind a beautiful, yellow Sydney summer.

For the first time in my life I found myself out of work for 11 weeks on the trot. I was out of work at Christmas and it didn't even snow. It just drizzled. Boring, miserable rain.

Did I do the right thing? I could have a million-dollar holiday home in Sydney now if I'd said yes. Who knows, I might even have ended up in *Neighbours*.

I went to quite a few parties with Elton back in England and remember, at one of them, smooching and snogging Liza Minnelli. We got on very well together. Elton was always a very nice guy, a bit drugs 'n' rock 'n' roll, but then we all were. It was a period when it was not frowned upon and was almost the norm for someone to offer you a joint. It was a funny old time and there was always a bit of coke around if you wanted it.

At this time I was very friendly with George Best, who had started playing for Fulham, and Angie, Calum Best's mother, and Suzanne became really good friends. Tramp nightclub, in Jermyn Street, W1, which was then the in place, was one of our great haunts and that era became a kaleidoscopic blur of celebrities, cocaine snorted, champagne drank. It was quite the high life.

I had the use of a villa beside the Aloha golf course in Marbella, which was Sean Connery's second home, and Hurricane Higgins was one of my golfing, drinking, snorting pals. If you fancied more sedentary relaxation, there was a heavy gambling card school led by a certain Mo Ash, who had two pretty daughters, Debbie and Leslie, who was to do very well for herself as a girl behaving badly.

I was finally lifted from my gloom after turning my back on the Australian sun when I was picked up for *Marco Polo*, a 17-hour television series in which I played a monk, Father Damian, with a bald pate. Thankfully, it was a wig and I didn't have to shave off my own hair. So, with a decidedly firmer spring in my step, I set off for Cinecitta studios in Rome to join David Warner, an old colleague from RADA days, who was now based in America and doing rather well for himself as a film star.

He confessed that this was the first time he had been allowed back into Rome after breaking both ankles when, in a drunken haze, he had plunged two storeys after walking through a plate-glass window 15 years earlier. David still enjoyed a glass of red wine first thing in the morning and relied rather heavily on me to help him through the rest of the day's work. But he was a charismatic actor and if you saw him on screen in the series you would never know it.

Both David and I were in all 17 episodes and I was in Rome for eight weeks filming my part. One afternoon, one of the producers, a handsome Italian called Fabrizio Castellani told me a film director wanted to meet me to discuss a future project, the story of Columbus discovering America. It was to be a massive project, filming for over 18 months.

As the director didn't speak English and my Italian was very limited, the producer turned up for dinner with an interpreter. The director was very complimentary about my performance in *Marco Polo* and offered me the starring role of Columbus. At last this is the breakthrough I was waiting for, I thought, as we shook hands and Fabrizio said they hoped to start filming later that year.

I met the director twice more in London to discuss the vast, 18-inch-thick scripts he had sent to me. Everything looked set fair for my new cinematic voyage. But in show business you can never take anything for granted.

When I went to meet the director for the third time at his Park Lane hotel, expecting to finalise contracts, I found Fabrizio looking rather glum. The director opened the conversation by holding up a photograph of a Renaissance painting of Columbus and, through Fabrizio, told me, 'This is what I want Columbus to look like.' He then held up a picture of Gabriel Byrne, looking exactly like the painting.

And that was how I was told I was no longer going to play Columbus. In the fickle world of entertainment you haven't got the part until you have signed the contract, and I hadn't signed.

He offered me a smaller role which would have meant working for nine months as one of the crew, but out of chagrin I declined the offer.

Gabriel Byrne sailed off to America in the *Santa Maria* and, after finishing the role, stayed there and is now what I wanted to be: a movie actor.

That's the gamble you take. And I must confess that I like a gamble, especially at the races.

One afternoon Suzanne and I were in the champagne bar at Ascot with a group of friends, the Ryder Cup golfer Sam Torrance, John O'Leary and a professional Irish gambler called Ron, who was almost a caricature of a racecourse man. A big jovial fellow with tickets festooned from his lapels, he always wore a trilby perched jauntily on his massive head, and he knew everybody. That afternoon he had a hot tip for a horse in the third race and he walked me down from the bar, past the bookies, along by the parade ring, beyond the unsaddling enclosure, until we reached a horse being unloaded from its box.

On our journey Ron had said a cheerful 'hello' to all and sundry and was obviously very popular. As the trainer supervised the unloading, Ron stood motionless, like a Labrador watching its prey, until the trainer caught his eye and gave a very slight inclination of his head.

'We're on,' Ron murmured to me under his breath. The signal obviously meant the horse was going for a win.

The only competition was a top jockey's mount and, as one of O'Leary's friends was an acquaintance of his, he had been dispatched to the jockeys' area to find out whether he felt his horse had a good chance. We arrived back in the bar to be told that the jockey had said his horse should be out with a milk float, not racing at Ascot – so our tip was secure. I put, for me, the massive sum of £50 on the horse and I'm sure the others bet far more on this dead cert.

The race was certainly exciting. In the final furlong, our horse was in the lead, but just yards from the finishing line the same jockey, bum high in the air, sailed up into contention with his legendary flair and the two horses crossed the line appearing, from my position in the stand, almost too close to call. Not close enough. The jockey's nag won by a neck.

That was not the only time I lost with Ron. He gave me many tips over the next two years, ringing me from Dublin or Los Angeles. For some reason he had taken a shine to Suzanne and myself. He was very generous and treated us to the three-day Irish meeting at Cheltenham, insisting that he paid for everything. But not once did any of his 'dead certs' win.

I wondered how he made his money. I found out two years later when I was told that Ron had been arrested in Amsterdam for murder. He had been involved in a drug-land argument and had shot a rival narcotics baron. His gambling persona and his acquisition of celebrity pals was all a front. He was a major drugs smuggler and was last heard of in a Dutch prison. He always travelled with his wife, an enormous woman, who looked rather like a Russian doll with her voluminous skirts.

My experience with *Marco Polo* hadn't dampened my appetite for films but, I must confess, the way movies happen never ceases to amaze me.

The public think that they are thought out with so much care and planning by the producers and writers, but the truth is that unless they are monster epics like a Bond they are put together on the back of an envelope. Someone says they have some money they don't mind losing – and there you go.

There was certainly more than a touch of improvisation and make-it-up-as-you-go-along about my next film, an American teen adventure flick about a group of guys and pretty girls who head for Mexico for paragliding, surfing, wind surfing. Initially called *California Cowboys*, it had a cast including John Wayne's son Ethan.

The director was Gordon Hessler, who knew from past experience that he could trust me to do the job, remember my lines, not get drunk and help carry the movie.

And that is how it turned out. I played the commandant of a Mexican prison nicknamed 'El Diablo', 'the Devil', and in the end they were so knocked out by my performance they changed the film's title to *Escape From El Diablo*.

Although it was set in Mexico, it was made – as were so many films – in Spain. We used the same castle as my beloved Sophia Loren had used to film the epic *El Cid*. Suzanne drove to Heathrow to see me off on the same plane as Roberto, the producer. Suzanne, as always, looked stunningly glamorous as she kissed me goodbye.

As I sat down I found I was seated next to Roberto, who asked, 'Who is that beautiful girl you were kissing?'

'My girlfriend,' I replied.

Five minutes' silence...

'Is she an actress?'

'Yes.'

Five minutes' silence...

'I think she could be very good. I think she should be in the film.'

'In what part?' I asked.

'We'll create one.'

And they did. Suzanne was cast as my character's girlfriend, a nightclub singer. In fact, I wrote the sexy little number she sang to great effect in the film.

Suzanne and I had a great time but I have never seen the film. It was released in America but not in the UK. Possibly it was a disaster. I had a letter from the writer thanking me for my performance. Mind you, it's probably circulating under some other title in a video shop near you.

The backstage manoeuvrings certainly didn't help. And what happened to Roberto, the producer, was typical of what happens on lots of films. On a violent stormy night, beneath a lowering purple-black sky as lightning flashed and thunder roared, there was a coup. Roberto was sacked.

I went into the hotel we were using as a base and a smart little man offered me his hand, 'Hello, Patrick, I'm the new producer.'

His name was Claudio and he was a Swiss banker.

'Oh, what happened to Roberto?' I asked.

'He is going to leave.'

Surprised, I asked, 'Does he know?'

'Not yet,' he replied.

There was to be a cast meeting that night and as I passed the large villa Roberto was using, a voice called out, 'Patrick, I have some friends I want you to meet.' The violent storm was the perfect setting for playing out this drama and I felt like Cassius in Shakespeare's *Julius Caesar* as I stood drinking champagne with Roberto and his pals, knowing that, like my friend Vincent Price, he was about to have a knife plunged into his back. I felt a twinge of 'Et tu, Patrick.'

I felt sorry for Roberto, he had done nothing wrong. It was his baby. I knew he had been working on the project for two years.

With *El Diablo*, and behind Roberto's back, rushes had been sent back to America to raise more money. The new backers, who were simply a financing company, insisted on many new people becoming involved, including a new producer, and changes to the film, including the name – so Roberto had to go.

Suzanne had had her own problems with films three years before, when she was cast in the Jackie Collins morality tale-cum-sex comedy *The World is Full of Married Men*.

Directed by Robert Young, the film starred Anthony Franciosa and Suzanne and I went to many meetings with Jackie in Hampstead talking about the script. They offered me a part but I said no. I didn't like the smell of it. They were very keen on persuading Suzanne to sign up as the star, a girl who slept around and had a very good time, but they assured her there wouldn't be any nudity. Suzanne was an obvious choice because she had played a disco dancer in the earlier Jackie Collins film *The Stud* and was the saucy star of *Carry On Emmanuelle*.

They started the five-week shoot at Pinewood and Suzanne did her first scene on the very first afternoon. On the second day she had to do a scene where she came out of a bathroom, sat down at a mirror and combed her hair. As they were shooting Suzanne from behind, the director told her to take her wrap off – so Suzanne asked for nipple covers. When they went to shoot the scene the cameraman said he could see the nipple covers. The director said he could also see them and asked Suzanne to take them off.

'If you can see the nipple covers you can see my breasts and it is in my contract that I am not doing nudity,' Suzanne told Young.

'In that case I suppose you had better put your dressing gown back on,' he said.

When Suzanne came home, she told me what had happened and I said, 'They're trying to get away with as much as they can.'

At eight o'clock the next morning, as she came out of make-up, Suzanne was approached by one of the producers, who said, 'Miss Danielle, you had a problem yesterday and wouldn't do what the director asked.'

'No,' she said. 'He wanted to show me naked and it's in my contract that I won't do nudity.'

The producer then told her that she had to do what the director said and they produced a new contract, one line of which said, 'There will be no shots of open or closed vaginary...' Their word, not mine. But the 'no' had been very crudely crossed out.

Suzanne then rang her agent to say she wouldn't do it. She then rang Equity, who said they were on her side.

They stopped filming for two days. The film company told Suzanne she was putting all the cast and crew out of work and that they had an American actress ready to go in her place. Equity, weak as ever, let the film continue, 'to save all the other actors' jobs'. The American girl, who we later discovered was a soft-porn actress, took over.

They embarrassed Suzanne, who ended up with half her salary, which was not very much.

Suzanne was a quite forward young lady, very ambitious and very talented, but being very beautiful can sometimes work against you in the entertainment world. With her fabulous figure – it wasn't without cause that she was known as 'the Body' – too many producers and directors couldn't see beyond this to the talent that lay beneath and I think her career suffered as a result.

But for years we were a gilded couple, the prime target to take part in lavish fashion shoots and join in celebrity sporting events.

There was a constant flow of invitations to play golf or cricket in the most wonderful surroundings like Wentworth and Lord's, which schoolboys only dream of. While we were burning the candle every night it was great fun to be mixing with Sam Torrance, Ian Woosnam, John O'Leary and suchlike.

And there were the parties, the booze and, always available, the drugs. But, because it was so available, you never used to do it so much, or perhaps I was just a little bit more sensible. I have always liked to be in control of myself and have never wanted to be completely drunk or take too much coke or too much dope. Back then it was more of a recreational thing than now. But sadly it could get out of hand and lead to the most tragic consequences, as happened with Paul Raymond's lovely daughter Debbie, who died from an overdose.

Debbie and Paul were great friends of Suzanne and I and often after an evening out we would end up at Paul's amazing apartment above the famous Caprice restaurant, just off

Piccadilly. Paul was a lovely, sociable chap and there would always be lots of everything around. The atmosphere was wonderfully relaxed and we used to sit writing the rude letters and answers that appeared in his *Men Only* magazine.

There would be peels of laughter from the girls as we made up all sorts of incredible stories or pleas for help like, 'My boyfriend's dick is too big for me – can it be shortened?' They were so ridiculous, yet, to our amazement, they would be printed.

It was great fun and a very naughty, sexy atmosphere. But the fun began to get out of hand, particularly with Debbie. As Suzanne's best friend, she used to come round to our house in Gerrards Cross a lot. She had just split from David Wilkie, the swimmer. It was a shock to see her at ten o'clock in the morning with a line of cocaine. Like anyone with an addiction, she would try to encourage us to do it too so that she wouldn't feel guilty. I have known a few alcoholics in my time and they were always trying to make you have a drink with them so that they could be forgiven and feel normal. So it was with Debbie.

At the time we didn't realise how addictive and harmful cocaine is. We just thought, Well, Debbie has a lot of money – her father is a multi-millionaire – and she can afford it. We thought she was just having a good time. So did she. So no one would say, 'Debbie, don't do it.' We couldn't see the harm in it. A lot of her friends even thought, Lucky her.

Not so lucky.

We knew she was on a crazy journey but it was the rock 'n' roll culture of the time and we just thought she was having fun. It's still a burden to me that I'm not sure that we did as much as we could to prevent her death. It was only when Debbie died that I realised you could become a cocaine addict.

And now, looking back, I feel that perhaps I was having too

much of what could loosely be called fun. Maybe I was getting into the spirit with too much enthusiasm. Also, all these outside influences were having an increasing impact on my and Suzanne's personal relationship.

We had been together for seven years and, while there wasn't actually an itch on either side, times were changing.

Suzanne hadn't been working as much as she would have liked and was not getting the kind of offers she fancied in England, so she took off to crack Hollywood.

This seemed to be a good point at which to end what had been a wonderful relationship. We mutually agreed that we didn't want to end up, as so many couples do, hating each other.

I don't think either of us felt the famous seven-year itch but we both knew in our hearts we might end up scratching each other and leaving scars.

17

Like a Boy in a Sweet Shop

NOW WAS TO begin a period in my life when, if I'd not already fulfilled every man's dream by sleeping with Suzanne, I was about to fulfil their ultimate fantasy. I was embarking on a journey where I lived the dream.

I was quite well-off, not bad-looking in a 'tall, dark, handsome' bachelor fashion and had quite a decent 'pad' in Gerrards Cross. For the first time in my adult life I had no commitments. I had a variety of television and theatre work lined up and could have affairs – and did – without compunction or guilt.

I chased a various assortment of girls, and caught a lot of them. I was the proverbial boy in the sweet shop and I was happy to indulge myself in all the liquorice all-sorts.

In those carefree bachelor days, I was never without a new girl on the horizon. At the time I had a predilection for Page Three girls – those glorious, sunny girls with their fabulous bodies and huge smiles – and luckily I knew just the person to help me meet them. She was one of the agents who looked after the Page Three models and when a new girl appeared in the *Sun* or the *Star* I would ring her up and say, 'Do you think so-and-so would like to go out for a drink?' Invariably she would say, 'I'm sure she would.' So I had what you might call my own special Page Three casting director.

I was very good friends with the photographer John Paul and his beautiful Page Three girlfriend Angie Layne. John had asked me to do a personal appearance for him and I persuaded Angie and her best friend, glamour model Linda Lusardi, to be my backing singers on a song I had written. After rehearsing, the three of us had a lot of fun together and one day we were fooling around being kissy-cuddly friendly in Rags, a small members' only club opposite Curzon Street, when, to avoid the photographers who were always trying to catch me with a different girl, we decided to move on to George Best's club, Blondes. I thought we would be all right there as my friendship with George stretched back to the Sixties, when we had played charity football matches together.

Then, on one never to be forgotten occasion, we had played against the victorious England World Cup squad. That match will live with me for ever. I've always been a keen sportsman and this was something out of my wildest dreams – the moment when you think you must have died and gone to sporting heaven.

The atmosphere inside the White City Stadium was electric. Twenty thousand cheering, chanting fans roared their approval as the nation's heroes trotted out of the tunnel to play their first game together since they had lifted the famous trophy. And I was there on the pitch, playing opposite them.

They were all there, the immortal names: Bobby Moore, Jackie Charlton, George Cohen ... and in one magical, adrenalin-pumping moment, as the crowd roared, the ball was at my feet. This was my chance for glory. Fully convinced in those few giddy seconds that I too could be a star, I raced towards the goal with Jackie Charlton in seemingly hot pursuit. It must have looked good from high up in the stands. For, as I ran with the ball, there was Jackie running alongside, apparently trying to tackle me.

Sadly the reality was far less glamorous. Instead of going for the ball, Jackie was simply keeping pace with me, urging me on in his broad Geordie accent, 'Keep goin', Pat, keep goin'.' Then, as I approached the goal area, his voice took on a fresh urgency as he roared, 'Shoot, you fool... *Shoot!*'

This was my moment for soccer stardom. The goal was at my mercy as Gordon Banks, bless him, deliberately dived the wrong way. But with the sweat pouring from me, my stomach tightening like a vice, and urged on by the jubilant crowd, I smashed the ball ... *outside* the post!

Back at George Best's club – named after the two famous blondes Jilly Johnson and Nina Carter – the three of us were in the bar sharing a bottle of bubbly, when George gave a dazzling display of the high-speed skills that had made him a legend on the pitch.

I was sitting with Linda on my left and Angie on my right – they both had their arms draped round me – and that was when suddenly George charged across the bar to the table in front of us and, with a great smash of broken glass, wiped the drinks off the table. George had saved me from one more unwanted appearance in the papers, for a paparazzi had a camera on the table underneath his napkin and had been taking pictures of us. Fortunately, someone had told George, who angrily seized the camera and ripped out the film as his bouncers marched the photographer out of the club, still asking in vain for his camera back.

The luscious Linda is still a friend and I'm happy to say is alongside me in *Emmerdale*, playing Carrie. She'd better watch out, I think Rodney's got his eye on her.

The lovely Angie, whom I visited many times in hospital, sadly died of breast cancer. She was such a fantastic person. She asked me if God had punished her for using her body to make money. I assured her he didn't work that way.

As time went by, it became increasingly difficult for me to escape from my playboy image. I found myself on the wrong end of the paparazzi yet again after a chance meeting with a stunning girl I dated against all the odds while I was doing a play in Aberdeen. It was during the North Sea oil boom, when Aberdeen was awash with millionaires, and just outside the city there was a Gold Members' club, the Shell Club, which catered strictly for mega-rich oil men.

On the play's last night, the two brothers who owned the theatre invited me to the club for dinner. As we arrived we were welcomed by one of the most beautiful girls I have seen in my life, a South American called, surprisingly, Lucy. She was working there and the brothers, realising just how much I was enamoured with her, urged me to try to date her.

'Go for it, Patrick,' they chorused. 'Everyone tries to get off with her because she's so beautiful, but they never succeed.'

That was a challenge I couldn't resist. Turning on my Charlie Charm, I drifted over to the girl and starting chatting her up.

As she was from South America, she didn't know me from Adam, but I gave her the full Mower works and we got on extremely well. As I was going back to London the next day, I said, 'You must come down and I will take you out.'

Smiling provocatively, she said she might just do that and gave me her phone number.

Back in London I phoned her and she said she would love to come and stay with me the following weekend – and I had only spoken to her once.

When she arrived, I took her to Sheekey's, a charming, discreet restaurant off St Martin's Lane. But it wasn't discreet for long. We were just sitting down at our table when, out of the blue, a man I had never seen before walked up to us, pulled out a camera and – *click* – took a picture and ran for it. Lucy couldn't believe her eyes; it was so strange and alien to her.

She had an even bigger surprise the next day when she saw the picture of us together in the papers under the heading 'Patrick Mower's new girlfriend'.

She was absolutely flabbergasted and asked me why it had happened. I explained who I was and I think she found it a little unnerving. We had a nice weekend and the following week she sent me a beautiful bunch of flowers, saying what a wonderful time she had had. I told her that I too had had a wonderful time, but I never saw her again because of the distance involved. It was a shame because she was sensational, but I couldn't just pop up to Aberdeen at the drop of a hat.

It may seem strange now that people would follow me around just for the chance of a snatched picture, but at the time I was obviously to them a means of making money and there was always a different girl on my arm.

There were even plans to make a television series about me and the girls in my life. Back then I could have fielded a full cricket team of girlfriends!

I should explain that they were girls for all seasons – and all for different reasons. One would be purely for sex, another for taking out to dinner, while I would date yet another for her interesting conversation. They were all sexual relationships but of different kinds.

I would devote a lot of time pondering, who shall I have this evening; who's on the menu for dinner. As Richard III says, 'I'll have her, but I will not keep her long.'

It was an amazing time. But I was a bachelor and what man in my situation wouldn't have made the most of it. I'm afraid that is when Mr Hyde completely took over and the caring Dr Jekyll was placed firmly in the bottle.

I also made sure there was lot of sexy fun wherever I went – even when playing in the Pro-am before a major tournament at La Manga with Eamonn D'Arcy and John O'Leary.

I was staying in a villa overlooking the eighth hole on the course with two stunning girls. One was Debee Ashby, the Page Three girl with very big boobs who later went out with Tony Curtis for a while, and the other was the beautiful Rhoda. I have always taken my golf seriously but with two such beauties to hand, I decided this was a golden opportunity to spice up the Pro-am. So I persuaded the girls to put on their sexiest outfits and come out with a tray of iced champagne as I approached the eighth hole.

The weather was perfect, hot and sunny, but with a slight breeze keeping it comfortable. And the golf wasn't going too badly either – until the girls came tripping across the fairway in miniskirts and with their amazing breasts thrusting from skimpy little tops.

As their hips swung provocatively on high heels, the effect was explosive and I cherish it to this day. I shall never forget the faces of the other golfers – their eyes out on stalks – as they gazed in sheer awe at the two young goddesses. Play swiftly ground to a halt, for the other golfers were unable to take their eyes off the girls as they swayed towards me with the champagne. Eamonn couldn't believe his eyes and the boys still talk about it.

After we had all had a glass I told the girls to offer champagne to all the other golfers as they came through and that little light relief made the whole tournament.

Rhoda even presented the prizes, but it was my champagne beauties at the eighth hole who won the day.

It took great dexterity and fleetness of foot – not to mention the odd fib – to manage so many affairs at once and make sure the girls never met each other. I think three of them knew there were other girls around but we were having so much fun they were prepared to go along with it. With the rest of the girls, though, I had to juggle my diary very carefully.

I worked out a reasonably simple formula to ensure that I didn't fall out with any of them – by only meeting each girl on her allotted day and at a specific time.

But even with the best planning, no matter how methodical, there can be complications – that unforeseen occurrence when the unexpected happens and you suddenly find yourself in a situation you can't control.

And I finally got caught out when one of the girls, Susan – a fiery beauty with a hard cockney accent – came to stay at my new home in Denham at the same time as my mother.

I was playing Newmarket with Suzie and my mother, who was 80 at the time, when the door bell rang. Excusing myself, I went to answer it and found, to my horror, that my worst nightmare had finally occurred. Standing on my doorstep was my old flame Annie.

She told me that she had caught the last train to Denham and asked if it was OK if she stayed the night. In the circumstances I had little option other than to, somewhat reluctantly, agree.

The moment Annie joined us in the sitting room I realised there was going to be trouble as the cockney beauty made it very clear that she took a very dim view of another girl turning up.

Flashing my most winning smile, I explained the situation in an attempt to ease the tension and, for a few moments, thought everything would be all right. I couldn't have been more wrong. After ten minutes of desultory small talk, my cockney charmer stood up and said, 'I'd better be going.'

'I thought you were staying the night,' I said.

'So did I,' she spat, 'I want to go *now*.'

'OK,' I agreed, 'I'll take you home.' We then went out to my big, very wide and very powerful Mercedes and set off.

As we drove down the road, she turned towards me, her lips trembling in barely suppressed rage. Finally, in a tight, angry accusation, she snapped, 'You *knew* she was coming and thought I was going to go.'

Trying to calm her down, I explained yet again that I was as surprised as she was by Annie's arrival. She really had turned up out of the blue.

Looking at me with an even more intense stare, she said, 'Yeah,' in a dismissive tone that made it obvious she didn't believe a single word I was saying.

She then turned away from me and, looking out of the window, brought her fist up.

We were bowling down the road at 80 miles per hour when suddenly, without any warning, she lashed out at me with her fist.

Her attack could have been fatal. Luckily I saw the blow coming out of the corner of my eye and reacted quickly enough to catch her fist with my right hand. With my left hand I fought to keep control of the car as she struggled to free her right hand. Pumping the brakes, I slowed to a halt and blessed my fast reaction, because if she had landed the blow she could have killed us both.

It had been a terrifying 30 seconds, but she acted as though nothing had happened. Turning on me again, she snarled accusingly, 'You knew she was coming,' adding in a menacingly cold whisper, 'You be careful, my dad killed someone...'

The way she said it, I knew she wasn't joking. But I also knew I had to be very careful how I reacted to this latest twist in an evening that had gone from the mundane to the bizarre. Summoning all the nonchalance I could muster, I casually asked, 'Oh, is he in jail?'

Glowering, she growled, 'No.'

'Why not?' I queried.

'Because no one knows about it – except you.'

It was a cold, calculated threat to keep me in line and, knowing something of her background, I realised that she wasn't fooling. But that was the kind of relationship we had and I soon saw her again, but I made sure no one came along on that date.

The last time we spoke was when she phoned me from an Arab country to tell me she was being held prisoner. She had gone there two years earlier with an Arab boyfriend but when she wanted to leave he had taken her passport away – and she wanted me to go out and rescue her.

Beneath her lovely face she was a pretty tough cookie and for once I resisted playing the gallant knight and confess that I didn't go. She may still be there, for all I know, but I doubt it. She could handle herself in any situation.

Strangely enough, another of my old amours went to Japan as a dancer and was trapped in the same way. She started as a legitimate nightclub dancer but soon the bosses told her she would have to dance topless or have sex with the customers to pay her way. They insisted that she owed them a lot of money for her flight and the flat they had provided – and they wanted their money back.

To increase the pressure, they also took her passport away.

She went topless as instructed but still couldn't satisfy them.

They tightened the screw even tighter by insisting she still wasn't earning enough and the only way she could get free was to become, in effect, a prostitute by sleeping with the customers.

She also phoned me, not to be rescued but for money. I saved her.

It's a really dirty racket in which the girls become sex slaves. Because no matter what the girls do the gangsters won't give them their passports back and just keep on claiming the girls owe more and more money until they can't even afford to pay their rent.

Money will do strange things to some girls, as I discovered to my cost when model Cherie broke the unwritten code of our group and did a 'kiss and tell' on me with a vengeance.

Cherie, a very pretty girl, was part of the glittering gang, including major stars like Rick Parfitt of Status Quo, who helped put the sparkle into the London night scene as we partied in Tramp, Stringfellows and Rags. And it was in this last club one night that I was introduced to Cherie. I took her out to dinner, she visited my home in Buckinghamshire and we had a lot of fun. So when I went to the Spanish villa I rented at Alla Maria to do some writing I invited Cherie along.

I was there for three weeks and had a different girl come out each week. None of the girls was a special girlfriend: it was all on the understanding that they would come out for a week and have a good time with no strings attached. And Cherie and I did have a good time.

Two weeks later, however, her mother telephoned me to say that Cherie had been offered £5,000 to write a story about me for one of the tabloids.

I rang Cherie and asked, 'What are you going to write?'
She said, 'I don't know, they are going to tell me.'
Because Cherie was part of our group and there were a lot of

stories that could have been told, I warned her, 'If you break the fraternity bond and tell secrets out of school, you'll be ostracised.'

'What does that mean?' she said. So I told her.

She said she wouldn't do it. But three days later her mother told me Cherie had now been offered £10,000, an awful lot of money in those days.

I again phoned Cherie, but she went ahead with a fabricated story under the banner headline 'Mower Hit Me For Sex' and, needless to say, I haven't spoken to her since. I don't think the others have either.

At the time I was trying to lead a non-public life, but the press still wanted news about me, knowing they could always then publish a picture of a pretty girl alongside.

I have always been good copy, but one extraordinary story – and certainly my strangest sexual adventure – escaped them.

Having a reputation for loving beautiful girls can land you in some pretty strange situations, as I discovered one afternoon when I dropped into McCreedy's, an actors' drinking club. I was revelling in my bachelor status and thoroughly enjoying my image as a Man about Town with a taste for the finer things in life.

I was standing at the bar having a drink with a bunch of other actors, including Lewis Collins – who was giving the impression of trying to live up to his screen reputation as a tough-guy hero in *The Professionals* – when a photographer came over.

'Patrick, I have someone who would like to meet you,' he said nodding towards a very beautiful girl who was sitting at a table with Cleo Rocos, who as Miss Whiplash provided the glamour, along with the laughs, on the Kenny Everett shows.

This was a period in London when one knew who the beautiful girls were and what actresses were around, but I had never seen this girl before. Smiling towards her, I said to the photographer, 'Who is she?'

He said she was a new girl in town called Robyn, adding, 'She would like to meet you.'

She was an absolutely stunning girl with long, black hair. I walked over and did my Charlie Charm bit, taking her hand and kissing it.

The photographer ordered a bottle of champagne, which struck me as rather unusual because in McCreedy's it was normally pints of beer.

She was very brown and the photographer said she had just come back from shooting a Smirnoff commercial in Hawaii and I teased, 'Have you got any white bits?' She laughed, shaking her head, and I joked, 'Oh well, I may have to prove you're lying.'

We got on famously and eventually I asked her where she was living. When she told me Church Street, Kensington, I asked her if she would like to share a cab as I too was living in the area.

Sitting in the back of the cab we had a little kiss, as one does, and I can still remember my hand sliding up over her wonderful breasts and getting rather passionate.

When we got to the corner of Church Street, we got out of the cab and started walking up it holding hands.

In retrospect, I recall thinking how tall she was. She was wearing heels, but she was about six foot. I was also struck by how broad her hands were.

We went to her flat, where we were met by another girl, who turned out to be her sister. Her sister, who was also very good-looking, gave me a whisky. It was in the days when a bit of marijuana was passed around and we had a smoke before going into Robyn's bedroom, where I, well, started to seduce her.

As we progressed, in my dreamy state I heard her sister say, 'Maybe you should use a little of this KY.' Looking up, I saw her sister standing in the doorway and thought, Well, this is going to be interesting!

But her sister disappeared and I carried on doing what I was doing. And, judging by the heavy moaning and groaning, it all seemed highly satisfactory. We then smoked a bit more dope and I remember looking up admiringly as this lovely body walked out the door.

As I lay there I could hear the voices talking quite loudly, and it was the strangest conversation. Robyn's sister was saying, 'How was it? Did it hurt?'

And she said, 'No.'

Then her sister asked, 'Did you have an orgasm?'

Robyn replied, 'No, I don't think so. I don't really know what you're supposed to feel.'

It was really weird, but I didn't think too much of it and carried on smoking.

I took Robyn's phone number and went on my merry way.

Three days later, I phoned her and we met for coffee. She was such a beautiful girl; one of those exceptional ladies everyone turns round to look at – tall, statuesque, wonderful figure – which was why she had been chosen to take part in one of those highly prized limited-edition calendar shoots. She was so good-looking she even made it as a Bond girl in *For Your Eyes Only*.

As we chatted over coffee, she told me she had something difficult to tell me. She asked me whether I had realised that she had been a virgin.

I said, 'Well, I could tell you were not very experienced. Is that what you wanted to tell me?'

'No' – she paused – 'this is so difficult. I'm afraid I used you last night, Patrick, but I wanted to thank you for being so kind to me.'

And then, in the cold light of Kensington High Street, she dropped her bombshell.

'There's going to be an exposé in the paper.'

'Oh no,' I stormed. 'What're you doing – a kiss-and-tell on me?' I stood up.

'No, Patrick, wait, you've got it wrong – someone is doing a tell on me.'

'Why should they do that?' I asked.

'Because, because...' She looked down and then back up at me. I felt as if the ground had turned to rubber beneath my feet as she told me, 'A year ago I was a *man*!'

I was absolutely stunned as she went on to explain that our lovemaking was the first time she had ever had sex with anyone. She said she had chosen me because I was a heartthrob, a man's man, and she had wanted it to be with a proper, lusty man, not some male model.

But now everything had been ruined because someone had found out about her true identity and it was coming out in one of the papers.

Nowadays it wouldn't be such a big deal; we've even had a transsexual winning the Eurovision Song Contest. But then it was really sensational and I feared I would be dragged into it. The disclosure ruined her career but, thanks to Robyn, my name never appeared.

The last time I ran into her she was dining in Madame Jo Jo's in Soho and she still looked sensational.

But there, I have to confess, Macho Mower has made love to a man.

Golf has certainly provided me with some memorable putting moments – and I don't just mean on the green.

One such occurred as I was leaving Gran Canaria at the end of a celebrity Pro-am golf trip with Jimmy Tarbuck, Tim Brooke-Taylor, Gareth Hunt, Kenny Lynch, John Conteh and a host of professional footballers.

During the trip I had had a very special interlude with one of the travel reps, so before we flew out I went along to her office to say goodbye and we ended up having one final sexual escapade.

It was rather cramped in her office so, hitching her skirt up, she leaned back against the wall for support. After I had been pleasuring her for some minutes she started to tremble uncontrollably – and so did I.

The floor heaved and the walls shook … An earthquake had struck – right at the peak of the action.

Shuddering, she clung to me even tighter, breathlessly sighing, 'Oh, Patrick, I know you are a fantastic lover, but that is the first time the earth has moved for me!'

I replied, 'It moved for me too!'

It was the only earthquake they had ever had on the island, but it did wonders for my reputation.

18

Stuck in the Middle

LIKE NERO, WHO didn't notice that Rome was burning, my career was taking second place to my philandering. I was enjoying myself too much.

On the rare occasion when I woke up alone, I asked myself the age-old question: 'Are you happy? Is this what you really want?'

I began to understand that it was not so much a case of not being happy – although I wasn't seeing my children as much as I should, through my fault, not theirs – as a realisation that I was at a crossroads again.

And I was in danger of going down another wrong path – and this time it seemed to be pointing downwards.

I realised that, although I was seeing Simon and Claudia occasionally, I had let them down, and this hurt me as much as I am sure I had been hurting them. Again I realised that my behaviour had been sybaritic and totally self-indulgent – not even caring for some of the young ladies I had taken advantage of.

I took myself off to the villa beside the Aloha golf course in

Spain – this time on my own – and, with only the occasional bottle of *cerveza*, contemplated my navel for a few weeks.

My agent sent me a tape of the musical *Chicago* and said he would leave the script at the airport for me to collect. I listened to the part of Billy Flynn, thought, No, and didn't bother to pick up the script. The production transferred to the West End to acclaim and continuing glory and it is now the part I would give my eye teeth to play.

While I was there I drew up a list of the things my perfect woman, like Sophia Loren, should have. Long, black hair, olive complexion, large eyes, full breasts that were real and hips to match, a great sense of humour and, above all, very sexy.

I was determined to find her.

I went home and remained celibate.

I was in a very happy touring production of the Ray Cooney farce *Wife Begins at Forty* when my co-star, Linda Hayden, who is now married to theatrical producer Paul Elliott, asked me if I would like to go out for dinner after the show and meet a friend of hers.

On arriving at the restaurant I was confronted by long black hair, dark eyes, olive complexion – all the boxes were ticked. Her name was Louise English, the very same Louise I had seen cavorting with Benny Hill as one of his Angels to the admiration of every lusty man in England.

It was as if I had placed my wanted advert for the perfect woman in a shop window and Linda had spotted it.

Although Louise played a saucy wench in the hilarious Benny Hill sketches and was often seen rather scantily clad, off screen she appeared almost demure. So demure that, when her dinner partner left the table and I was in like Flynn, asking for her telephone number, she replied, 'I'll have to ask Harry.'

Luckily, Harry turned out to be merely her walker.

Two weeks later, having stolen Louise's number from Linda's phone book, I persuaded her that my reputation was a thing of the past and I would be eternally grateful if she would have lunch with me.

That was the start of a whirlwind romance – more of a hurricane really, as within three months I found myself engaged to be married.

Louise was lovely and I soon discovered that in real life she was even more modest than I had at first supposed. So modest that when we went on holiday to the sun she was too shy to go topless.

Although Louise still retained her flat in St John's Wood, most of the time she was with me in Gerrards Cross, while Audrey and the children had continued to live on three floors of the five-storey house in Pembroke Gardens, on which I still held the lease.

All this time Audrey and I had kept a 'Mr and Mrs' bank account, and one day she told me that the Kensington house was coming up for sale and I was being offered first refusal.

I consulted my accountant and told him that I intended to buy the Pembroke Gardens house. He informed me that because its value was likely to be high, for tax reasons it would have to be my primary residence, or I would have to pay capital gains. So I would have to sell my home in Gerrards Cross first.

I started the negotiations. I sold the Gerrards Cross house, and, borrowing money from my friendly bank manager, bought Audrey a house in Twickenham and moved back into Pembroke Gardens. All the time Audrey and I had held the lease on that home, the block of Georgian houses had been under threat of demolition. But now that threat was lifted and suddenly the properties were being called desirable again. My house had the largest garden in Kensington and an enormous basement.

Apart from the three floors Audrey and the children had used, the rest of the house had been left empty since I had departed. Now Audrey and the children had also moved out, the house was to all intents and purposes empty, apart from the one room I occasionally used as I was now virtually living with Louise in St John's Wood because, for reasons of her own, she refused to set foot in my marital home.

I put the house on the market with the best estate agents in Knightsbridge, De Groot Collis. I had my own special representative, Yolanda, and she was very special. A stunning Dutch-American with long blonde hair. We were to become friends and she helped me to make my first million. So for two months property developers, millionaires, three separate Saudi princes, along with their builders and architects, came to see this highly desirable residence opposite David Hockney's studios in the heart of Kensington.

They all poked and prodded, looking for whatever builders look for, generally treating it as a derelict house, apart from the one floor I was using as an apartment where occasionally Claudia might stay also.

So everything was fine in the state of Denmark – but it was soon to turn very rotten.

At the time I was appearing in Ray Cooney's *Run for Your Wife* with Ernie Wise and had almost committed to a sale at £960,000, when Yolanda rang to say an Israeli millionaire had heard about the house. He wanted to send his representative, with a photographer, to look at it and then email the pictures back to him in Israel. He was prepared to offer a quick £1 million, if it could be organised for that afternoon. I explained that I was doing a matinee but I arranged for Claudia to let them in.

That evening I was called to the stage door to find a reporter from the *Sun* asking if he could talk to me about my house in

Kensington. Having many years' experience of the tabloids, I heard alarm bells ring and made my excuses.

In the interval a representative of the Press Council arrived in my dressing room with a proof of the next day's *Sun*'s front page and centre spread. The headline, in three-inch high letters, read 'Star Lives in £1 Million Tip' and showed ten pictures of various rooms in a state of general disarray with old mattresses littering the place.

The Israeli 'millionaire', turned out to be a spotty cub reporter, Piers Morgan – who went on to become the editor of the *Daily Mirror* – and his photographer a snapper from the *Sun*.

Ernie quipped, 'The only other time the *Sun* had headlines that big was when Prince Andrew's father-in-law, the Major, had been caught going into a brothel – so you're in good company, Patrick.'

The Press Council representative implored me to make a stand, with their help, against what was becoming more and more intrusive journalism. He said, 'Don't worry. This is only a proof. By the time the paper comes out something far more interesting will have happened to take over the front page. Unfortunately for me, nothing more interesting did happen and the story, to my fury, was published in full.

Stupidly, I didn't take the Press Council's advice to work with them and instead went to a lawyer and sued for intrusion by false entry to my house.

This was well before Elton John's successful battle over false rent-boy allegations – and Elton could afford to take them on. I had to pay for my lawyer and, as the case went along, the *Sun* told my lawyer they would fight, arguing the story was of public interest.

The one mistake the *Sun* made was to print a picture of 'Patrick's bedroom' which showed one of the unused rooms that hadn't had an incumbent for ten years.

After ten days and £10,000 poorer, I was advised by all and

sundry to let the matter drop. In later editions of the paper, the picture of my alleged bedroom had been changed for another photograph. Years later I was told this was the main issue on which we could have won.

Yolanda sold the house and I asked the bank to put the money into my account for one day. So that, plus what was left of my Gerrards Cross house, added up to £1 million. I still have a copy of my account. So, like Rodney Blackstock, I have been a millionaire – if only for a day. I've been promised Rodney will regain his wealth – so let's hope life mirrors art.

I finished at the Criterion and, anxious to get away, accepted a wonderful role in Dublin's fair city.

Louise, meanwhile, accepted a part in another touring production – and the whirlwind romance was blowing itself out. When we both returned to England, there wasn't a hint of breath that could resuscitate our relationship.

After the break-up with Louise, I did quite a bit of touring to pay the rent and then headed to Los Angeles for six months to try to ignite the film career that had never really caught fire.

I had many promises, but I was stuck in the middle as it was a time in my life when I was not a big enough star to have leading roles but too big a name to play smaller parts. Although I was considered for leads, I didn't have enough cachet or the 'Marquee' to convince producers and I thought that if I accepted small roles it would not help my career while I was waiting for the big role.

After six months I returned home with my film-star ambitions, if not in ashes, definitely smouldering.

I recorded an episode of *Minder* called 'A Number of Old Wives' Tales', in which my character, Clive Cosgrove, had six wives. I wonder why they thought of me.

With the proceeds of the Pembroke Gardens house, I bought

a little house in Denham Village and it was while I was there that I met Samantha Corby through my friend, her father Colin, a film cameraman known in the business as the 'Silver Fox'. It started out as a friendship but we fell for each other – Samantha, that is, not Colin. It took us both by surprise.

But I was even more surprised when Samantha and I ran into my old chum Ollie Reed at a glittering black-tie showbiz dinner to celebrate the 500th edition of Thames TV's *This Is Your Life*.

As it was being held in the Whitbread Brewery in the City of London, it was hardly surprising that Ollie was roaring drunk when he came to join our table.

No change there. I'd seen Ollie drunk as a skunk before, but this time the wicked glint in his eye wasn't for mischief but trouble.

Ollie could be articulate, intelligent and charming but he always courted trouble and loved a fight.

David Jacobs said to me, 'I see you've drawn the short straw – you've got Ollie on your table.'

Ollie arrived with his wife, and, recalling our Elphick days, I introduced him to the others, but he just glared at me over his moustache.

He kept saying, 'Carpentier.' I thought he'd said something rude, but I soon gathered he was talking about the famous French boxer of old called Georges Carpentier.

My broken nose had obviously triggered something in his addled brain. He was rolling up his sleeves and squaring up to me with his fists. Then he grabbed a glass of wine and downed it in one as if it was a Scotch. The glass shattered as he put it down on the table and he was too drunk to even reach another bottle.

He then called me a cunt and started bad-mouthing the other celebrities, who included boxers John Conteh and Alan Minter, as posing wankers.

I've always believed the best way to deal with drunken

loudmouths is to ignore them. I've known quite a few policemen and they say the only things they are frightened of are mad dogs and drunks, because you can't reason with either of them. And I've faced my share of mad dogs.

Ollie then weaved his way round to my side of the table and said, 'Shall we do it here or shall we go outside?'

I knew that every eye in the room was on us. I thought I'd be in a better position standing up, so I rose to face him. He pressed his forehead against mine – Ollie had the eyes of a crazed dog. He was excited, his breaths coming in short pants. He was like a wild animal. I swear that for him it was almost sexual. He had a blood lust he was longing to satisfy.

Then he swung a punch, playful perhaps, but with quite a lot of life behind it. I have been in a few fights. And one trick you learn is, if the hands start to move, watch the head. So when he swung the punch that just grazed my chin, I knew the head would not be far behind. I stepped back so his head fell short of his target – my nose. All my sporting instincts told me 'now an uppercut to his jaw' but, when you are at a black-tie function like that where everyone was important enough to have been on *This Is Your Life*, you don't want to spoil it.

If I hit him, I thought, I'm going to start something that will ruin everything. And I'll probably end up dead because this is a wild animal. He could turn into those Alsatians I'd encountered in the past and bite me.

I'm no coward, though. I would have hit him if he'd landed a proper punch. I'd be dead but at least my honour would have been intact.

But, before anything else could happen, Ollie was completely overpowered by the best bunch of bouncers I'll ever have. Henry Cooper, John Conteh, Pat Jennings, Geoff Hurst, stuntman

Nosher Powell, even dear old Frank Carson – all helped to escort him, roaring like a lion, away out of the hall.

Everyone gets out of order sometimes, but that night Ollie was disgusting and I felt so sorry for his wife, Josephine, who was an angel throughout, looking at him with a loving yet pitying look. She told me that Ollie hadn't been on the town beforehand – he was drunk when he woke up.

Dennis Waterman and I found ourselves in another fine mess when we were signed up for the world premiere of *Bing Bang*, a new play written by Keith Waterhouse, the creator of the immortal *Billy Liar*, and directed by Ned Sherrin.

Sadly, this was no *Billy Liar* and it was heading for a spectacular *Bang* before we even finished rehearsals. Ned's choice for a rehearsal room seemed to be driven by one factor – that it was near a Michelin five-star restaurant, and, notwithstanding claret costing £40 a bottle, vast quantities of wine were downed at lunchtime.

This tended to make the rehearsals go far better after lunch than before, but Dennis and I soon discovered the story – a bittersweet comedy drama about writer's block based on the writing partnership of Bob Monkhouse and Denis Goodwin – was a block, period. It was more of a drama without much comedy, and the audiences felt so too. So did the critics. The reviews were stinking.

So I suggested to Ned and Dennis that there should be more longueurs between Dennis and I on stage, to which Dennis muttered the immortal line, 'Yeah, but I don't want to be on stage any long–er. I want to do it as quickly as possible and get away to the pub.'

Needless to say, it never made the West End.

I did another 'Pre-West End tour' of a rather tedious thriller called *Verdict* with Fiona Fullerton and, during one sleepy Matinée, when there was a knock at door and I said my line

'Who can that be?', a voice from the audience called out, 'We don't care, for god's sake let them in.'

It also wasn't the best of times when I linked up with the former screen hardman Lewis Collins in the touring production of another two-hander, *Who Killed Agatha Christie?*

I had known Lewis for years and we'd downed many a drink together, but, although the play proved tremendously successful, the tour turned into a bit of a nightmare.

At the time, Lewis was slightly impecunious so, at his behest, I started giving him lifts in my car to the various theatres we were playing. But I found some of the negativity he brought into my Mercedes was too much to cope with. He struggled with inner demons and questioned his *raison d'etre*, and I think he was going through a difficult period in his life, which made him somewhat gloomy.

Being the happy, personable, sorted chap that I am, I eventually told him I thought it would be better for both of us if he found his own way to the assorted venues, where I would be happy to meet him on stage.

It's an old saying that an actor with a low golf handicap is an actor who doesn't work very much – and I was worried that my handicap was getting lower.

I always enjoyed doing pantomime, being in my element with the dancers, and needed no urging to accept the role of King Rat opposite Les Dawson in what was to be Les's last panto, in Plymouth.

Les, a very intelligent and intellectual man behind the clown mask, had always been a good friend and we spent many happy hours swapping old theatre tales. He had his lovely wife, Tracey, and their new baby with him and I would keep cave on his dressing-room door as Les, false breasts pushed down over his white vest to his ample belly, shared a fag with his good mate Peter Cartwright. Les was a true comic genius and underrated actor. A wonderful bon viveur who exuded great bonhomie and underlined that great truth 'In vino veritas'.

Apart from my golf handicap I had another worry. I noted that this was the fourth year on the trot I had performed in panto. And, while panto is a very underrated art form which requires a lot of skill as you tread the tightrope of engaging the audience, keeping the show rolling along and putting bums on seats, this was not how I had planned my career, even though the money was good and the chorus girls eager to please.

So what was I to do about it?

I suppose I was leading a typical semi-successful actor's life, doing the occasional television appearance, the occasional theatrical role and, if lucky, the occasional film.

Little did I know when I accepted a six-week tour of a well-crafted thriller, *Murder by Misadventure*, that I was to reach the final, and most important, crossroads in my life.

I have fallen in and out of love in all its many hues. All my affairs were special; some extra special. They shall remain so. But they were to be eclipsed.

I was to meet Anya.

19

Floating on Air

'BEGINNERS, PLEASE.' THE Tannoy woke me from my reverie. Rather grumpily waiting to do a matinee, I had been listening to the most wonderful laughter bouncing up the stairs from the stage door. She sounds happy, I thought as I left my dressing room. Looking forward to jousting once more with the delightful Derren Nesbitt in *Murder by Misadventure*. We were at the Liverpool Playhouse and I couldn't resist having a peep at the source of the merriment, and instead of going on to the stage I continued down the stairs.

Neil Armstrong may have made an important 'small step' on the moon but that could never equal the importance of my extra four steps. Because there she was. At the stage door was my Sophia Loren. Admittedly, she wasn't soaking in water, but she was perfect in every other detail. I had found my dream girl.

I'd just had time to persuade her to join me for a cup of tea after the performance before Derren called, 'Patrick, come on! The curtain's up, I'm going to start without you.'

I discovered her name was Anya Pope, an art student at Liverpool University who was helping out backstage. It was love at first sight, a life-transforming experience which has brought me the deepest joy ever since.

I noticed her eyes first. They are amazing – and the moment I looked into them I knew she was the person for me. Something special happened.

It was a bolt from the blue and I'm a very lucky man. Cupid's arrow struck us both at the same time and it's still embedded. I am still head over heels in love with her. I only have to leave her for a few hours while working to find I'm missing her.

She is a lovely person and everything a man could want – the sexiest, most beautiful girl in the world, and the fact that Anya is 33 years younger than me – the same age as Claudia and two years younger than Simon – has never been a problem for us. As Anya has candidly declared, 'The age gap doesn't matter. I fell in love with Patrick the first time I met him. We are very similar, like one person. We have the same thoughts and the same interests. Patrick made me a woman. I am glad he was my first lover and he will be my last.'

That feeling is mutual. At first we were just friends because Anya was living with her parents in the Wirral in Cheshire, while I was still living in Denham, and our phone bills were astronomical because we'd talk about anything and everything. But finally we were properly together when we stole away on holiday to Crete.

Three months later, after Anya had left college, she came to London to find work – and so that we would be closer. A month after that, she moved in with me in Denham. I know that was a big decision for her to take, but it felt so right and eventually I won over her parents, Ray and Sheila, who had understandably been wary of me because of my reputation.

And to prove our love for each other we had matching tattoos done on our shoulders. They show two entwined wedding rings – a symbol of togetherness.

Meeting Anya was like starting a new life. And looking back at my bachelor days, and all the other women, it is almost as if it had happened to another person. Now I feel as if I've packed two lives into one. Soon after Anya moved in with me, I was persuaded to take on the really challenging role of Mellors, the gamekeeper who bewitches Lady Chatterley, in a pre-West End production of DH Lawrence's classic *Lady Chatterley's Lover*. I was playing opposite Irina Brook, the very beautiful daughter of the famous Peter Brook. Foolishly I had believed that we were going to do an intelligent, articulate and intellectual interpretation. We soon discovered that what the audience wanted – and what the audience expected – was naked humping on stage.

There was certainly plenty of flesh on display as Irina and I were totally naked for the sexier sections of the production and the reaction of some of the audience provided a little comic relief for both of us. As customers with overdeveloped sensibilities left the front stalls in disgust at the sight of naked bodies on stage, their exits were covered by the clatter in the rows behind as furtive men in raincoats eagerly moved forward to claim their now vacant seats.

Anya came to every performance and admitted she felt nervous for me every night, but I have always kept myself in good shape and stripping off didn't worry me. I even got some decent reviews, including wags who commented, 'Patrick Mower shows off his obvious talents' and 'Patrick Mower more impressive in more ways than one', which did my prowess as a lover a power of good. But my professional credibility, I fear, suffered somewhat, although it was a pleasure simulating sex with the lovely Irina.

As Irina and I were both completely naked it was a rather hot production and the West End beckoned. But we never got there as the producers wanted to be even more controversial. It was a very potent production about the class struggle and, while the powerful sexual chemistry between Mellors and Lady Chatterley was an integral part of the play, it was not the main thrust, if you will pardon the expression. To make a West End opening viable, the producers wanted Irina and I to go further, and we refused. So Charles Spencer and the other West End critics never had the joy of seeing my attributes.

In Denham, Anya and I were surrounded by other stars. Sir John and Lady Mills lived round the corner while neighbours included Robert Lindsay, Rosemary Ford, Cilla Black and Paul Daniels and Debbie McGee.

And before long we had an addition to our family. Anya had been looking for a miniature horse for a long time and so I bought her a palomino Falabella called Honeybee Rascal, who soon became totally domesticated. He lived on our back lawn but many a time we would return home to find he had pushed the French windows open and was fast asleep on the carpet. Anya, a very talented artist and illustrator, was commissioned by the BBC to write a television series about his exploits. We are both now, with young Maxim's help, adapting her scripts into a children's book. It is going to be brilliant.

One summer's evening, our neighbours were entertaining friends when Honeybee Rascal lived up to his name. He followed their 'Dulux dog' indoors and proceeded to trot nonchalantly past them as they sat at the dinner table. They then went on up the stairs and into a bedroom. The guests couldn't believe their eyes and there was much hilarity as Anya was called and took command. But, as anyone with any knowledge of horses knows, you can take them to water but you can't get them to walk down stairs. It was a good job they had six guests that evening to help carry Honeybee back down.

Honeybee Rascal became such an integral part of our family that, when I accepted the role of Bela Zangler, the creator of the Ziegfeld-style 'Zangler Follies' in the major Gershwin musical production *Crazy for You*, he came too – as, of course, did Anya.

It was a massive show with a cast of a hundred and we were on the road for a year. I travelled in my Mercedes 350SL and Anya followed in her specially adapted minivan with integral horsebox. The three of us had the most wonderful adventure, staying on average for three weeks in all the major cities.

I finally felt, now that Anya had come into my life, that I was a complete human being.

The role of Zangler was very satisfying and the show was tremendously successful, winning standing ovations everywhere we went. Finally we arrived in Edinburgh. And that was to prove the magical moment when I committed myself to a new life with the woman from whom I knew that I never wanted to be parted.

On New Year's Eve, as I held her in my arms, crushed on all sides by the vast multitude of New Year revellers celebrating the arrival of 1996 beneath the city's famous Castle Rock, we kissed – and Anya was literally levitated by the mighty throng pressing ever tighter. As we were enveloped by the romantic skirl of the Black Watch pipers and the pealing of bells, we knew that we could be no closer. We were one – physically and emotionally.

By now I too had been swept aloft, suspended in space in the crush. As we hugged each other ever more tightly I asked, 'Will you marry me?'

'Try and stop me,' Anya laughed, her eyes dancing with delight.

We both took another swig of pure Islay single malt to toast our future. We were literally floating on air – and still are.

When I finally got a short break in the theatre schedule, I whisked Anya to paradise.

I was determined our wedding should encapsulate all the feelings I felt for my beautiful bride, and what better place than 'Paradise Island' – Mauritius, in the Indian Ocean.

There we finally sealed our love for each other in a wedding ceremony performed by the island's registrar and witnessed by our two very good friends, Robert and his beautiful Japanese partner, Wakki. A simple marriage in the sun in which we alone mattered. Paradise indeed.

Life could only improve.

It also got a lot more complicated when we took *Crazy for You* to the New Theatre in Cardiff.

Over the years I had received fan mail from people claiming to be my aunt or my cousin or my sister and, recalling Richard Burton's warning that once you are famous you suddenly find that you are related to half of Wales, I took no notice.

But one woman, who became known to my agent and myself as 'Megan of Porth', took to writing letters asking me to get in touch. She then started ringing my agent urging him to persuade me to get in contact. Thinking she was some young lady who was after my body, I didn't. But finally, under pressure from my agent, I rang her, and the conversation went like this:

'Can I speak to Megan, please?'

'Megan speaking.'

'It's Patrick Mower.'

'Oh, thank you for calling. It is just that you are becoming really famous and there are some things about yourself you ought to know before they do *This Is Your Life*.'

In fact I had already done the show with Eamonn Andrews in the dim, distant past, when I was 28.

'Listen, what is it?' I asked somewhat testily.

'Please don't put the phone down,' Megan implored. 'Let me tell you, to prove I know what I'm talking about. Your father's name is Archie and he had a brother, Walt. Your uncle was Bythan Price and you have a brother called Donald.'

'I have *two* brothers,' I interjected.

'Well.' She paused.

'What do you mean, "Well"?'

'Well, I know about that.'

'Listen, I think I have had enough of this.'

'No, please don't put the phone down. I am your sister!'

She then gave me the short version of how we were related.

'My father lived in a one-up, one-down miner's cottage. He had four daughters and his wife was upstairs giving birth. He called upstairs to the midwife, "Is it a boy or a girl?" He was told it was a girl. "Fuck it, I'm off," he slurred. And he was.'

Megan's story came as a major shock and so I rang Don and told him about the additional complications, with Derek being a Stanton Mower while Don and I were both Archie Mowers.

This riddle needed solving so I agreed to meet Megan and asked her to bring her sisters along. We all met backstage at the New Theatre and it was quite a reunion. They were terribly charming ladies and much older than me.

But as I looked into their eyes the song from *A Chorus Line* revolved in my head: 'I felt nothing. I felt nothing. I reached right down to the bottom of my soul and I tried. And I felt nothing!'

Not many years later, as I looked down at my father lying dead in hospital with the oxygen mask still attached to his face but with the bellows no longer moving, that same theme ran through my mind. I felt nothing.

My father's brother Walt died of silicosis and associated lung diseases and, although my father's official cause of death was heart failure, his health obviously wasn't helped by his heavy smoking and the years underground.

Unfortunately, my half-sisters didn't know anything about Derek being a Stanton other than that they had been told my father had only two sons. At the time we all met, my father was still alive so we were reluctant to try to sort it all out.

Don and I decided the news of the sisters was a ticking time bomb for our mother and so, until the day she died she had no knowledge that my father was, in fact, a bigamist. So, having enjoyed my sisters' company, I didn't pursue the relationship too vigorously for fear of the truth getting out, which I knew would have ruined my mother's life.

Peggy, my dear old mother, only died six years ago. A wonderful lady, she was full of life to the end. Don, Anya and I were at her bedside in the John Radcliffe Hospital in Oxford and we knew her time was near. But, even at the age of 93, lying in her little nightdress, she still had the twinkle in her eye which she had passed on to me and was still an outrageous flirt.

When the male nurse minced in to change her sheets and said in his high-pitched voice, 'Come on, Peggy, let's lift up your legs,' she gave me that little saucy look and raised her eyebrows as if to say, 'I think I'm *in* here, Patrick!' That look summed up my mother's personality entirely and is something I will always remember. I think she's responsible for me getting into a lot of illicit scrapes!

As deaths go, it was the best you could hope for. Don and I sang a song at her funeral; she would have loved that.

Don, who used to be married to an Iranian, still lives in Oxford. I joked that he was an arms dealer and we laughed about that for years – until he discovered he was being followed by Special

Branch. When he came out of the Army, he stayed in the Reserve and is always volunteering to go and sort people out in Africa and other hot spots. As for Derek, he moved to Australia many years ago, and there are now legions of Mowers living there.

Cardiff was to provide another milestone in my life as my film career finally got the boost I had been waiting for.

My exploits in Europe had been remembered once more. I received a script from the Italian producer Roberto Bertolucci for a film called *Monella*, in which I was offered the role of the French chef Andre, who, of course, has a mistress whose daughter is also in love with him.

It was a fantastic role. Incredible. Perfect for me. And once again the gods were shining on me. My character was not required on set until two weeks after I finished the run of *Crazy for You*. Once last chance at film stardom. What could go wrong?

But there is, they say, 'No business like show business.'

Unfortunately for me, the heavens opened over northern Italy and what was formerly Yugoslavia. Gallons of water swept down from the Alps, washing out the locations for the first three weeks of filming. So the production company brought my schedule forward by those three weeks.

Disaster!

I went to the producer of *Crazy for You* to ask to be released from my contract for the last two weeks of the show in Southampton. My understudy was brilliant, more than capable of stepping into my beard and wig. But the producer flatly refused to let me go, arguing that I was an integral part of the show and couldn't be released. What a load of bollards! He was just being a pig.

I am normally a finely tuned engine, but being denied the chance of a starring role in a major movie by a petty, spiteful, jumped-up, pseudo-producer took its toll on my motor.

Maybe if I had done what my brain was telling me to do and kicked the living daylights out of him, I would have felt better, but in the New Theatre in Cardiff the energy that had been supporting me for 12 months deserted me.

It had never happened to me before and it has never happened since, but I collapsed on stage. My body just cut out.

I remember drifting slowly down past the beautiful long limbs of fishnet-stockinged legs and lying gazing upwards as the band played on. Actually, the 20-piece orchestra didn't play on for much longer. They realised what had happened and, like me, the show stopped.

I was carried to my dressing room and announcements were made as the famous smelling salts we've all seen in so many movies were applied. Somebody slapped me around the face. A doctor was called. Anya was called. An ambulance was called and arrived. A heart attack was suspected. Luckily, as it turned out, it wasn't. Doctors verified that I had had a mental and physical collapse. My body had shut down with the strain and the pain of losing my film.

The pain, however, was short-lived. My doctor's hand – or was it God's – wrote my certificate stating that he would not be responsible if I performed in front of 2,000 people, but that, with medication, there seemed to be no reason why I should not fulfil my role in the film – which I did.

The film also provided Anya and myself with a second honeymoon. Italy is an incredible land for lovers; the countryside, the colours, the vibrancy of the people, the deep blue of the sea, the food, the wine; even the language dances. And Anya accompanied me for the whole of the shoot, during which we drank our fill of the country's wonders. We filmed by Lake Como – which alone was paradise as I had my own villa – Milan, Venice and finally Rome.

It was a dream come true: to be with the person I loved and to be a film star at last, and one perfect evening in our suite in a luxury hotel in the Villa Borghese, off Rome's Via Veneto, we made love. We both knew that Anya had conceived – and nine months later our most wonderful son, Maxim, completed our happiness.

The one thing I hadn't taken into account when I accepted the role of Andre was the director, Tinto Brass. Tinto was a Hitchcockian figure with his constant cigar and open-necked shirt flowing over his enormous waistband; always ready to feel, without permission, the quality of any female breast.

He was the notorious director who, when making the beyond-excess *Caligula* with John Gielgud, Peter O'Toole, Helen Mirren and Malcolm McDowell, signed up young soldiers from the local barracks to play Romans and engaged hookers from the Via Venetto to play the wenches. As the red wine flowed in the famous orgy scene, the soldiers were told they could avail themselves of the girls because the hookers had been paid for their services.

This prompted one of Gielgud's classic unscripted performances. As he descended the stairs into the orgy and began his oration while walking past the copulating couples, Gielgud stopped in mid-speech and, with the camera still rolling, uttered the immortal words, 'Oh my God, they are fucking. Oh God, I can't say "fucking" on camera. They are fornicating. Oh my God, they are fucking fornicating!'

Our plot was basically about my mistress's daughter, Lola, played by the delicious Anna Ammirati, getting married to the local baker while actually being in love with me. She believes me to be her father.

The mistress finds the daughter and myself in an innocent but compromising situation and, in a fit of pique, tells me that I am not after all the girl's father. On the wedding day I have my wicked way with Lola while the groom is dancing. At the party my mistress reveals that she was lying and her daughter really is my child. Oh hell!

A wonderful part, although I knew from Tinto's history that it would be a bold and daring film. In my many conversations with Tinto, whom I found to be incredibly intelligent and knowledgeable, he assured me that the film would be – as Kenny Everett always said – in the best possible taste.

My mistress was played by one of Tinto's favourite actresses, Serena Grande, who had the most enormous breasts I have ever seen. They were each as big as a football and I had many memorable scenes rolling on and falling off these two enormous melons, which, she assured me, were natural – and indeed they felt natural.

All the girls in the film managed to have their tops removed or to be filmed from one of Tinto's favourite camera angles – with the camera on the floor shooting up between their legs. This particular shot reminded me of the equally outrageous Peter Langan and his famous restaurant off Piccadilly that he co-owned with Michael Caine. Whenever I dined there with Suzanne Danielle, Peter would plonk his bottle of champagne on the table and then slide down on to his back beneath the table and lie looking up Suzanne's skirt.

But Tinto cared. He talked constantly about how to improve a scene and create the right atmosphere. He took Anya and I to his beautiful villa overlooking the incredible vista of Rome and I spent many hours with him examining his library of pornography. He was obsessed by the erotic and the sensual and saw nothing wrong in it. Nor do I. He tries to create these senses on screen and as Andre was, surprise, surprise, also a photographer of erotic pictures, I found myself doing one of the strangest scenes in my life – caressing a naked girl showing off her beautiful bare bum as she kneeled over. The girl was obviously chosen for the perfection of her rear end and I had to deliver a long eulogy, in Italian, about the perfection of her cheeks and, indeed, orifice while caressing that glorious behind.

Unfortunately when I saw the film, or at least a particular version, I realised the finished product did not necessarily look like the scenes we shot. In the film the baker/bridegroom goes to a hooker before his wedding night to be given some experience – a scene I actually saw being filmed in Rome – and at no time was he fully naked. When I saw the film, not only was he naked but his manhood was very proud indeed and, although still beautifully shot, he certainly had his wicked way with the wench.

In that version, luckily, Andre didn't do any inserts, if you know what I mean, but since working with Tinto I have heard many a tale of the things that happen in his private cutting room. Andre was a very sensuous man and his studio was adorned with many erotic artefacts, including enormous erect phalluses, from Tinto's own collection. I had a cigarette holder entwined with naked girls doing naughty things. I am dreading the Japanese version.

But I have my fingers crossed because Tinto confided that he had chosen me to play Andre because, in his mind's eye, I was his alter ego.

It's strange how in show business careers can go in circles. Months later I found myself once more teamed up with Edward Woodward. I was also back in Cape Town, plotting to blow up the world. It was another glorious, luxurious location and I made the most of it.

I also thought about my future.

On my return I filmed the psychological thriller *The Asylum*, playing a deranged brain surgeon complete with manic glint and goatee. The film was shot all around the south of England and I realised that more and more of my work opportunities were no longer London-based. So there was no real reason to stay in Denham.

We took another step towards creating the perfect life.

Maxim was now two. And still being a country boy at heart, I raised my sights to more distant horizons. It was time for pastures new.

We took our time and looked for suitable properties. We visited many palatial and non-palatial Georgian and pseudo-Georgian properties until we found our lovely gated Georgian house in six acres of grounds, deep in the Lincolnshire Wolds. It was perfect and has brought us the greatest pleasure ever since. There is plenty of room for the now seven horses and three dogs and Anya's carriages. Sponsored for the last two years by Tunnocks Biscuits, she is one of the best carriage drivers in the country.

While completing *The Asylum*, I became aware of the smell of Palmolive in the air. Soap suds were bubbling away under the surface.

My agent, Barry Burnett, told me he had had an 'off the record' enquiry as to how I would feel about being in a soap.

'Oh dear. Which one?'

'As Barbara Windsor's love interest in *EastEnders*.'

'Mmmmmm!'

Three days later, Barry phoned me again and said, 'I've had another enquiry about you being in a soap.'

'What's this?' I asked.

'They're going to regurgitate *Crossroads* and they've asked if you would be interested in playing the new manager of the Crossroads Motel.'

'Wasn't that the series where the scenery used to shake?' I said.

'That's the one,' said Barry adding, 'and, by the way, *EastEnders* have gone in a different direction.'

I don't know if the bongo drums of the bush telegraph beating between Shepherd's Bush and Nottingham were being picked up in Yorkshire. But, seven days later, Barry called again. This time he could hardly get the words out for laughing.

'You're not going to believe me, Patrick, but they want to see you for a part in *Emmerdale*.'

My first reaction to this news was one of regret that my mother was not still alive. *Emmerdale* was Peggy's favourite programme and she never missed an episode. Many a time when she stayed in my house we would sit on the sofa and watch it together. I would laugh and she would cry.

My part was to be Rodney Blackstock, a womanising good-time Charlie from a rough background who'd made money, spent it and then made some more – and had a great time doing it.

Sounds familiar, I thought. Could be autobiographical.

So I did a screen test for the role at the *Emmerdale* studios in Leeds and I loved it. Rodney and Patrick got on like a house on fire. Thankfully, Keith Richardson and the then Series Producer, Kieran Roberts, agreed it was a perfect match. Kieran has now gone on to be Controller of Drama at ITV Productions in Manchester.

Keith Richardson, as well as being the Executive Producer of *Emmerdale*, is also Controller of Drama at Yorkshire Television. He is one of the most respected TV drama producers in the UK, being responsible for *Harry's Game*, *Shipman*, *Heartbeat*, *The Royal* and many more fabulous shows.

I'd had a meeting with Keith a few years earlier when I

returned from one of my sorties into the American market and found him to be a most genial fellow. Within the inner sanctum at ITV he is known variously as 'Tartan Leader', 'the Guv'nor' and 'the Godfather'. I'm happy to say that Keith has become a good friend as well as my boss. His knowledge of single malt never ceases to amaze me and with his help I am learning to tell my Lagavulin from my Laphroaig without ending up under the table. I don't always succeed.

20

Emmerdale

EVERY MORNING AS I step through the doors at Burley Road into the reception at *Emmerdale*, I think of my mother.

'Here I am again, Mater,' I say. 'Let's see what Rodney gets up to today, shall we?'

She always made a point of seeing all my stage work, all my TV and most of my films – except the ones I kept quiet about!

But for her the pinnacle of my career would have been me appearing in her beloved *Emmerdale*. She adored it. Like Anya's parents, Ray and Sheila today, she never missed an episode. She was desperate for me to be in it.

Watching it with her one evening, I remarked that I was at RADA with Helen Weir, the actress then playing Jack Sugden's wife.

'Oh were you really, Patrick?' She was terribly impressed. 'Shall I write to her and remind her? I'll tell her you're my son. She might be able to get you a job in *Emmerdale*.'

I told her not to, but knowing my mother she probably did. You never know, maybe Helen passed the letter to Keith Richardson and ten years later he found it in his in-tray!

The show has a following like no other I have ever been involved with. Ten million viewers tune in six nights a week. Their loyalty and passion for the programme is phenomenal. *Emmerdale* even has its own fan club, with members as far afield as New Zealand, Canada and Finland.

I discovered its incredible popularity when I did a personal appearance in Cork earlier this year. The crowds were amazing. I even heard screams. It reminded me of my glory days in the Seventies.

Joining *Emmerdale*, however, was not all plain sailing. I was already under contract to Jim Davidson to star with Julie Goodyear in the pantomime *Snow White* at Manchester's Opera House. To get round the problem, *Emmerdale*'s bosses agreed that I could do three months in the soap before fulfilling my obligation to the panto and then return to Yorkshire later in the New Year.

Normally when a contract arrives for film, television and theatrical roles, my agent will discuss the salary and of course the billing. On *Emmerdale*, he was informed, there are no stars. The show is the star. And I was very happy with that.

My arrival in *Emmerdale* attracted quite a lot of press attention, but, because of my imminent departure to panto land, Rodney Blackstock did not arrive with as much of a bang as I would have liked.

Even seasoned old-timers like me have been known to turn into nervous teenagers on meeting their heroes. I recall running into John Cleese in Kensington High Street. He stopped and said, 'Hello, Patrick.' I said, 'Hello, John.' We shook hands and after a few moments of silence, he said, 'I've never met you before, but I'm a fan.' I said, 'I've never met you before, but I'm a fan.' He said, 'Goodbye.' I said, 'Goodbye.' And we went our separate ways.

Not that I was nervous as Rodney shook Jack Sugden's hand on my first Monday morning acting in the Woolpack, but I had been watching Clive Hornby playing Jack for nearly 30 years. Who was Jack and who was Clive? Luckily, Rodney could tell the difference.

It was easier with Elizabeth Estensen, who plays Diane, my ex-wife, and Billy Hartman, the stalwart Terry Woods. The three of us had been in a musical version of Pirandello's *The Servant of Two Masters*, so we had an immediate rapport. Billy has a very fine singing voice which, sadly, he no longer uses. What a waste.

It's a shame that in the whole of my 35 years as an actor this was the first time I'd worked for Yorkshire Television. I was delighted to discover that it lived up to its reputation for being one of the nicest and friendliest companies to work for. Sue Jackson, the Head of Casting, whispered in my ear at the BAFTA awards that she had always fancied me. Maybe it would have been better if she had admired my acting talent rather than my long locks.

There are 50 regular characters in *Emmerdale*, so dressing rooms are limited. I was squashed in with one of the most famous families in TV land – the Dingles.

How proud my mother would have been as I changed my trousers, rubbing buttocks with Steve Halliwell, who plays Zak Dingle, and sharing laughter and disgust with Mark Charnock (Marlon) as another obnoxious fart caused the rear end of Andy Devine's trousers to flutter as he got into character as Shadrach Dingle. Wafting the smell away, Jeff Hordley, who lent his dark, brooding looks to Cain Dingle, grimaced across at me, 'Patrick, welcome to *Emmerdale*.'

I soon learned how quickly things happen in a 'continuing drama'. I discovered that I had the beautiful Samantha Giles as my daughter, but another Blackstock offspring was to arrive on set to put the cat among the pigeons. This was the fiery blonde Nicola, played by the equally fiery Nicola Wheeler. Much later, when the storyline demanded it, a Blackstock son would appear. Seeds of the father? My own, I mean.

The writers can do anything in *Emmerdale* land. They can write you in; they can write you out. They can make you gay; they can make you straight. Luckily, at the moment Rodney is in and is straight. He has been in the village now for over five very happy years.

After my first three months, I bade adieu to *Emmerdale* and left for my panto to cries of 'Look behind you, Patrick!' from the cast as they waved me off.

My part in *Snow White* was the wicked witch's henchman who has to cut out Snow White's heart in the forest. Jim Davidson assured Barry that my character would have two songs and the whole part was being written especially for 'Patrick Mower'.

At the press call for photographs the day before rehearsals, I met Julie Goodyear lurking behind her cigarette holder and the young lady playing Beauty and was given the 'new' script. Rehearsal call was ten o'clock next morning and as I flicked through the script in my hotel it became obvious that there were no songs and indeed no changes at all had been made. I immediately phoned Barry, who in turn rang Jim, who said, 'It must be a mistake.' He would have the amended script for the next day's rehearsal.

The next morning I attended the most hilarious read-through imaginable. Snow White's seven dwarfs were played by a tumbling troupe of Scandinavian dwarves, none of whom spoke

English. 'I'm Schneezy, I'm Sdopy and I'm Schappy' got the wrong kind of laughs.

Not a great beginning – and it got a lot worse. Julie, having been told that there was no smoking in the rehearsal room, would say her three lines and then, accompanied by her assistant, withdraw to another room to light up.

I refused to say my lines because the new script had yet to rear its head, so the gay stage manager, the Irish lady director – whose frayed fingernails and bright-red eyes foretold problems to come – and Beauty proceeded to read all the characters – dwarfs and all.

Phone calls rang back and forth. I spoke to Jim myself. We had shared many a drink and girlfriend over the years, and he assured me that the new script was forthcoming. I retired to my hotel. No script arrived. I offered to make my part up. Rehearsals were cancelled. We were due to open in eight days.

Would I do an interview with the *Daily Telegraph*? 'Can I tell them we have no script?' The interview was cancelled. I worried that the director would have a nervous breakdown. Julie and her cigarette holder and female companion puffed away in another room. Schneezy Schneezed and Schleepy was ill. It was now Snow White and the Five Dwarves. What a shambles.

So I quit, or, as we say in showbiz, I walked. As regards Julie, in the few dealings I had with her I found her sociable, talented and living up to the image of the icon that she was.

As for Jim, I told him what he could so with his next production! He's a great bloke, but before I ever worked with Jim again I'd want to cross the T's and dot the I's, and add plenty of 0's on to the end!

But there were consolations. Anya, Maxim and I left the chaos in Manchester and zoomed off to sample the joys of Jamaica and had the most glorious time in the Caribbean sun.

So on my return it was a sun-tanned Rodney Blackstock who strode back into the Woolpack... to be whacked hard around the ear by my new daughter, Nicola. As I picked myself up off the floor, and the ringing in my head subsided, I thought, I'll have to make sure she's with me next time there's any chance of bumping into Oliver Reed.

Being a Virgo, always seeking perfection, I have always found it very difficult to hold back if I see or feel something is being done in a production that I think could be corrected. My motives have always been altruistic. But in my early days at *Emmerdale* I think I might have trodden on some toes.

It took dear old Stan Richards – whose woolly cap is still preserved, along with the show's many awards in the foyer of the *Emmerdale* studios – to point me in the right direction. There is also a plaque to his memory where he sat at the Woolpack Bar.

One day he put his arm round me as we were leaving the studio. He had become quite frail and very shaky on his legs. I thought it was just for support, but it turned out to be an arm of friendship. 'I want to buy you a pint, Patrick – and put you straight,' he said through his droopy moustache.

A very good pianist and former stand-up comic on the club circuit, Stan was very much like the character he portrayed on screen and could be as abrasive, cynical and short-tempered as Seth. Which was not unusual, as something I've noticed now that I'm in my sixth year in *Emmerdale* is how the characters on screen do tend to get closer to the real persons portraying them – perhaps because of the sheer speed of the filming turnaround.

On our second pint in his Barnsley local, Stan made his point, 'Patrick, you have bags of talent and bags of enthusiasm. Keep 'em both for your own performance.'

I took his advice, and now only offer mine when asked – but I still occasionally have to bite my tongue.

Towards the end of his life, Stan was very ill and used to come and do one scene in the morning and then go home. He told me that *Emmerdale* had become his life and he wanted to do it no matter how much of a strain it had become. He thought that if he stopped his life would stop. And it did. His funeral in February 2005 was a very poignant affair; the end of a chapter. Every member of the cast attended and many kind words were spoken and many tears shed. A much-loved soap personality, Stan's 'Seth Armstrong', was up there with Hilda Ogden and Ena Sharples – characters the viewers had taken to their hearts and who were in their unique ways irreplaceable.

The most important lesson I have learned about being in a soap is how little control one has over one's destiny. About three years ago Rodney Blackstock had a heart attack. Talk about the Sword of Damocles hanging over my head.

Round about September a strange phenomenon happens at *Emmerdale*. A haunted look starts to appear in cast members' eyes. One day in the Green Room someone will dare to vocalise what everyone else is thinking, 'It's new contract time.' No one replies but everyone will be thinking, Is it me for the chop?

This is the way it works. The phone rings in the Green Room. Kathleen Beedles, our Producer, has a PA, Estelle. It will be Estelle on the phone, saying, 'Kelvin Fletcher, please come up and see Kath.' And so it starts. One by one, like lambs to the slaughter, actors are called up.

Nobody in *Emmerdale* gets a contract lasting longer than one year. Not even dear old Clive Hornby, after all these years. Each October he is on tenterhooks the same as everyone else. Will he be asked to do another year?

Like naughty sixth-formers who have been caught with their hand up nurse's skirt we go to receive the headmistress's decision.

Some actors brazenly say, 'I don't think I will do another year anyway,' just in case they don't get offered one. As they come back down the stairs saying, 'I told her what she could do with the job,' we all know they have been given the sack.

Behind her desk, Kath Beedles may appear young to be the Producer of one of the nation's most popular programmes, but beneath her youthful, reserved exterior she is incredibly creative and talented. Kath is passionate about the content and quality of each and every show. There, that should get me another year! But, sincerely, I have great respect for her. She will go far. Watch out Michael Grade!

One of my closest friends in the show is Richard Thorp, who plays that splendid character Alan Turner. He is also something of an institution. He greets you with, 'Have you heard this one?'

Everyone in turn goes, 'Oh no,' because Richard will have told you the same joke already that day. But he is a lovely man. A dedicated biker – he still has a customised Harley-Davidson – he used to be a Rank film star, and still has an eye for the ladies.

'I don't mind them rolling on top of me, but they complain when I roll on top of them,' he beams, his eyes twinkling above his massive girth.

He starred in *Emergency Ward 10*, Britain's first popular soap, which drew 24 million viewers a night.

I actually met Richard in those far-off days. I vividly remember John Alderton, who was to marry Pauline Collins, at RADA announcing to our admiration that he was joining *Emergency Ward 10*. One afternoon while visiting John on the set I had the honour of meeting the show's handsome young star. It was Mr Thorp. Richard says he remembers meeting me, but I think he's being kind.

Rodney, on his arrival in the show, started having affairs with most of the cast – female, I am glad to say – but of course only on the screen. Luckily, he was called upon to kiss most of them. Some with real lips, some with pneumatic lips.

In my career I have had the arduous task of kissing many very beautiful girls and some not so beautiful. Some clean-shaven, some with moustaches, but whether it was on stage, in films or on television, always with enthusiasm. Even if I didn't like the actress or she didn't like me, we kissed as if we were in love or lust – with real passion. But of course it's all pretence.

There was also some 'pretend' acting when the bosses decided *Emmerdale* would be the vehicle for a soap stars' reality show. People all over Britain took part in televised auditions in a bid to win three-month contracts with *Emmerdale* in which they would appear as a new family.

The reality show was very successful but there was a feeling among some of the cast that the show was not only demeaning to *Emmerdale* but to the acting profession by making it appear so easy to become a successful actor. At the time, *Emmerdale* was building itself up to compete not only with *Coronation Street* but also with the mighty *EastEnders*, and it was felt that the whole soap stars idea might be self-destructive. Keith Richardson and Steve Frost asked me, because of my experience, to participate in the selection process. I appeared in a few shows giving acting advice and so on. When the winning contestants joined the show they came in and worked mainly with my character so I could keep an eye on them. I had reservations about the whole thing but hope I made their stay as pleasant as possible. And to be fair they were not bad actors.

One story called for a drunken Rodney to inveigle the mother, Sandy Walsh, into his bedroom and then attempt to have his way with her. And Sandy was all too willing.

Unbeknown to us, however, my daughter, Nicola, was under

the bed. Why, I can't remember – this is *Emmerdale*! Maybe she was emptying the chamber pot.

Sometimes I feel Rodney is turning into a character from one of the *Carry On* films and hear myself saying, 'Hellooo!' in a Leslie Phillips voice. And we certainly did our best to emulate the best *Carry On* traditions as 'Leslie Phillips' removes 'Hattie Jacques's' large bra, which drops over the edge of the bed on to the head of the highly embarrassed daughter. Luckily, this whole scene was played on Nicola's face because the next moment I put my feet either side of her head – to be quickly followed by my trousers. It was a very funny scene – stolen by Nicola.

One of my favourite amours in *Emmerdale* was with that highly accomplished comedic actress Sherrie Hewson. Who can forget her iconic waterbed scene with Reg Holdsworth in *Coronation Street* when their passion destroyed the bed, sending the contents cascading on to Curly Watts in the flat below?

In *Emmerdale*, Sherrie's character, Lesley, was fatally attracted to Rodders, gazing wistfully at him with baleful puppy eyes as she lusted after him like a poodle on heat. Unfortunately, one of the best scenes we ever did together will never be seen, unless it appears on one of those out-takes programmes.

It was one of those drunken nights when both our characters were very much in their cups and Lesley, fortified by two bottles of wine, decided it was time to mount the unsuspecting Mr Blackstock. With Rodders three parts to the wind, first his jacket is removed. Then shirt buttons fly in all directions and, before he knows where he is, he is on top of the spread-eagled Lesley as she cries, 'Take me, Rodney. Take me, take me.'

It was hilarious. The crew collapsed in laughter, fortunately after the director had said, 'Cut.' Many hands were shaken in congratulations, but, to our surprise and dismay, when the show was aired we found the scene had been cut and instead of ending on Sherrie and myself it closed on the beautiful, frownless face of Patsy Kensit. Was our scene too saucy? Was it too *Carry On*? Or was it simply the allure of Miss Kensit – the face that launched a thousand commercial breaks.

Patsy, with her sparkling presence and obvious sex appeal, was, I thought, a terrific addition to the cast as Sadie. Very professional on screen and self-effacing off camera, with no airs and graces at all, she was very popular. Patsy became a very good friend of mine and we had a special bond, swapping stories of how we had both been targets for unsavoury tabloid tales. In that respect, we were like peas in a pod and we compared many a note on where we were and where we had been in our careers. I also knew from my many conversations with her about our families how hard she was finding the filming schedule.

As a parent of a young child myself, I realised how painful it was for her with two young children to be working in Leeds while her family remained in London, particularly as our normal weekend finishing time was 7.45pm on Friday evening – and we would normally be due back at 7.15 on Monday morning.

Even though it had been impressed upon us when we joined that there were no stars in *Emmerdale*, I felt that, as Patsy had made such an impact in the show, she deserved to see more of her family. So I encouraged her to chance her arm and ask if she could be let off early on a Friday and come in later on a Monday. She was at first reluctant, not wishing to abuse her position, but later she plucked up courage, and as a result her children saw more of her.

I have had many different girls while playing a ladies' man and have found that producers and directors don't always get it right when they choose a girl as your soul mate who they think will reflect your taste. But when Steve Frost told me he was bringing in the beautiful Emily Symons from *Home and Away* I was delighted.

Sadly, our pleasant on-screen affair was short-lived after Emily's character, Louise Appleton, discovered Rodney in bed with his ex-wife Diane. In the show Rodney has always held a torch for Diane and knows that if he can ply her with enough drink the likelihood is that she will forget all his past misdeeds and the flames will start to flicker – and Rodney is not the one to put them out.

Those flames, however, received a severe dousing when her young sister Val (the brilliant Charlie Hardwick) arrived on the scene. Diane discovered that Rodney had been having an affair with Val while still married to her. Of course this being a soap, the progeny of that illicit union appears 30 years later in the form of their gay son, Paul. He is played by the maddeningly handsome Matthew Bose.

I am incessantly in Kath's office complaining that not only is Matthew taller and younger than me, he is also better-looking and this has got to stop!

Matthew, being a couple of years older than his screen persona, is a most delightful, erudite individual, having spent a few years in Hollywood. It is a great compliment to have him as my son. He is, in fact, not too far removed from my own son, Simon, now thankfully a teacher in Bangkok – good riddance! Because Simon too is taller, better-looking and obviously much younger than me. Only kidding, Sambo!

Matthew and I care deeply about our characters' relationship and both believe that given the chance we could say more on screen about the difficulties and trials of a very heterosexual father discovering that he has a gay son, and vice versa. There must be many parents and children going through similar situations as, indeed, my own father would have done, thinking

I was, as he would have called it, 'a poof'. No doubt he would be shot nowadays for using words like that, but that was the language of his time. I suppose he must have agonised over me and my acting career while supping many a pint. People didn't talk about 'things like that' in those days.

Back in the show, with ice replacing Diane's earlier flames, Rodney, never one to miss a trick, promptly starts another affair with Val.

I have worked with a lot of very fine actors in my career, including Dame Maggie Smith, now rated one of England's greatest, and I have no hesitation in saying that Charlie would put up a good fight with Maggie. She has that rare quality of power, comedy and pathos, sometimes all in one line. When actors perform without any fuss they can on occasion be taken for granted. On stage I always perform for the hardest critic and I hope that when people see Charlie on screen they can appreciate the talent behind the ease.

Lorraine Chase, playing the nutty Steph Stokes, as mad as a hatter – Lorraine, that is – also made a play for Rodney when she detected the rustle of £50 notes. As soon as Rodney became a millionaire, she bought him champagne, and in three days he proposed and she accepted. They became engaged, she moved in and went through his drawers – the ones in the cabinet, that is; she had already been in the others. To her horror, she found the cupboard was bare. Rodney had no money, so at the engagement party she dumped him. That's showbiz, folks.

I enjoyed working with Lorraine because she always gave 100 per cent, even if most of that 100 per cent was to make sure she was 'All right, Jack', but I was experienced enough to make sure my character was also in focus as well as hers. But I fear other, less experienced actors allowed themselves to be overshadowed, not necessarily to anyone's benefit. In fact, the way Lorraine outplayed some of the weaker members of the cast for her own character's advantage was sometimes quite awesome.

I had met Lorraine many times before on celebrity junkets before she joined *Emmerdale* and she has always been famous for opening her mouth and letting words come out without too much thought. Usually it's charming and endearing.

But it wasn't so endearing to some in the Green Room on her first day. She light-heartedly said to the whole cast in a loud cockney accent, ''Ello ev'ryone, I'm Lorraine Chase. It's no good any of you tellin' me who you are, 'cos I don't watch the show, so I wouldn't know.'

Faces turned back to their scripts and sandwiches.

At the speed we shoot *Emmerdale* – 12 half-hour episodes in a ten-day filming block – there is no room for any actors to have egos. Egos get in the way.

Millionaire Rodney's ego, however, received a massive boost when the lovely Kelly Windsor came into his colourful life. Was it his charm, his good looks? And then the infamous question Debbie McGee was asked comes to mind: 'What did you ever see in the millionaire Paul Daniels?'

Sixty-year-old Rodders found the gorgeous 26-year-old Kelly had fallen in love with him. What a result! Kelly is played by the delicious Adele Silva, who has been voted one of the sexiest girls in Britain. Her curvaceous half-clad form is forever gracing the pages of the 'red tops' and she's the pin-up darling of *Loaded* and the other 'lads' mags'. To Rodney's delight, Kelly graced him with her charms for over nine months. Lucky me! Nice work if you can get it.

Rodney and Kelly's humour and warmth were encapsulated as they saw in the New Year 2006, both outside and in the hot tub.

Rodders raises his champagne glass to her, saying, 'Happy New Year, Gold Digger!'

'Happy New Year, Gold Mine!' she replies.

Both Adele and I expected to receive a barrage of 'Dirty Old Man' accusations and letters from 'Disgusted of Dagenham' protesting at the affair, but the critics, the newspapers and, luckily for me, the *Emmerdale* writers all thought the characters suited each other. Mind you, Rodney is only 36 in his mind. But then so am I!

Disaster, however, was just around the corner for Rodney. The producers felt he was having too easy a life as a millionaire and decided to make him lose his fortune and go back to where he started – with nothing. I've been promised, though, that he will work his way back up again. We all thought that as soon as Rodney lost his money the kittenish Kelly would take her Brigitte Bardot body off. To everyone's surprise, it was Rodney she was after, not his money. But dear old Rodders said he would rather they part as friends than end up arguing over cash. Money may not buy happiness but it certainly helps.

Kath Beedles had called me into the office to tell me that, although she liked the relationship between Adele and myself and thought it was very touching, she wanted to break it up. She preferred Rodney as a loose cannon among the ladies of *Emmerdale* and wanted him to go back to his little black book. And long may he continue to flick through the pages.

Rodney, or Hot Rod as he has been called many times in the show, certainly lost no time in scribbling in the name of Carrie, played by my very old friend Linda Lusardi.

Linda stopped being a glamour model 15 years ago and I have seen her in many fine performances on stage. She has worked constantly to prove herself as an actress and has earned the right to be judged as such. It was a delight to catch up with her again and I welcomed her with open arms. I did give her the odd tip on the dos and don'ts, but, heeding old Stan's words, left her to do the breaststroke alone.

We have many beauties in *Emmerdale*.

At our recent Pageant to celebrate 500 years of the village of Emmerdale, while dressed as Sir Walter Raleigh – question not, dear reader – I had the pleasure to meet again the stunning mezzo-soprano Katherine Jenkins. With his usual charm Tim Fee had persuaded her to appear at the famous *Emmerdale* Aberdeen charity weekend in 2006. We raised many thousands of pounds and I was lucky enough to have dinner with Katherine, who, as well as having a fantastic voice, is a true beauty. And Welsh with it! We talked of the Valleys.

Emmerdale is famous for its explosive incidents – and it lived up to its reputation when the Queen came to join the celebrations for the show's 30th anniversary.

Whether she was persuaded to come or, as we like to think, she is a closet fan, I don't know, but she duly arrived. I should have suspected the worst when things started to go slightly off key from the moment her limo purred into the village.

Emmerdale Village is a work of art. The houses are real bricks and mortar with real foundations and the roads are finished in tarmac. The doors and windows work but when you step inside there is nothing there. They are shells in which you flick a switch and all the lights come on; you flick another switch and the chimneys smoke. It is very impressive and was constructed under the eagle eye of our Line Producer, my dear friend Tim Fee.

Tim, who had spent many years at the English National Ballet – not in tights, I hasten to add – has become a very good friend. He and I empty many a glass of malt as we regale each other with our showbiz escapades. And now Tim's eye was very proud indeed as he waited to show Her Majesty around his beloved Emmerdale.

But as the Queen's limousine slid to a halt her equerry got out the wrong side, getting his sword stuck in the process. Her Majesty was left to open her door herself. *Quelle horreur!* But what was that? Was it a bird, was it a plane? No, it was Mr Fee. Luckily the hours Tim had spent watching his dancers from the wings came in extremely handy as he bounded balletically across the road and came gallantly to the Queen's aid.

I had the honour of being the first member of the cast to be presented to her and as I took her hand she said, 'Oh, I know you.'

Tim said quickly, 'This is Patrick Mower.'

Her Majesty replied, 'Of course it is.'

I suppose, as I've been an actor for over 40 years, she would have seen me in something. Earlier this year I introduced myself to Tony Blair, saying, 'You won't know me but...'

'Of course I know you, Patrick,' he interrupted. 'You're part of my life.'

Gosh!

Back at the village, the heavens opened and I made some quip to Her Majesty about Mr Fee controlling everything in Emmerdale but obviously not the weather. She chuckled and was ushered inside the B&B.

Maybe the Queen was simply being polite in her remark to me, or maybe she had a very good memory. I had actually met her once before with Prince Philip when Eric Morecambe, in his capacity as president of the Lords Taverners, had introduced me to them in the Long Room at Lord's.

Naturally, with its reputation for eccentric incidents from lightning strikes to plane crashes, a stunt was arranged to impress Her Majesty. The post office was to be blown up!

It was blown up all right – in a more spectacular style than anticipated.

The Queen, standing 50 yards away on the steps of the Woolpack, showed the cool control we have seen so often on television. As a tremendous explosion sent pieces of plywood hurtling into the assembled photographers, Her Majesty remained absolutely motionless and expressionless.

Liz Estensen and Mark Charnock, who demonstrates a wonderful light-comedy touch as Marlon the chef, were standing either side of her, and they both leaped – open-mouthed – a foot into the air. I dived flat on my face to avoid having my head severed by a Walls Ice Cream sign.

In the replay we later watched on television it was as though the Queen had received special SAS training for any guerrilla attack – that she, as head of our Armed Forces, must remain unflappable. She certainly was. She never moved a muscle. 'If you can keep your head when all about you...'

The stunt had gone wrong, but the Queen simply remarked, 'That was fun. Do you do it every day?'

Bearing in mind my advice to Patsy, I certainly make sure I see Anya and eight-year-old Maxim as much as possible – by making the 100-mile drive from my rural retreat in Lincolnshire to the *Emmerdale* set and back again every day. It is more to Audrey's credit than mine that Simon and Claudia have both turned into the highly intelligent, witty and charming people they are. They are both tremendous fun to be with. Simon happily made me a grandfather nine years ago with his son William, and then with four-year-old Elise. A soon-to-be headmaster, he is now teaching in the lap of luxury in Bangkok. I am amazed that my beautiful Claudia still hasn't been ensnared by one of her beaus. He'll have to be a very special prince charming. She has forsaken her marketing job to become a charity project fundraiser.

Having Maxim has been an amazing experience and I would

recommend any older man to have a child. We have even talked about having more children – we would have loved a little girl. But the reason we didn't is because Maxim is so perfect.

Now I have the contentment that everyone wants. Work is important, but it isn't my whole life any more. I don't see age as a problem. If anything, I am a better parent for being older and I keep fit with exercise, swimming and golf, and we are lucky enough to have a tennis court at home.

Watching Maxim grow and develop, or just playing football and cricket with him, are the things that mean the most to me now. He is such a wonderful child.

Emmerdale has also brought me a new generation of fans. I still do get flattering letters from the ladies. But, as I always have, I take it with a pinch of salt. Even the weatherman gets fan letters.

I was playing golf with the weather forecaster Michael Fish once and at the bottom of the fairway there were four women of a certain age waiting. They were all saying, 'Here he comes, here he comes.' So I brushed my hair back and got ready to sign a few autographs. Then they rushed up and went straight to Michael. Now, he wasn't the most handsome man in the world, but they thought he was the cat's whiskers because he was on TV. I've been around too long to be concerned. I often hear people arguing about where they remember me from.

Someone will say, 'Oh, he was in *Target*,' and another will say, 'No, it was *Special Branch*.' Then someone will come in with, 'Rodney from *Emmerdale*.' I don't mind what they remember me for – it's just nice to still be asked for my autograph. When they stop asking will be the time to worry.

On a more serious note, I certainly had cause to worry three years ago. I was told I was losing my sight in both eyes. It was the most terrifying thing I have had to face. Of all the senses, I think sight is the most valuable. I have always loved nature –

flowers, birds, trees. And my sport – cricket, football, golf. And my children, Maxim, Simon, Claudia – and of course Anya! In a millisecond these images flashed through my mind. To lose them, to never be able to see them again.

I was, of course, distraught. When I told Anya, we both cried. I feared I would not have the wonderful pleasure of seeing Maxim grow up.

I had first noticed my sight was failing in a tennis match against my old mate Ken Farrington, who played Tom King in *Emmerdale*. Ken was beating me and I honestly thought it was because the net was sagging low at one side. It looked like it was wiggling. So I went and checked the height and it was OK. I just thought I must be tired. But the problem grew worse. On holiday in Florida with Anya and Maxim I had an eye test and was told that I had grains of dirt behind the eyes. The optician advised vitamins and sold me some driving glasses.

But things didn't get any better. When I was reading, the letters kept moving around on the page and lines just weren't straight. Playing golf, my ball looked misshapen. It was disorientating and I thought that perhaps I had had a stroke without realising. This threw me, so I confided in Anya and she said I had to see a doctor. Another specialist diagnosed macular degeneration. This condition, although not common, is something that can affect eyes as one grows older. So I was not too worried.

However, an examination at Moorfields Eye Hospital in London revealed a much more serious problem. When they said I had to see a surgeon that afternoon, I was scared. He told me I had a condition called pre-retinal glial membrane – a layer of scar tissue on the retina which was crinkling continuously and messing up my vision – and I needed an operation.

When he showed me the device he would use it looked to me